THE PARADOX OF ACTING

and

MASKS OR FACES?

The Paradox of Acting

by DENIS DIDEROT

and

Masks or Faces?

by WILLIAM ARCHER

Introduction by Lee Strasberg

A DRAMABOOK

Advisory Editor, Eric Bentley

HILL AND WANG, INC. · New York · 1957

The Publisher wishes to express his appreciation to Mr. Wilson Follett for his extensive editorial work in the preparation of this volume.

Library of Congress Catalog Card No. 57-5838

Manufactured in the United States of America

William Archer (1856-1924) was a distinguished Scottish critic, author, and translator. Educated as a lawyer, he never practised. He was dramatic critic for the *London Figaro,* 1879-1881, and later for *The World* and other papers. Archer made a great success with his melodrama, *The Green Goddess,* produced in the United States in 1921 and in London two years later. Archer himself considered his translating and editing of Ibsen's works to be one of the chief labors and privileges of his life.

Denis Diderot (1713-1784) is primarily known for his monumental *Encyclopedia.* He wrote several plays in the sentimental vein which were accompanied by his *Paradoxe sur le comédien* in which he presented the fundamentals of a new drama—the drama of real life as opposed to the conventional drama of the classic French theatre. The *Paradoxe* was not published until 1830, many years after the author's death.

CONTENTS

CONTENTS

INTRODUCTION

It is difficult to discuss with exactitude the problem of acting. The object of the discussion—the actor's performance—is a fluid and fleeting process that leaves no lasting record by which the audience can test its recollection. Unlike an El Greco painting, a Monteverdi madrigal, or a Shelley ode, the performance lives and dies anew each night. Our response to the actor is a total one; it does not distinguish easily between the actor as a personality and the role he is playing. It is difficult to tell where the playwright's contribution stops and the actor's begins. The famous French director and actor Jacques Copeau points out the difficulty of formulating anything definitive about the actor's art when he says: "Those who see only the grimaces and tricks of the actor refuse to see anything creative in his art. Others, aware only of his all too human frailty, relegate him to the dust heap and demand the marionette in his place."

The difficulty of definition has not prevented a long list of theatre people from attempting it, from Luigi Riccoboni to Stanislavski. Talma, Iffland, Henry Irving, Coquelin, Salvini, Rachel, Joseph Jefferson, Forbes-Robertson, and many others have had their say. The eighteenth century, through much of which the stage was dominated by individual virtuosos, is particularly rich in the theoretic discussions. Men of all-around genius, among them Voltaire, Lessing, and Goethe, found it natural to participate actively in the drama, considered the theatre culturally important, and wrote about its problems brilliantly and sometimes profoundly. Of all such writings the most widely known is Diderot's treatise in the form of a dialogue, *Paradoxe sur le comédien*. It has been out of print for many years and is now happily made available once more in Walter Herries Pollock's fine translation as *The Paradox of Acting,* together with its answer, the pragmatic investigation by William Archer of the assumptions of Diderot.

Denis Diderot, 1713–84, coeditor of the *Encyclopédie* (1751–65), and the most prolific of its contributors, played a major part in his century's intellectual revolution. In his plays Diderot broke away from the conventions of the classic French stage and tried to create a new genre, bourgeois drama. His plays were not particularly successful with the public, but they influenced Gotthold Ephraim Lessing and, through him, the development of drama in the nineteenth century. Diderot also influenced Lessing with his *Observations sur Garrick,* in which he blocked out the main ideas later developed in *Paradoxe sur le comédien.*

The *Paradoxe* itself was not printed until 1830, forty-six years after the death of its author; it is known to have been written in the 1770's, retouched and added to from time to time, and finally reworked about 1778. Because of its polemic brilliance, because it is the view of an "outsider" and, therefore, perhaps easier to assimilate, it has remained to this day the most significant attempt to deal with the problem of acting. Any discussion of acting almost invariably touches on Diderot's famous paradox: to move the audience the actor must himself remain unmoved.

The Paradox of Acting is a theoretic essay. It expresses Diderot's idea of what acting should be—not what it is; it presents a theory of acting, a basic analysis, rather than an actor's experiences in the process of creation. It was written in response to other writings of the period which maintained the emotionalist point of view. Yet, Diderot had on various occasions supported this same emotionalist point of view and cited evidence differing from the opinions expressed in the *Paradox.* In fact, he had so completely reversed his opinions that some students have doubted that the *Paradox* is actually his.

At all times Diderot had a high opinion of the actor's art: it demands, he said in the *Encyclopédie,* article *Comédien,* "a great number of qualities that nature so rarely unites in the same person, that one can count more great writers than great actors." Of the genius he said, article *Génie:* "In the heat of the enthusiasm he [the genius] doesn't worry about nature, nor the continuity of ideas; he is transported into the situation of the personages he must act; he takes on their character; if he experiences in the highest degree the great passions . . . he creates the sublime." In another essay, the *Second Entretien,* he writes: "Happily an actress of limited judgment, of ordinary understanding but of great sensibility, understands without difficulty a situation of the soul, and finds, without thinking, the accent which leads to the different sentiments that constitute the situation, which all the sagacity of the philosophers is unable to unravel." Similar comments, descriptions of sublimely inspired moments on the stage can be found in his writings, especially in his letters to the young actress Mlle. Jodin. In the period of transition, before he had fully accepted the thesis developed in the *Paradox,* he argued for a balance between feeling and judgment. In one of the letters to Mlle. Jodin he says at one point:

An actor who has only sense and judgment is cold; one who has only verve and sensibility is crazy. It is a peculiar combination of good sense and warmth which creates the sublime person; and on the stage as in life he who shows more than he feels makes one laugh instead of affecting one. Therefore never try to go beyond the feeling that you have; try to find the true point.

Shakespeare expressed a similar point of view in his familiar lines:

In the very torrent, tempest, and as I may say, whirlwind of your passions, you must acquire and beget a temperance, that may give it smoothness.

In the *Paradox,* Diderot is concerned with expounding the antiemotionalist point of view, and it differs sharply from his earlier one. But Diderot obviously knew better than those of his adherents who followed him literally. These older (or rather younger) ideas "made much more sense," remarks Jacques Copeau, who is responsible for many of the innovations in the modern French theatre.

What caused Diderot to change his views we do not know. Perhaps it was the actors' insensitivity to the new type of play he was writing. His caustic remarks on the character of his contemporary actors certainly indicate disappointment and bitterness. The excesses of "emotionalist" theory and practice may have led Diderot to exaggerate his own views.

Felix Vexler in his essay "Studies in Diderot's Esthetic Naturalism" has logically reasoned that "Diderot's plea against feeling is in reality directed only against morbid and useless 'sensibility,' against the show of emotion that bears no relation to the circumstances that provoke it and is barren of pragmatic results." Diderot, Vexler continued, was moved to inveigh against the misguided sentimentalists and the followers of Rousseau, "who because they thought themselves possessed of 'sentiments' and 'genius' felt they could dispense with the quest for beauty and with social duties."

Diderot rejected not the idea of enthusiasm or inspiration, but of "false" enthusiasm. He had come to believe that these feelings arise not as a sudden thrust of emotion, undisciplined and overwhelming, but rather at moments of tranquillity and reflection.

The *Paradox* is thus a challenge to the actor to recognize the high nature of his art, a plea that he discipline and control the flow of his imagination and feeling. In an era which worshiped the actor of sudden inspiration and delighted in thrilling bits of stage business, Diderot called on the actor to recognize his responsibility to the play and the playwright, to the "whole" of the theatre. This demand for actor's discipline, for a technique of emotional experience, is an essential of any acting theory or practice. Here is the real historical significance of Diderot's contribution. With this demand Diderot becomes one of the pioneers of the modern concept of the theatre. This explains Stanislavski's recognition of Diderot's essay as one of the important contributions to acting theory.

The classic rejoinder to Diderot's *The Paradox of Acting* is William Archer's *Masks or Faces?* first published in 1888. Archer, a brilliant critic and practical man of the theatre who defended the "new drama" of the late nineteenth century and edited the collected works of Ibsen, undertook a systematic test of Diderot's theories. He circulated a carefully framed questionnaire on the issue, emotion versus cold calculation, among the prominent actors and actresses of the period. The questions and the fascinating and varied replies he received constitute the marrow of *Masks or Faces?* Thus in this book we leave the area of theoretic and personal opinion for the concrete investigation and exploration of facts.

Some present-day theories of acting suggest that the actor's creative processes differ for different styles of plays, that while one approach may be right for the realistic play, another is necessary for the classic or poetic play. Does this imply that a painter or musician working in the modern idiom feels less keenly or is less involved in his work than one working in the more conventional realistic style? An ancient Greek actor, working in a theatre quite different from ours, still felt it necessary to carry an urn containing the ashes of his dead son onto a scene where he was to deliver a funeral oration. A Japanese actor, working in a theatre dedicated to formal results, tells how his teacher made him walk in his bare feet for hours in the snow in order to prepare him for a part on the stage.

The two essays reprinted in this volume bring the discussion down to where it belongs—an analysis of the actor's basic creative processes regardless of the material he is working on. The greatest theatre practitioners have agreed on the actor's basic problem. Talma's formula of sensibility and intelligence, Joseph Jefferson's "the warm heart and the cool mind," and Stanislavski's division of the actor's work into two spheres—the actor's work on himself and the actor's work on the role—are cut from the same cloth. In the process of learning, one aspect of the actor's art may be emphasized temporarily at the expense of the other, but before a complete and convincing image can be created on the stage both must be mastered.

Over 200 years ago in 1745 an anonymous poet described the contrasting errors into which actors fall:

Some who would Gaiety and Passion show,
With smart, lisp'd catch make half formed word to flow;
Swift Rolls of jargon sound, a rapid flood,
With not one Word distinctly understood:
Others to seem articulate and clear,
With dull, loud, slow, plain Sound fatigue the ear;
All words, all lines, the same grave Cadence keep,
And drowsy lull invisibly to sleep.

This was written long before Stanislavski, the "Method," and the Actor's Studio could be blamed for putting an audience to sleep. The actor's basic problem has remained the same throughout the ages. He is the only artist whose basic raw material is himself; he uses his own muscles, brain, emotions, voice, speech, and gesture to identify with and create another human being. "The struggle of the sculptor with his material," Jacques Copeau has well said, "is nothing compared to the resistance that his body, his blood, his extremities, his mouth and all his organs offer to the actor." From this, and not from any problem of realism or style, springs the actor's eternal problem. And according to Shakespeare it is a "monstrous" one:

> Is it not monstrous that this player here
> But in a fiction, in a dream of passion,
> Could force his soul so to his own conceit. . . .

How to "force his soul to his own conceit"—here is the basic goal of the actor, and all his techniques are directed to a way of achieving it.

LEE STRASBERG

THE PARADOX OF ACTING

and

MASKS OR FACES?

THE PARADOX OF ACTING

Translated by Walter Herries Pollock

PREFACE

It is the nature of a paradox that it should deal with extremes. Diderot's entertaining work is an apt illustration of this truth. Having persuaded himself that sensibility should have no part in an actor's functions, he goes on to prove that it is one of the misfortunes, and even one of the vices, of the human mind. He is almost as angry with it as Sir Peter Teazle is with everything that sounds like a sentiment. 'Sensibility cripples the intelligence at the very juncture when a man needs all his self-possession.' Sensibility is the 'disposition which accompanies organic weakness.' It 'inclines one to being compassionate, to being horrified, to admiration, to fear, to being upset, to tears, to faintings, to rescues, to flights, to exclamations, to loss of self-control, to being contemptuous, disdainful, to having no clear notion of what is true, good, and fine, to being unjust, to going mad.' A number of illustrations, real or imaginary, drawn ostensibly from his own experience, enable the philosopher to show that whenever he was unequal to an emergency, whenever a repartee was not ready on his tongue, he was the victim of sensibility. On one occasion he did not lose his head, but was able to reproach a man for refusing help to a starving brother; and this he sets down to the habit of cool reflection, and not to the impulse of indignant humanity. In a word, it is impossible, according to Diderot's theory, for sudden feeling of any kind to find just and adequate expression. Even the orator can never be swayed by real emotion, but must produce his finest effects, must move the multitude at his will, by a simulated fervour which is the outcome of care and calculation.

This is a paradox, indeed; but it is no business of mine to

5

vindicate human nature against the philosopher's fantasy.
The basis of his speculation is the character of actors, and as
he is sufficiently inaccurate in painting this, there is no
necessity to follow him through all the variations of his
theme. Diderot had the highest opinion of acting as an art.
The great actor, he said, was even a more remarkable being
than the great poet. Yet the actor was in some respects a
worthless creature, without character or even individuality,
and wholly lacking in moral sense. The actors of Diderot's
day were not only devoid of sensibility on the stage; they had
not a particle of sentiment in private life. They were often
seen to laugh, never to weep. They were 'isolated, vagabonds,
at the command of the great,' and had 'little conduct, no
friends, scarce any of those holy and tender ties which associate us in the pains and pleasures of another, who in turn
shares our own.' This picture may have had some truth then;
nobody will pretend that it is true now. The stage in
Diderot's time did not enjoy that social esteem which makes
public spirit and private independence. Actors were the
hangers-on of the Court; actresses were, in too many cases,
worse than hangers-on. 'Want of education, poverty, a libertine spirit,' says Diderot, 'made actors slip on the sock or the
buskin;' and to the libertine spirit he frankly confesses when
speaking of his own early desire to enter the theatrical profession. 'The stage is a resource, never a choice. Never did
actor become so from love of virtue, from desire to be useful
in the world, or to serve his country or family; never from
any of the honourable motives which might incline a right
mind, a feeling heart, a sensitive soul, to so fine a profession.'

When such an assumption is essential to a paradox, it is
plain that ingenuity and plausibility are at their most auda-
cious climax. For Diderot's position is nothing short of this—
that, though wholly destitute of moral qualities, the accomplished actor must, by sheer force of imitation, absorb into
himself for the purposes of his art the moral qualities he sees
in others. This is not with him an affair of feeling, but of
argument. He 'must have penetration and no sensibility; the
art of mimicking everything, or, which comes to the same
thing, the same aptitude for every sort of character and
part.' The obvious answer to this is, that an actor's aptitude,
however great may be his versatility, must have limits. He

cannot, any more than another man, be born without a temperament, and though his talent may be many-sided, his natural idiosyncrasy will impel him more strongly in one direction than in another. It was necessary for the purpose of his paradox that Diderot should assume that sensibility must be a wild, ungovernable emotion, absolutely fatal to the nerve of all who are afflicted by it. The one example Diderot gives of a dramatic artist guided by sensibility leaves no doubt of this. Mlle. Dumesnil, he tells us, 'comes on the stage not knowing what she is going to say; half the time she does not know what she is saying: but she has one sublime moment.' Therefore Mlle. Dumesnil was not a great actress. But Talma thought she was. It is of this actress, as well as of Le Kain, Molé, and Monvel, that he says, 'It was only by a faithful imitation of truth and nature that they succeeded in creating those powerful emotions in an en-lightened nation which still exist in the recollections of those who heard them.' For an actress to come on the stage not knowing what she is going to say is not the way to give a faithful imitation of truth and nature. 'The extravagant creature who loses her self-control has no hold on us; that is gained by the man who is self-controlled.' But is there no such thing as inspiration? 'Certainly there is,' replies the philosopher. 'You may have your sublime moments, but they must come when the man of genius is hovering between nature and his sketch of it, and keeping a watchful eye on both. Cool reflection must bring the fury of enthusiasm to its bearings.' Exactly; but this is scarcely the bearing of the paradox, for why should not the man of sensibility exercise cool reflection and a watchful eye when the ideas suggested by his emotions are subjected to the test of his judgment? When Macready played Virginius after burying his loved daughter he confessed that his real experience gave a new force to his acting in the most pathetic situations of the play. Are we to suppose that this was a delusion, or that the sensibility of the man was a genuine aid to the actor? Bannister said of John Kemble that he was never pathetic, because he had no children. From this I infer, that Bannister found that the moral quality derived from his domestic as-sociations had much to do with his own acting. And John Bannister was a great actor. Talma says, that when deeply moved he found himself making 'a rapid and fugitive observation on the alteration of his voice, and on a certain spasmodic vibration it contracted in tears.' Has not the actor who can thus make his own feelings part of his art an advantage over the actor who never feels, but makes his observations solely from the sensibility of others? Untrained actors, yielding to excitement on the stage, have been known to stumble against the wings in impassioned exit. But it is quite possible to feel all the excitement of the situation and yet be perfectly self-possessed. This is art which the actor who loses his head has not mastered. It is necessary to this art that the mind should have, as it were, a double consciousness, in which all the emotions proper to the occasion may have full sway, while the actor is all the time on the alert for every detail of his method.

'I call sensibility,' says Talma, 'that faculty of exaltation which agitates an actor, takes possession of his senses, shakes even his very soul, and enables him to enter into the most tragic situations, and the most terrible of the passions, as if they were his own. The intelligence which accompanies sensibility judges the impressions which the latter has made us feel; it selects, arranges them, and subjects them to calculation. It aids us to direct the employment of our physical and intellectual forces—to judge between the relations which are between the poet and the situation or the character of the personages, and sometimes to add the shades that are wanting, or that language cannot express: to complete, in fine, their expression by action and physiognomy.' That, in a small compass, is the whole matter. It would be impossible to give a more perfect description of the art of acting in a few words. Talma does not assume that the intelligent actor who does not feel cannot be an admirable artist. 'The inspired actor will so associate you with the emotions he feels that he will not leave you the liberty of judgment; the other, by his prudent and irreproachable acting, will leave your faculties at liberty to reason on the matter at your ease.' Nor need it be contended that the actor of sensibility must always feel—that, as Diderot suggests, he must wear himself out by excess of soul. It may be that his playing will be more spirited one night than another. It is possible to see in the writings of the greatest novelists where the pen has flagged, and where the deftness of the workman is more conspicuous than the inspiration of the man of genius. But the actor who combines the electric force of a strong personality with a mastery of the resources of his art, must have a greater power over his audiences than the passionless actor who gives a most artistic simulation of the emotions he never experiences.

It will be observed that Diderot lays great stress upon the divorce between Nature and the Stage. He was thinking of the stage of Racine, and not of the stage of Shakespeare. He quotes Garrick to the effect that 'an actor who will play you a scene of Shakespeare to perfection is ignorant of the first principles of declamation needed by Racine.' Garrick made a revolution in English declamation by showing that Hamlet's advice to the players might be literally obeyed. But to French critics of that day this was rank heresy. They would not admit that it was the function of tragic poets and actors to hold the mirror up to Nature. Diderot points out that people do not speak on the stage as they do in the street. Every jealous man does not utter laments as pathetic and eloquent as Othello's, but these are none the less human because they are couched in splendid diction. They move the hearer because they are the utterance of a man's agony. But to Diderot the creations of Racine were out of this sphere of human emotion. They were grand ideal types, which could not express themselves in simple language; they required an artificial declamation, in which anything like a natural tone would have been a sacrilege. So the chances that the sensibility of the actor would be in keeping with the stilted method he was expected to adopt were necessarily few.

If actors feel, how is it, asks our author, that they can quarrel or make love on the stage all the while they are conducting some scene of great pith and moment, by which the audience is deeply moved? Diderot illustrates this difficulty with much wit. It is sufficient to reply, that the experience of the actor is often superior to the perceptions of his audience; and that to feel love or aversion for a character in a play it is not necessary to entertain one sentiment or the other for the actor or actress who represents that character. The whole soul of an actor may be engaged in Hamlet's revenge upon Claudius, but he need not on that account feel any desire to slay the excellent gentleman who enacts the king.

Perhaps it will always be an open question how far sensibility and art can be fused in the same mind. Every actor has his secret. He might write volumes of explanation, and the matter would still remain a paradox to many. It is often said that actors should not shed tears, that real tears are bad art. This is not so. If tears be produced at the actor's will and under his control, they are true art; and happy is the actor who numbers them amongst his gifts. The exaltation of sensibility in art may be difficult to define, but it is none the less real to all who have felt its power.

HENRY IRVING

THE PARADOX OF ACTING

The First Speaker. Let us talk no more of that.

The Second Speaker. Why?

The First. It is the work of a friend of yours.[1]

The Second. What does that matter?

The First. A good deal. What is gained by accepting the alternatives of holding his talent or my judgment cheap, of going back on the good opinion you hold either of him or of me?

The Second. That will not be the result; and were it so it would make no hole in my friendship for both of you, founded as it is on firmer grounds.

The First. May be.

The Second. It is so. Do you know of what you just now remind me? Of an author I know who fell on his knees to a woman he loved to beg her not to go to the first night of a piece of his.

The First. A modest man, and a prudent.

The Second. He was afraid that her affection might hang on the amount of his literary fame.

---

[1] The work referred to was *Garrick, ou les Acteurs Anglais*, a translation by Antonio Fabio Sticotti of an English pamphlet. The translation appeared in Paris in 1769. Sticotti was one of the *Comédiens du Roi de la Troupe Italienne*, was famous in the parts both of Pierrot and of Pantalon, and was popular in private life. A most interesting account of the Italian company in Paris, and of how by degrees they came to act in French and to play French pieces, will be found in M. Campardon's book, *Les Comédiens du Roi de la Troupe Italienne*. (Paris: Berger-Levrault et Cie.)

I have, with considerable trouble, procured a copy of Sticotti's work in a second edition published, without his name on the title-page, in Paris by 'J.P. Costard, Libraire, Rue Saint Jean-de-Beauvais. M.DCC.LXX.' It is a free version, with many additions, of *The Actor, or a Treatise on the Art of Playing*. (London: Printed for R. Griffiths, at the Dunciad in Pater-noster Row. MDCCLV.)

11

The First. Like enough.

The Second. That a public check might lessen him somewhat in his mistress's eyes.

The First. That loss of love would follow on loss of reputation. That strikes you as absurd?

The Second. It was thought to be so. The box was taken; he had a complete success; and you may guess how he was embraced, made much of, caressed.

The First. He would have been made all the more of if the piece had been hissed.

The Second. I am sure I am right.

The First. And I hold to my view.

The Second. Hold to it by all means; but remember that I at least am not a woman, and that I am anxious you should explain yourself.

The First. Absolutely?

The Second. Absolutely.

The First. I should find it much easier to say nothing than to veil what I really think.

The Second. Of course.

The First. I shall be uncompromising.

The Second. That is just what my friend would like you to be.

The First. Well then, as I must speak—his work, crabbed, obscure, complicated, bombastic as it is in style, is yet full of commonplace. A great dramatic artist will not be a bit the better, a poor actor not a bit the less inefficient, for reading it. It is Nature who bestows personal gifts—appearance, voice, judgment, tact. It is the study of the great models, the knowledge of the human heart, the habit of society, earnest work, experience, close acquaintance with the boards, which perfect Nature's gifts. The actor who is merely a mimic can count upon being always tolerable; his playing will call neither for praise nor for blame.

The Second. Or else for nothing but blame.

The First. Granted. The actor who goes by Nature alone is often detestable, sometimes excellent. But in whatever line, beware of a level mediocrity. No matter how harshly a beginner is treated, one may easily foretell his future success. It is only the incapables who are stifled by cries of 'Off!

off!'[2] How should Nature without Art make a great actor when nothing happens on the stage exactly as it happens in nature, and when dramatic poems are all composed after a fixed system of principles? And how can a part be played in the same way by two different actors when, even with the clearest, the most precise, the most forceful of writers, words are no more, and never can be more, than symbols, indicating a thought, a feeling, or an idea; symbols which need action, gesture, intonation, expression, and a whole context of circumstance, to give them their full significance? When you have heard these words—

'Que fait là votre main?'
'Je tâte votre habit, l'étoffe en est moelleuse'
['Your hand—what does it there?'
'It feels your robe; 'tis soft and pleasant to the touch']

what do you know of their meaning? Nothing. Weigh well what follows, and remember how often and how easily it happens that two speakers may use the same words to express entirely different thoughts and matters. The instance I am going to cite is a very singular one; it is the very work of your friend that we have been discussing. Ask a French actor what he thinks of it; he will tell you that every word of it is true. Ask an English actor, and he will swear that, '*By God,* there's not a sentence to change! It is the very gospel of the stage!' However, since there is nothing in common between the way of writing comedy and tragedy in England, and the way of writing stage poems in France; since, according to Garrick himself, an actor who will play you a scene of Shakespeare to perfection is ignorant of the first principles of declamation needed for Racine; since, entwined by Racine's musical lines as if by so many serpents whose folds compress his head, his feet, his hands, his legs, and his arms, he would, in attempting these lines, lose all liberty of action; it follows obviously that the French and the English actors, entirely at one as to the soundness of your author's principles, are yet at variance, and that the technical terms of the stage are so broad and so vague that

[2] Cf. Lord Beaconsfield's 'You *shall* hear me one day,' at the end of his first unsuccessful and derided speech in the House of Commons.

men of judgment, and of diametrically opposite views, yet find in them the light of conviction. Now hold closer than ever to your maxim, '*Avoid explanation if what you want is a mutual understanding.*' [3]

The Second. You think that in every work, and especially in this, there are two distinct meanings, both expressed in the same terms, one understood in London, the other in Paris?

The First. Yes; and that these terms express so clearly the two meanings that your friend himself has fallen into a trap. In associating the names of English with those of French actors, applying to both the same precepts, giving to both the same praise and the same reproofs, he has doubtless imagined that what he said of the one set was equally true of the other.

The Second. According to this, never before was author so wrong-headed.

The First. I am sorry to admit that this is so, since he uses the same words to express one thing at the Cross-roads of Bussy and another thing at Drury Lane. Of course I may be wrong. But the important point on which your author and I are entirely at variance concerns the qualities above all necessary to a great actor. In my view he must have a deal of judgment. He must have in himself an unmoved and disinterested onlooker. He must have, consequently, penetration and no sensibility; the art of mimicking everything, or, which comes to the same thing, the same aptitude for every sort of character and part.

The Second. No sensibility?

The First. None. I have not yet arranged my ideas logically, and you must let me tell them to you as they come to me, with the same want of order that marks your friend's book. If the actor were full, really full, of feeling, how could he play the same part twice running with the same spirit and success? Full of fire at the first performance, he would be worn out and cold as marble at the third. But take it that he is an attentive mimic and thoughtful disciple of Nature, then the first time he comes on the stage as Au-

---

[3] This was a favourite aphorism of Grimm, to whom the first sketch of the *Paradoxe* was addressed *à propos* of *Garrick, ou les Acteurs Anglais*. It is given in vol. viii. of M. Assézat's edition. (Paris: Garnier frères.)

gustus, Cinna, Orosmanes, Agamemnon, or Mahomet, faithful copying of himself and the effects he has arrived at, and constantly observing human nature, will so prevail that his acting, far from losing in force, will gather strength with the new observations he will make from time to time. He will increase or moderate his effects, and you will be more and more pleased with him. If he is himself while he is playing, how is he to stop being himself? If he wants to stop being himself, how is he to catch just the point where he is to stay his hand?

What confirms me in this view is the unequal acting of players who play from the heart. From them you must expect no unity. Their playing is alternately strong and feeble, fiery and cold, dull and sublime. To-morrow they will miss the point they have excelled in to-day; and to make up for it will excel in some passage where last time they failed.[4] On the other hand, the actor who plays from thought, from study of human nature, from constant imitation of some ideal type, from imagination, from memory, will be one and the same at all performances, will be always at his best mark; he has considered, combined, learnt and arranged the whole thing in his head; his diction is neither monotonous nor dissonant. His passion has a definite course—it has bursts, and it has reactions; it has a beginning, a middle, and an end. The accents are the same, the positions are the same, the movements are the same; if there is any difference between two performances, the latter is generally the better. He will be invariable; a looking-glass, as it were, ready to reflect realities, and to reflect them ever with the same precision, the same strength, and the same truth. Like the poet he will dip for ever into the inexhaustible treasure-house of Nature, instead of coming very soon to an end of his own poor resources.

What acting was ever more perfect than Clairon's?[5] Think

---

[4] This was, according to good authority, the case with Talma in his earlier days; and was certainly so with M. Mounet Sully in his earlier days. Both actors learnt by experience the unwisdom of relying upon inspiration alone.

[5] Mlle. Clairon was born in Condé in 1723, and received her first impulse to go on the stage from seeing Mlle. Dangeville taking a dancing lesson in a room of which the windows were opposite to those of the attic in which Clairon's ill-natured mother had locked her up. She made her first appearance with the Italian company at the age of thirteen; then made a great success in comedy parts in the provinces; and at the age of eighteen came back to Paris. Here she appeared first at

over this, study it; and you will find that at the sixth performance of a given part she has every detail of her acting by
heart, just as much as every word of her part. Doubtless she
has imagined a type, and to conform to this type has been
her first thought; doubtless she has chosen for her purpose
the highest, the greatest, the most perfect type her imagination could compass. This type, however, which she has
borrowed from history, or created as who should create some
vast spectre in her own mind, is not herself. Were it indeed
bounded by her own dimensions, how paltry, how feeble
would be her playing! When, by dint of hard work, she has
got as near as she can to this idea, the thing is done; to preserve the same nearness is a mere matter of memory and
practice. If you were with her while she studied her part
how many times you would cry out, *That is right!* and how
many times she would answer, *You are wrong!*

Just so a friend of Le Quesnoy's[6] once cried, catching him
by the arm, 'Stop! you will make it worse by bettering it—
you will spoil the whole thing!' 'What I have done,' replied
the artist, panting with exertion, 'you have seen; what I
have got hold of and what I mean to carry out to the very
end you cannot see.'

I have no doubt that Clairon goes through just the same
struggles as Le Quesnoy in her first attempts at a part; but
once the struggle is over, once she has reached the height
she has given to her spectre, she has herself well in hand, she
repeats her efforts without emotion. As it will happen in
dreams, her head touches the clouds, her hands stretch to
grasp the horizon on both sides; she is the informing soul of
a huge figure, which is her outward casing, and in which her
efforts have enclosed her. As she lies careless and still on a
sofa with folded arms and closed eyes she can, following
her memory's dream, hear herself, see herself, judge herself,
and judge also the effects she will produce. In such a vision
she has a double personality; that of the little Clairon and of
the great Agrippina.

---

the Opera; then, in September 1743, at the Français, where she took every one by
surprise by choosing to play Phèdre, and playing it with complete success. For
twenty years from this time onwards she remained queen of the French stage. She
left the stage in 1788 and died in 1803.
[6] This is a mistake of Diderot's. The person referred to is Duquesnoy the Belgian
sculptor.

The Second. According to you the likest thing to an actor, whether on the boards or at his private studies, is a group of children who play at ghosts in a graveyard at dead of night, armed with a white sheet on the end of a broomstick, and fending forth from its shelter hollow groans to frighten wayfarers.

The First. Just so, indeed. Now with Dumesnil[7] it is a different matter: she is not like Clairon. She comes on the stage without knowing what she is going to say; half the time she does not know what she is saying: but she has one sublime moment. And pray, why should the actor be different from the poet, the painter, the orator, the musician? It is not in the stress of the first burst that characteristic traits come out; it is in moments of stillness and self-command; in moments entirely unexpected. Who can tell whence these traits have their being? They are a sort of inspiration. They come when the man of genius is hovering between nature and his sketch of it, and keeping a watchful eye on both. The beauty of inspiration, the chance hits of which his work is full, and of which the sudden appearance startles himself, have an importance, a success, a sureness very different from that belonging to the first fling. Cool reflection must bring the fury of enthusiasm to its bearings.

The extravagant creature who loses his self-control has no hold on us; this is gained by the man who is self-controlled. The great poets, especially the great dramatic poets, keep a keen watch on what is going on, both in the physical and the moral world.

The Second. The two are the same.

The First. They dart on everything which strikes their imagination; they make, as it were, a collection of such things. And from these collections, made all unconsciously, issue the grandest achievements of their work.

Your fiery, extravagant, sensitive fellow, is for ever on the boards; he acts the play, but he gets nothing out of it. It is in him that the man of genius finds his model. Great poets, great actors, and, I may add, all great copyists of Nature, in

[7] Mlle. Dumesnil was born in 1713—not, as M. de Manne says in his *La Troupe de Voltaire*, in 1711. She came to Paris from the provinces in 1737, and made her first appearance at the Français in the same year as Clytemnestra in *Iphigénie en Aulide*. She was admitted the following year, left the stage in 1776, and died in year XI. of the Republic.

whatever art, beings gifted with fine imagination, with broad judgment, with exquisite tact, with a sure touch of taste, are the least sensitive of all creatures. They are too apt for too many things, too busy with observing, considering, and reproducing, to have their inmost hearts affected with any liveliness. To me such an one always has his portfolio spread before him and his pencil in his fingers.

It is we who feel; it is they who watch, study, and give us the result.[8] And then . . . well, why should I not say it? Sensibility is by no means the distinguishing mark of a great genius. He will have, let us say, an abstract love of justice, but he will not be moved to temper it with mercy. It is the head, not the heart, which works in and for him. Let some unforeseen opportunity arise, the man of sensibility will lose it; he will never be a great king, a great minister, a great commander, a great advocate, a great physician. Fill the front of a theatre with tearful creatures, but I will none of them on the boards. Think of women, again. They are miles beyond us in sensibility; there is no sort of comparison between their passion and ours. But as much as we are below them in action, so much are they below us in imitation. If a man who is really manly drops a tear, it touches us more nearly than a storm of weeping from a woman. In the great play, the play of the world, the play to which I am constantly recurring, the stage is held by the fiery souls, and the pit is filled with men of genius. The actors are in other words madmen; the spectators, whose business it is to paint their madness, are sages. And it is they who discern with a ready eye the absurdity of the motley crowd, who reproduce it for you, and who make you laugh both at the unhappy models who have bored you to death and at yourself. It is they who watch you, and who give you the mirth-moving picture of the tiresome wretch and of your own anguish in his clutches.[9]

You may prove this to demonstration, and a great actor will decline to acknowledge it; it is his own secret. A middling actor or a novice is sure to contradict you flatly; and of some others it may be said that they believe they feel, just as it has been said of some pious people that they believe

[8] This was so with Goethe, to take an instance; and not improbably so with Shakespeare.

[9] Cf. inter alia Horace, Satires, Book I., Sat. IX.; and Les Fâcheux.

they believe; and that without faith in the one case and without sensibility in the other there is no health.

This is all very well, you may reply; but what of these touching and sorrowful accents that are drawn from the very depth of a mother's heart and that shake her whole being? Are these not the result of true feeling? are these not the very inspiration of despair? Most certainly not. The proof is that they are all planned; that they are part of a system of declamation; that, raised or lowered by the twentieth part of a quarter of a tone, they would ring false; that they are in subjection to a law of unity; that, as in harmony, they are arranged in chords and in discords; that laborious study is needed to give them completeness; that they are the elements necessary to the solving of a given problem; that, to hit the right mark once, they have been practised a hundred times; and that, despite all this practice, they are yet found wanting. Look you, before he cries *'Zaïre vous pleurez,'* or *'Vous y serez ma fille,'* the actor has listened over and over again to his own voice. At the very moment when he touches your heart he is listening to his own voice; his talent depends not, as you think, upon feeling, but upon rendering so exactly the outward signs of feeling, that you fall into the trap. He has rehearsed to himself every note of his passion. He has learnt before a mirror every particle of his despair. He knows exactly when he must produce his handkerchief and shed tears; and you will see him weep at the word, at the syllable, he has chosen, not a second sooner or later. The broken voice, the half-uttered words, the stifled or prolonged notes of agony, the trembling limbs, the faintings, the bursts of fury—all this is pure mimicry, lessons carefully learned, the grimacing of sorrow, the magnificent aping which the actor remembers long after his first study of it, of which he was perfectly conscious when he first put it before the public, and which leaves him, luckily for the poet, the spectator, and himself, a full freedom of mind. Like other gymnastics, it taxes only his bodily strength. He puts off the sock or the buskin; his voice is gone; he is tired; he changes his dress, or he goes to bed; and he feels neither trouble, nor sorrow, nor depression, nor weariness of soul. All these emotions he has given to you. The actor is tired, you are unhappy; he has had exertion without feeling, you feeling without exertion. Were it otherwise the player's lot would be the most wretched on earth: but he is not the person he represents; he plays it, and plays it so well that you think he is the person; the deception is all on your side; he knows well enough that he is not the person.

For diverse modes of feeling arranged in concert to obtain the greatest effect, scored orchestrally, played *piano* and played *forte,* harmonised to make an individual effect—all that to me is food for laughter. I hold to my point, and I tell you this: 'Extreme sensibility makes middling actors; middling sensibility makes the ruck of bad actors; in complete absence of sensibility is the possibility of a sublime actor.' The player's tears come from his brain, the sensitive being's from his heart; the sensitive being's soul gives unmeasured trouble to his brain; the player's brain gives sometimes a touch of trouble to his soul: he weeps as might weep an unbelieving priest preaching of the Passion; as a seducer might weep at the feet of a woman whom he does not love, but on whom he would impose; like a beggar in the street or at the door of a church—a beggar who substitutes insult for vain appeal; or like a courtesan who has no heart, and who abandons herself in your arms.

Have you ever thought on the difference between the tears raised by a tragedy of real life and those raised by a touching narrative? You hear a fine piece of recitation; by little and little your thoughts are involved, your heart is touched, and your tears flow. With the tragedy of real life the thing, the feeling and the effect, are all one; your heart is reached at once, you utter a cry, your head swims, and the tears flow. These tears come of a sudden, the others by degrees. And here is the superiority of a true effect of nature over a well-planned scene. It does at one stroke what the scene leads up to by degrees, but it is far more difficult to reproduce its effect; one incident ill given would shatter it. Accents are more easily mimicked than actions, but actions go straighter to the mark. This is the basis of a canon to which I believe there is no exception. If you would avoid coldness you must complete your effect by action and not by talk.

So, then, have you no objection to make? Ah! I see! You give a recitation in a drawing-room; your feelings are stirred; your voice fails you; you burst into tears. You have, as you

say, felt, and felt deeply. Quite so; but had you made up
your mind to that? Not at all. Yet you were carried away,
you surprised and touched your hearers, you made a great
hit. All this is true enough. But now transfer your easy tone,
your simple expression, your every-day bearing, to the stage,
and, I assure you, you will be paltry and weak. You may cry
to your heart's content, and the audience will only laugh. It
will be the tragedy outside a booth at a fair.[10] Do you suppose that the dialogue of Corneille, of Racine, of Voltaire, or,
let me add, of Shakespeare, can be given with your ordinary
voice and with your fireside tone? No; not a bit more than
you would tell a fireside story with the open-mouthed emphasis fit for the boards.

The Second. Perhaps Racine and Corneille, great names
as they are, did nothing of account.

The First. Oh, blasphemy! Who could dare to say it? Who
to endorse it? The merest word Corneille wrote cannot be
given in everyday tone.

But, to go back, it must have happened to you a hundred
times that at the end of your recitation, in the very midst of
the agitation and emotion you have caused in your drawing-
room audience, a fresh guest has entered, and wanted to hear
you again. You find it impossible, you are weary to the soul.
Sensibility, fire, tears, all have left you. Why does not the
actor feel the same exhaustion? Because there is a world of
difference between the interests excited by a flattering tale
and by your fellow-man's misfortune. Are you Cinna? Have
you ever been Cleopatra, Merope, Agrippina? Are these same
personages on the stage ever historical personages? Not at
all. They are the vain images of poetry. No, nor even that.
They are the phantoms fashioned from this or that poet's
special fantasy. They are well enough on the stage, these
hippogriffs, so to call them, with their actions, their bearing,
their intonations. They would make but a sorry figure in
history; they would raise laughter in society. People would
whisper to each other, 'Is this fellow mad? Where in the
world does this Don Quixote come from? Who is the in-

---

[10] *'Ce ne sera pas une tragédie, ce sera une parade tragique que vous jouerez.'* [It
will be not a tragedy that you enact, but samples of a tragicomedy.]

Parade tragique is the brief sketch of a tale of horror given by strolling players
outside their booth by way of tempting spectators to the fuller performance to be
given inside.

ventor of all this stuff? In what world do people talk like this?'

The Second. And why are they not intolerable on the stage?

The First. Because there is such a thing as stage convention. As old a writer as Æschylus laid this down as a formula—it is a protocol three thousand years old.

The Second. And will this protocol go on much longer?

The First. That I cannot tell you. All I know is that one gets further away from it as one gets nearer to one's own time and country. Find me a situation closer to that of Agamemnon in the first scene of *Iphigenia* than that of *Henri IV.*: when, beset by fears only too well founded, he said to those around him, 'They will kill me; there is nothing surer; they will kill me!' Suppose that great man, that superb and hapless monarch, troubled in the night-watches with this deadly presentiment, got up and knocked at the door of Sully, his minister and friend—is there, think you, a poet foolish enough to make Henri say—

'Oui, c'est Henri, s'est ton roi qui t'éveille;
Viens, reconnais la voix qui frappe ton oreille?'
(Ay, it is Agamemnon [Henri], 'tis thy King
That wakes thee; his the voice that strikes thine ear.)

Or to make Sully reply—

'C'est vous-même, seigneur? Quel important besoin
Vous a fait devancer l'aurore de si loin?
A peine un faible jour vous éclaire et me guide,
Vos yeux seuls et les miens sont ouverts. . . .' [11]
[Is't thou indeed, my lord? What grave concern
Has made thee leave thy couch before the dawn?
A feeble light scarce lets me see thy face,
No eyes but ours are open yet in Aulis. . . .]

The Second. Perhaps Agamemnon really talked like that.

[11] There were believers in poets quite foolish enough for this long after Diderot's time. It was precisely because this sort of diction was dropped for a more natural one in *Hernani* that the play, from its first scene, raised such a storm among the classicists—as he who will may read in the pages of Théophile Gautier. The lines quoted are from the speeches of Agamemnon and Arcas in the opening of Racine's *Iphigénie*, the name Henri being substituted for Agamemnon. The English version is from *The Dramatic Works of Jean Racine: A Metrical English Version*, by Robert Bruce Boswell (London: George Bell and Sons, 1901).

The First. No more than Henri IV. did. Homer talks like that; Racine talks like that; poetry talks like that; and this pompous language can only be used by unfamiliar personages, spoken from poetical lips, with a poetical tone. Reflect a little as to what, in the language of the theatre, is *being true*. Is it showing things as they are in nature? Certainly not. Were it so the true would be the commonplace. What, then, is truth for stage purposes? It is the conforming of action, diction, face, voice, movement, and gesture, to an ideal type invented by the poet, and frequently enhanced by the player. That is the strange part of it. This type not only influences the tone, it alters the actor's very walk and bearing. And hence it is that the player in private and the player on the boards are two personages, so different that one can scarce recognise the player in private. The first time I saw Mlle. Clairon in her own house I exclaimed, by a natural impulse, 'Ah, mademoiselle, I thought you were at least a head taller!'

An unhappy, a really unhappy woman, may weep and fail to touch you; worse than that, some trivial disfigurement in her may incline you to laughter; the accent which is apt to her is to your ears dissonant and vexatious; a movement which is habitual to her makes her grief show ignobly and sulkily to you; almost all the violent passions lend themselves to grimaces which a tasteless artist will copy but too faithfully, and which a great actor will avoid. In the very whirlwind of passion we would have a man preserve his manly dignity. And what is the effect of this heroic effort? To give relief and temperance to sorrow. We would have this heroine fall with a becoming grace, that hero die like a gladiator of old in the midst of the arena to the applause of the circus, with a noble grace, with a fine and picturesque attitude. And who will execute this design of ours? The athlete who is mastered by pain, shattered by his own sensibility, or the athlete who is trained, who has self-control, who, as he breathes his last sigh, remembers the lessons of the gymnasium? Neither the gladiator of old nor the great actor dies as people die in their beds; it is for them to show us another sort of death, a death to move us; and the critical spectator will feel that the bare truth, the unadorned fact, would seem despicable and out of harmony with the poetry of the rest.

Not, mark you, that Nature unadorned has not her moments of sublimity; but I fancy that if there is any one sure to give and preserve their sublimity it is the man who can feel it with his passion and his genius, and reproduce it with complete self-possession.

I will not, however, deny that there is a kind of acquired or factitious sensibility; but if you would like to know what I think about it, I hold it to be nearly as dangerous as natural sensibility. By little and little it leads the actor into mannerism and monotony. It is an element opposed to the variety of a great actor's functions. He must often strip it from him; and it is only a head of iron which can make such a self-abnegation. Besides, it is far better for the ease and success of his study, for the catholicity of his talent and the perfection of his playing, that there should be no need of this strange parting of self from self. Its extreme difficulty, confining each actor to one single line, leads perforce to a numerous company, where every part is ill played; unless, indeed, the natural order of things is reversed, and the pieces are made for the actors. To my thinking the actors, on the contrary, ought to be made for the pieces.[12]

The Second. But if a crowd of people collected in the street by some catastrophe begin of a sudden, and each in his own way, and without any concert, to exhibit a natural sensibility, they will give you a magnificent show, and display you a thousand types, valuable for sculpture, music, and poetry.

The First. True enough. But will this show compare with one which is the result of a pre-arranged plan, with the harmony which the artist will put into it when he transfers it from the public way to his stage or canvas? If you say it will, then I shall make you this answer: What is this boasted magic of art if it only consists in spoiling what both nature and chance have done better than art? Do you deny that one can improve on nature? Have you never, by way of praising a woman, said she is as lovely as one of Raphael's Madonnas? Have you never cried, on seeing a fine landscape, 'It's as good as a description in a novel?' Again, you are talking to me of

[12] Note by the publishers of the small popular edition in Paris:—'Our modern authors have ended in always writing their pieces for this or that actor. Hence the short life which their productions will have.' The practice, I may add, is, unfortunately, by no means unknown in England.

a reality. I am talking to you of an imitation. You are talking to me of a passing moment in Nature. I am talking to you of a work of Art, planned and composed—a work which is built up by degrees, and which lasts. Take now each of these actors; change the scene in the street as you do on the boards, and show me your personages left successively to themselves, two by two or three by three. Leave them to their own swing; make them full masters of their actions; and you will see what a monstrous discord will result. You will get over this by making them rehearse together. Quite so. And then good-bye to their natural sensibility; and so much the better.

A play is like any well-managed association, in which each individual sacrifices himself for the general good and effect. And who will best take the measure of the sacrifice? The enthusiast or the fanatic? Certainly not. In society, the man of judgment; on the stage, the actor whose wits are always about him. Your scene in the street has the same relation to a scene on the stage that a band of savages has to a company of civilised men.

Now is the time to talk to you of the disastrous influence which a middling associate has on a first-rate player. This player's conception is admirable; but he has to give up his ideal type in order to come down to the level of the poor wretch who is playing with him. Then he says farewell to his study and his taste. As happens with talks in the street or at the fireside, the principal speaker lowers his tone to that of his companion. Or if you would like another illustration, take that of whist, where you lose a deal of your own skill if you cannot rely on your partner. More than this, Clairon will tell you, if you ask her, that Le Kain[13] would maliciously make her play badly or inadequately, and that she would avenge herself by getting him hissed. What, then, are two players who mutually support each other? Two per-

[13] Le Kain made his first appearance at the Français in September 1750, as Titus in Voltaire's *Brutus*. His success was gained in spite of natural disadvantages in voice and personal appearance. He owed much to Clairon, but more to unceasing study and application. What helped him in the first instance to please critical taste was that, like Garrick, he was the first to venture on varying the conventional sing-song of declamation. Later he and Clairon reformed the stage costume. Much of interest will be found about him in the lately published pamphlet, *Talma on the Actor's Art*. He was great as a tragedian; good as a comedian. He died in February 1778.

sonages whose types are, in due proportion, either equal, or else in them the subordination demanded by the circumstances, as laid down by the poet, is observed. But for this there would be an excess, either of strength or of weakness; and such a want of harmony as this is avoided more frequently by the strong descending to the weak than by its raising the weak to its own level. And pray, do you know the reason of the numberless rehearsals that go on? They are to strike the balance between the different talents of the actors, so as to establish a general unity in the playing. When the vanity of an individual interferes with this balance the result is to injure the effect and to spoil your enjoyment; for it is seldom that the excellence of one actor can atone for the mediocrity, which it brings into relief, of his companions. I have known a great actor suffer from his temperament in this way. The stupid public said he was extravagant, instead of discerning that his associate was inadequate.

Come, you are a poet; you have a piece for the stage; and I leave you to choose between actors with the soundest judgments and the coolest heads and actors of sensibility. But before you make up your mind let me ask you one question. What is the time of life for a great actor? The age when one is full of fire, when the blood boils in the veins, when the slightest check troubles one to the soul, when the wit blazes at the veriest spark? I fancy not. The man whom Nature stamps an actor does not reach his topmost height until he has had a long experience, until the fury of the passions is subdued, until the head is cool and the heart under control. The best wine is harsh and crude in its fermenting. It is by long lying in the cask that it grows generous. Cicero, Seneca, and Plutarch, I take to represent the three ages of composition in men. Cicero is often but a blaze of straw, pretty to look at; Seneca a fire of vine-branches, hurtful to look at; but when I stir old Plutarch's ashes I come upon the great coals of a fire that gives me a gentle warmth.

Baron, when sixty years old, played the Earl of Essex, Xiphares, Britannicus, and played them well. Gaussin,[14] at fifty, bewitched her audiences in *L'Oracle et la Pupille*.

[14] Mlle. Gaussin was the daughter of Antoine Gaussin, Baron's coachman, and Jeanne Pollet, cook to Adrienne Lecouvreur. She made her *début* at the Comédie Française in 1731. She appeared in *Zaïre* and in *Alzire*, but she is best remembered in the part of Inès in *Inès de Castro*, a tragedy by the innovator La Motte.

The Second. She cannot have looked the part.

The First. No; and here you hit perhaps an insurmountable obstacle to getting a perfect stage performance. For that your player must have trod the boards many years, and sometimes a part calls for the blush of youth.[15] If there ever has been an actress who at seventeen could play Monimia, Dido, Pulcheria, Hermione, why then that is a miracle which will not be repeated.[16] However, an old player does not become ridiculous until his strength has quite left him, or until his fine art will not avail to outweigh the contrast between his real and his supposed age. As on the satge, so is it in the world, where people never fall foul of a woman's conduct unless she has neither talent nor other kind of merit enough to veil her failing.

In our days Clairon and Molé[17] played when they first

which was much laughed at at the time, though it made even the Regent weep. Mlle. Clairon thus described her sister-comédienne: 'Mlle. Gaussin had the loveliest head, the most touching voice. She had a noble presence, and all her movements had a childish grace which was irresistible; but she was Mlle. Gaussin in everything.' After a brilliant career, on the stage and in the world, this once famous actress, who counted statesmen, poets, and philosophers among her lovers, married an opera-dancer, who ill-treated her, and she died without a friend in 1767.

[15] Baron, when eighty years old, came back to the stage to play Rodrigue in the *Cid*. All went well until he had to say,—

'Je suis jeune, il est vrai, mais aux âmes bien nées
La valeur n'attend pas le nombre des années.'
[My years are few, but, Count, in high-born souls
Valor and youth full oft united are.

The Cid, translated into English blank verse by Florence Kendrick Cooper (D. Appleton & Co., 1901)]

The pit laughed once and twice. Baron came to the front and said: 'Gentlemen, I am about to begin again a third time; but I warn you, that if any one laughs I shall leave the stage and never come back again.' After this all went well, except that when he knelt to Chimène he could not get up again.

[16] This is an allusion to Mlle. Raucourt's first appearances in 1772. She was, as a matter of fact, nineteen at the time. The publishers of the French popular edition have this note on the passage: 'The instance of Rachel has given a triumphant lie to Diderot's assertion.' It may, however, be supposed that the annotators did not mean that Rachel had nothing of her art to learn at seventeen. In our own times, and in England, a very distinguished actor was in the habit of saying that no man could possibly play Romeo until he was past fifty, and that then he might perhaps be a little old for the part.

[17] Molé, born in Paris in November 1734, made his first appearance at the Français in 1754. He was an example, like Mrs. Siddons, of a player who triumphed completely over a first failure. Collé wrote of him in his *Journal*, judging him from his first appearances, that he had a good appearance and nothing more; no passion, no art, no ease, no grace. He was not admitted at first, but he went into the provinces, came back in 1760, and appeared successfully as Andronicus in Campistron's tragedy. From that date his success was assured. He was extremely versatile, and there is a story of him which tells for 'the man with the paradox.' Lemercier relates how he was carried away by Molé's acting, and rushed to congratulate him. Molé replied, 'I was not pleased with myself. I let myself go too much; I felt the situation too deeply; I became the personage instead of the actor

appeared like automata; afterwards they became fine players.[18] Why was this? Did they, think you, acquire more soul, sensibility, heart, in proportion as they grew older?

It is not long since, after ten years' absence from the stage, Clairon consented to a reappearance. If she played but moderately, was it that she had lost her soul, her sensibility, her heart? Not at all; what she had lost was the memory of her methods. I appeal to the future to confirm me.

The Second. What! you believe she will come back to the stage?

The First. Or die of boredom. What substitute is there for the great passions and the house's plaudits?

If such or such an actor or actress were as deeply moved as people suppose, tell me if the one would think of casting an eye round the boxes, the other of smiling to some one at the wing, and, as almost all of them do, speaking straight to the pit; and if the call-boy would have to go to the greenroom and interrupt a third player in a hearty fit of laughter by telling him that it's time to go and stab himself?

Come, I will sketch you a scene between an actor and his wife who detested each other; a scene of tender and passionate love; a scene publicly played on the boards, just as I am going to rehearse it, or maybe a trifle better; a scene in which both players surpassed themselves—in which they excited continual bursts of applause from pit and boxes; a scene interrupted half-a-score of times with our clapping of hands and exclamations of delight. Their triumph was won in the third scene of the fourth act of Molière's *Le Dépit Amoureux*. The actor plays Eraste, Lucile's lover. The actor's wife plays Lucile, Eraste's adored.

THE ACTOR

Non, non, ne croyez pas, madame,
Que je revienne encor vous parler de ma flamme.
   (THE ACTRESS. *I just advise you.*)

---

playing it; I lost my self-control. I was true to Nature as I might be in private; the perspective of the stage demands something different. The piece is to be played again in a few days; come and see it then.' Lemercier went, and just before the great scene Molé turned to him and said, 'Now I have got my self-control: wait and see.' Never, Lemercier adds, were art and art's effect more striking. Molé died in 1802.

[18] This was so, as many people well remember, in the case of Signor Mario, who, beginning by being a stick, ended by being so fine an actor that even without his exquisite voice and method of singing he would have been a great artist.

C'en est fait.
>   (*I hope so.*)
>   Je me veux guérir et connais bien,
Ce que de votre cœur a possédé le mien.
>   (*More than you deserved.*)
Un courroux si constant pour l'ombre d'une offense,
>   (*You offend me! You flatter yourself.*)
M'a trop bien éclairci de votre indifférence:
Et je dois vous montrer que les traits du mépris,
>   (*Yes, the deepest contempt.*)
Sont sensibles surtout aux généreux esprits
>   (*Yes, to generous minds.*)
Je l'avouerai, mes yeux observaient dans les vôtres,
Des charmes qu'ils n'ont point trouvés dans tous les autres.
>   (*Not for want of looking.*)
Et le ravissement où j'étais de mes fers
Les aurait préférés à des sceptres offerts.
>   (*You have made a better bargain.*)
Je vivais tout en vous;
>   (*That's not the case; you tell a lie.*)
>   Et je l'avouerai même
Peut-être qu'après tout j'aurai quoique outragé,
Assez de peine encore à m'en voir dégagé.
>   (*That would be a bore.*)
Possible que malgré la cure qu'elle essaie
Mon âme saignera longtemps de cette plaie.
>   (*Don't be afraid—mortification has set in.*)
Et qu'affranchi d'un joug qui faisait tout mon bien,
Il faudra me résoudre à n'aimer jamais rien.
>   (*You'll find a way out of that.*)
Mais enfin il n'importe; et puisque votre haine,
Chasse un cœur tant de fois que l'amour vous ramène,
C'est la dernière ici des importunités
Que vous aurez jamais de mes vœux rebutés.

The Actress

Vous pouvez faire aux miens la grâce tout entière,
Monsieur, et m'épargner encor cette dernière.
>   (The Actor. *Sweetheart, you are an insolent baggage, and
>   you shall live to repent this.*)

The Actor

Eh bien, madame! eh bien! ils seront satisfaits,

Je romps avecque vous, et j'y romps pour jamais,
Puisque vous le voulez, que je perde la vie,
Lorsque de vous parler je reprendrai l'envie.

THE ACTRESS

Tant mieux, c'est m'obliger.

THE ACTOR

                    Non, non, n'ayez pas peur
(THE ACTRESS. *Afraid of you? Not I!*)
Que je fausse parole! Eussé-je un faible cœur,
Jusques à n'en pouvoir effacer votre image,
Croyez que vous n'aurez jamais cet avantage
          (*Ill-luck, you mean.*)
De me voir revenir.

THE ACTRESS

                    Ce serait bien en vain.
(THE ACTOR. *My darling, you are an arrant wretch; but
I'll teach you to behave.*)

THE ACTOR

Moi-même de cent coups je percerais mon sein.
          (THE ACTRESS. *I wish to Heaven you would!*)
Si j'avais jamais fait cette bassesse insigne.
          (*Why not, after so many others?*)
De vous revoir après ce traitement indigne.

THE ACTRESS

Soit; n'en parlons donc plus.[19]

---

[19] The subjoined rendering is from *The Dramatic Works of Molière*, rendered into English by Henri Van Laun (New York: A. W. Lovering, publisher, n. d.). The asterisks indicate the points at which Diderot places the actress's interjections.

Eraste. No, no, madam, do not think that I have come to speak to you again of my passion; * it is all over; * I am resolved to cure myself. I know how little share I have in your heart. * A resentment kept up so long for a slight offence * shows me your indifference but too plainly, and I must tell you that contempt, * above all things, wounds a lofty mind. * I confess I saw in you charms which I never found in any other; * the delight I took in my chains would have made me prefer them to sceptres, had they been offered to me. * . . . My life was centred in you; * I will even own that, though I am insulted, I shall still perhaps have difficulty enough to free myself. * Maybe, notwithstanding the cure I am attempting, my heart may for a long time smart with this wound. * Freed from a yoke which I was happy to bend under, I shall take a resolution never to love again. * But no matter, since your hatred repulses a heart which love brings back to you, this is the last time you shall ever be troubled by the man you so much despise.

And so on, and so on. After this double scene—one of love, the other of marriage—as Eraste led his adored Lucile to the wing he squeezed her arm so hard as to tear his sweet wife's flesh, and answered her complaints with the bitterest insults.

The Second. If I had heard these two simultaneous scenes I don't think I should ever have set foot in a playhouse again.

The First. If you think this actor and actress were moved, let me ask you, was it in the lovers' scene, or the husband and wife's scene, or both? Now listen to another scene between the same actress and another player—her lover. While he is speaking his lines the actress says of her husband, *'He is a brute. He called me . . . I cannot repeat what he called me.'*

While she, in turn, gives her lines, her lover replies, *'Aren't you accustomed to it by this time?'*

And so on from speech to speech. 'Do we sup together to-night?' 'By all means; but how can we escape observation?' 'That you must manage.' 'If he finds out?' 'It will make no odds; and we shall have a quiet evening.' 'Whom shall we ask?' 'Whom you like.' 'The Chevalier, to begin with; he is our mainstay.' 'Talking of him, do you know I could easily get up a jealousy of him?' 'And I could as easily give you cause for it.'

Thus, then, these sensitive creatures seemed to you to be heart and soul in the speeches spoken out loud, which you heard, while really they were immersed in the speeches spoken under their breath, which you did not hear. You exclaimed to yourself, 'It must be admitted that she is a charming actress; no one listens so well as she does; and she plays with an intelligence, a grace, a conviction, a fine touch, a

---

Lucile. You might have made the favour complete, sir, and spared me also this last trouble. *

Eraste. Very well, madam, very well, you shall be satisfied. I here break off all acquaintance with you, and break it off for ever, since you wish it; may I lose my life if ever again I desire to converse with you!

Lucile. So much the better, you will oblige me.

Eraste. No, no, do not be afraid that I shall break my word! * For, though my heart may be weak enough not to be able to efface your image, be assured you shall never have the pleasure of seeing me return. *

Lucile. You may save yourself the trouble. *

Eraste. I would pierce my breast a hundred times * should I ever be so mean as to see you again, after this unworthy treatment. *

Lucile. Be it so; let us talk no more about it.

sensibility, by no means common.' I meanwhile laughed at your exclamations.

Well, this actress plays her husband false with another actor, plays this other actor false with the Chevalier, and plays the Chevalier false with yet another person, with whom the Chevalier catches her. The Chevalier plots a mighty vengeance. He takes his place in the lowest part of the stage-seats[20] (the Comte de Lauraguais had not then rid our stage of this arrangement). Stationed thus he looked forward to disconcerting the faithless wretch by his presence, and by his contemptuous looks to completely upsetting her, and getting her hooted by the pit. The piece begins; the traitress appears; she sees the Chevalier, and without any disturbance to her acting she says to him, with a smile, 'Ah! silly fellow, making a fuss for nothing!' The Chevalier smiles in his turn, and she goes on: 'You are coming to-night?' He makes no answer, and she continues: 'Let us make an end of this foolish quarrel; and do you order up your carriage.' And do you know in what scene she put in all this? It was in one of the most touching scenes of La Chaussée,[21] a scene in which the actress was convulsed with sobs and made us drop scalding tears. This startles you; yet it is an exact statement of fact.

The Second. It's enough to sicken one of the stage.

The First. And why, pray? If this kind of people could not achieve such feats, what business would they have on the stage? Now I will tell you a thing I have actually seen.

Garrick[22] will put his head between two folding-doors, and in the course of five or six seconds his expression will

20 'Aux balcons, sur les gradins les plus bas.' The meaning of the phrase may be best explained by the following quotation from Alfred de Musset's essay on Tragedy, written in 1838:—'How is it that the tragedies of Racine, fine as they are, appear, as it must be confessed they do, cold and formal, like stately statues half vivified? It is because, in 1759, the Count de Lauraguais procured the removal of seats for the audience from the stage, at a cost of thirty thousand francs. Now-a-days Andromache and Monimia stand alone in their vast peristyles, and have an area of sixty feet to walk about in. There are no more marquises to surround the actress and crack a joke with her after every tirade, to pick up Hermione's fan and criticise Theseus's stockings.'

21 Nivelle de la Chaussée, born in 1692, is looked upon as the founder of *drames* in France. Schlegel, speaking of Voltaire's *Enfant Prodigue* and *Nanine*, says that 'the affecting drama had been before attempted in France by La Chaussée.' Piron characteristically described La Chaussée's plays as 'Les Homélies du Révérend Père La Chaussée.' Among his best plays are *Le Préjugé à la Mode* (to which Mlle. Quinault is said to have contributed an act), *Mélanide*, and *La Gouvernante*. La Chaussée died in 1754.

22 Garrick spent six months in Paris in the winter of 1764-5, when Diderot made his acquaintance.

change successively from wild delight to temperate pleasure, from this to tranquillity, from tranquillity to surprise, from surprise to blank astonishment, from that to sorrow, from sorrow to the air of one overwhelmed, from that to fright, from fright to horror, from horror to despair, and thence he will go up again to the point from which he started. Can his soul have experienced all these feelings, and played this kind of scale in concert with his face? I don't believe it; nor do you. If you ask this famous man, who in himself is as well worth a visit to England as the ruins of Rome are worth a visit to Italy; if you ask him, I say, for the scene of the Pastrycook's Boy he will play it for you; if you asked him directly afterwards for the great scene in *Hamlet* he would play it for you. He was as ready to cry over the tarts in the gutter as to follow the course of the air-drawn dagger.[23] Can one laugh or cry at will? One shall make a show of doing so as well or ill as one can, and the completeness of the illusion varies as one is or is not Garrick.

I play the fool in this sort sometimes, and with success enough to take in men who have knocked about the world a great deal. When I go distracted over the pretended death of my sister in the scene with the Norman lawyer; when in the scene with the First Clerk of the Admiralty I confess to the paternity of the child of a captain's wife; I seem exactly as if I suffered grief and shame: but do I suffer either? Not a bit more now that the thing is in definite stage shape than originally in private company, where I invented these two parts before putting them into a stage play.[24] What, then, is a great actor? A man who, having learnt the words set down for him by the author, fools you thoroughly, whether in tragedy or comedy.

Sedaine produces the *Philosophe sans le Savoir*. I took more interest in the piece's success than he did; envy of

[23] Here is an odd slip on the part of Diderot, who seems to have mixed up Hamlet with Macbeth, and to have left the mistake uncorrected.

[24] This refers to the *Plan d'un Divertissement Domestique*, to *La Pièce et le Prologue*, and to the final form in which Diderot put the ideas of the rough sketch and the little piece, that final form being the play, *Est-il Bon, est-il Méchant?* The words are a close description of the part of M. Hardouin, in which Diderot sketched his own character. Baudelaire and M. Champfleury tried, many years ago, to get the play acted, the one at the Gaîté, the other at the Théâtre Français. It seems obvious from the text that Diderot, before either *La Pièce et le Prologue* or *Est-il Bon, est-il Méchant?* was written, was in the habit, as many people are now-a-days, of giving little dramatic sketches in private life, and that he himself played M. Hardouin in *Est-il Bon, est-il Méchant?* in private theatricals.

others' talents is not among my vices; I have enough indeed without it. I may call to witness all my brothers in literature, if, whenever they have deigned to consult me as to their work, I have not done all I could to give a fitting answer to this high mark of esteem. The *Philosophe sans le Savoir* trembles in the balance at the first and second performances, and I am very sorry for it; at the third it goes like wildfire, and I am delighted. The next morning I jump into a coach and rush to find Sedaine. It was winter and horribly cold, but I went everywhere where I could hope to find him. I am told he is in the depths of the Faubourg St. Antoine, and my driver takes me there. I rush up to him, I throw my arms round his neck, my voice fails me, and tears run down my cheeks. There you have the man of sensibility, the middling man. Sedaine, reserved and still, looks at me and says, 'Ah! Monsieur Diderot, you are splendid!' There you have the man of observation—the man of genius.

I told this story one day at table in the house of a man whose high talents marked him for the greatest place in the State—in the house of M. Necker.[25] There were many men of letters there; amongst them Marmontel, who is my friend as I am his. He said to me with an ironical air, 'Then, if Voltaire is overcome by the mere narrative of a pathetic incident, and Sedaine is undisturbed by the sight of a friend in tears, Voltaire is the ordinary man and Sedaine the man of genius.' This apostrophe put me out, and reduced me to silence, because the man of sensibility, like me, is wrapped up in the objection to his argument, loses his head, and does not find his answer until he is leaving the house. A cold and self-possessed person might have replied to Marmontel, 'Your observation would come better from other lips than yours, for you feel no more than Sedaine, and you too turn out fine work. You, being in the same line with him, might have left it to some one else to be an impartial judge of his talent. But, without preferring Sedaine to Voltaire, or Voltaire to Sedaine, can you tell me what would have come out of the brains of the author of the *Philosophe sans le Savoir,* of the *Déserteur,* and of *Paris Sauvé,* if, instead of passing thirty-five years of

---

[25] Necker was not Director-General of Finance till 1777. M. Assézat, the admirable editor of the *Œuvres complètes de Diderot,* points out that the reference proves that *Le Paradoxe sur le Comédien,* written in 1773, must have been afterwards retouched. It was not published until 1830.

his life in damping plaster and cutting stone, he had spent all this time, like Voltaire, like you and me, in reading and thinking on Homer, Virgil, Tasso, Cicero, Demosthenes, and Tacitus? We could never learn to see things as he does; he might have learnt to tell them as we do. I look upon him as one of the latest posterity of Shakespeare; of Shakespeare, whom I shall compare neither to the Apollo Belvedere nor to the Gladiator, nor to Antinous, nor to the Farnese Hercules, but rather to the Saint Christopher in Notre Dame—a shapeless Colossus, coarsely sculptured, if you will. Yet we might all walk between his legs and never a head reach to his thighs.'

Now here is another instance of a man reduced at one moment to flat stupidity by sensibility, and the next rising to sublimity by the self-possession following the stifling of his sensibility.

A man of letters, whose name I will hold back, had fallen into great poverty.[26] He had a wealthy brother, a theologian. I asked the poor brother why the rich one did not help him. 'Because,' he replied, 'he thinks very ill of me.' I obtained his leave to go and see the theologian. I went, was announced, and told the theologian I had come to talk about his brother. He took me by the hand, made me sit down, and then pointed out that a man of sense takes care to know the client whose case he takes up. Then he said, with some liveliness, 'Do you know my brother?' 'I think so.' 'Do you know his conduct to me?' 'I think so.' 'You do? Then you know . . .' and herewith my theologian sets off to tell me, with astonishing rapidity and energy, a whole chain of infamies, the one more revolting than the other. My senses feel confused; I am overwhelmed; I lack courage to plead for so vile a wretch as is presented to my view. Luckily the theologian, growing prolix in his philippic, gave me time to recover. By degrees the man of sensibility disappeared, and made way for the man of eloquence; for I may venture to say that on this occasion I was eloquent. 'Sir,' said I coldly to the theologian, 'your brother has done worse than this, and I admire you for concealing the worst of his infamies.' 'I conceal nothing.' 'To all you have told me you might have

---

[26] This is the recital of an actual incident. Mme. de Vandeul in her *Memoirs* gives the names and some additional circumstances.

added that one night, as you left your house to go to matins, he caught you by the throat, and drawing a dagger from beneath his dress was about to plunge it in your bosom.' 'He is quite capable of it; but I have not accused him of it because he never did it.' Then rising suddenly, and fixing a firm, stern look on my theologian, I cried in accents of thunder, and with all the force and emphasis indignation can give, 'And had he done it, would that be a reason for refusing your brother bread?' The theologian, overborne, overwhelmed, confounded, held his peace, walked about the room, came back to me, and granted me an annual allowance for his brother.

Is it at the moment when you have just lost your friend or your adored one that you set to work at a poem on your loss? No! ill for him who at such a moment takes pleasure in his talent. It is when the storm of sorrow is over, when the extreme of sensibility is dulled, when the event is far behind us, when the soul is calm, that one remembers one's eclipsed happiness, that one is capable of appreciating one's loss, that memory and imagination unite, one to retrace the other to accentuate, the delights of a past time: then it is that one regains self-possession and expression. One writes of one's falling tears, but they do not fall while one is hunting a strong epithet that always escapes one; one writes of one's falling tears, but they do not fall while one is employed in polishing one's verse; or if the tears do flow the pen drops from the hand: one falls to feeling, and one ceases writing.

Again, it is with intense pleasure as with intense pain—both are dumb. A tender-hearted and sensitive man sees again a friend he has missed during a long absence; the friend makes an unexpected reappearance, and the other's heart is touched; he rushes to him, he embraces him, he would speak, but cannot; he stammers and trips over his words; he says he knows not what, he does not hear the answer: if he could see that the delight is not mutual, how hurt he would be! Judge, this picture being true, how untrue are the stage meetings, where both friends are so full of intelligence and self-control. What could I not say to you of the insipid and eloquent disputes as to who is to die, or rather who is not to die, but that this text, on which I should enlarge for ever, would take us far from our subject? Enough has been said for men of true and fine taste; what I could add would teach nothing to the rest. Now, who is to come to the rescue of these absurdities so common on the stage? The actor? and what actor?

The circumstances in which sensibility is as hurtful in society as on the stage are a thousand to one. Take two lovers, both of whom have their declaration to make. Who will come out of it best? Not I, I promise you. I remember that I approached the beloved object with fear and trembling; my heart beat, my ideas grew confused, my voice failed me, I mangled all I said; I cried *yes* for *no;* I made a thousand blunders; I was illimitably inept; I was absurd from top to toe, and the more I saw it, the more absurd I became. Meanwhile, under my very eyes, a gay rival, light-hearted and agreeable, master of himself, pleased with himself, losing no opportunity for the finest flattery, made himself entertaining and agreeable, enjoyed himself; he implored the touch of a hand which was at once given him, he sometimes caught it without asking leave, he kissed it once and again. I the while, alone in a corner, avoiding a sight which irritated me, stifling my sighs, cracking my fingers with grasping my wrists, plunged in melancholy, covered with a cold sweat, I could neither show nor conceal my vexation. People say of love that it robs witty men of their wit, and gives it to those who had none before: in other words, makes some people sensitive and stupid, others cold and adventurous.

The man of sensibility obeys the impulse of Nature, and gives nothing more or less than the cry of his very heart; the moment he moderates or strengthens this cry he is no longer himself, he is an actor.

The great actor watches appearances; the man of sensibility is his model; he thinks over him, and discovers by after-reflection what it will be best to add or cut away. And so from mere argument he goes to action.

At the first performance of *Inès de Castro,* and at the point where the children appear, the pit fell to laughing. Duclos,[27] who was playing Inez, was angered, and cried to

27 Mlle. Duclos was born in 1670. Her first appearances were made, without much success, on the lyric stage at the Royal Academy of Music in Paris. In October 1693, she appeared at the Français as Justine in *Geta,* a tragedy by Péchantré. In 1696 she was definitely installed as understudy for Mlle. de Champmeslé in the leading tragic parts. She left the stage in 1733, and died in 1748.

the pit: 'Laugh, you blockheads, at the finest point in the piece!' The pit listened, and was silent; the actress went on with her part, and her tears and the spectators' flowed together. Tell me now, Can one pass and repass in this way from one deep feeling to another, from sorrow to anger, from anger to sorrow? I cannot think it; what I can very well think is, that Duclos's anger was real, her sorrow pretended.

Quinault-Dufresne[28] plays the part of Severus in *Polyeucte*. Sent by the Emperor to harry the Christians, he confides to a friend his real feeling about the calumniated sect. Common sense demanded that this confidence, which might cost him the prince's favour, his honours, his fortune, his liberty, perhaps his life, should be uttered in a low tone. The pit called out, 'Speak louder!' He replied, 'And do you, Sirs, speak less loud!' Had he really been Severus, could he so quickly have again become Quinault? No, I tell you, no. Only the man of self-possession, such as he no doubt had, the exceptional actor, the player who is before all a player, can so drop and again assume his mask.

Lekain-Ninias[29] enters his father's tomb, and there cuts his mother's throat; he comes out with blood-stained hands. He is horror-stricken; his limbs tremble, his eyes roll wildly, his hair stands on end. So does yours to see him; terror seizes on you, you are as lost as he is. However, Lekain-Ninias sees a diamond drop which has fallen from an actress's ear, and pushes it towards the wing with his foot. And this actor feels? Impossible. You will not call him a bad actor? Of course not. What, then, is Lekain-Ninias? A cold man, who is without feeling, but who imitates it excellently. It is all very well for him to cry out, 'Where am I?' I answer, 'Where are you? You know well enough. You

[28] Quinault-Dufresne was born in 1693, and made his first appearance at the Français as Orestes in Crébillon's *Electra*, in October 1712. In the month of December following he became an actor of leading parts, both in tragedy and comedy. He left the stage in March 1741, and died in 1759. One of his great parts on the stage was Le Glorieux, and in private life he was in the habit of strutting into the Café Procope and there enlarging upon his genius and his beauty. He married Mlle. Deseine, and it is told of him that after he left the stage he said to his wife, 'I, Quinault-Dufresne, who have conquered the world in the characters of Cæsar and Alexander, my name, alas, is only known to my parrot!'

[29] That is, of course, Le Kain as Ninias in *Sémiramis*.

are on the boards, and you are in the act of kicking a diamond drop off the stage.'

An actor has a passion for an actress; they come together
by chance in a stage scene of jealousy. If the actor is poor
the scene will be improved; if he is a real player it will lose:
in such a case the fine actor becomes himself, and is no
longer the grand and ideal type of a jealous man that he
has striven for. The proof that if this be so the actor and
actress lower themselves to everyday life is, that if they kept
to their stilts they would laugh in each other's faces; the
bombastic jealousy of tragedy would seem to them a mere
clowning of their own.

The Second. All the same there are truths of Nature.

The First. Yes, as in a statue by a sculptor who has given
a close transcript of a bad model. You may admire the
exactitude, but the whole effect is poor and wretched.

I will go further. A sure way to act in a cramped, mean
style, is to play one's own character. You are, let us say, a
tartufe, a miser, a misanthrope; you may play your part
well enough, but you will not come near what the poet has
done. He has created *the* Tartufe, *the* Miser, *the* Misanthrope.

The Second. And how do you make out the difference
between *a* tartufe and *the* Tartufe?

The First. Billard, the clerk, is a tartufe; Grizel, the abbé,
is a tartufe, but he is not *the* Tartufe. Toinard, the banker,
was a miser, but he was not *the* Miser. *The* Miser, *the* Tartufe, were drawn from the Toinards and Grizels in the
world; they contain their broadest and most marked features,
but there is in them no exact portrait of a given individual;
and that is why the real people don't recognise themselves in
their types. The comedy that depends on 'go,' even the
comedy of character, is an exaggeration. The fun of society
is a light froth, which evaporates on the stage; the fun of the
stage is an edged tool which would cut deep in society. For
imaginary beings we have not the consideration we are
bound to have for real beings.

Satire deals with *a* tartufe; comedy with *the* Tartufe.
Satire attacks the vicious; comedy attacks a vice. If there
had been only one or two *Précieuses ridicules* in the world

they would have afforded matter for a satire, but not for a comedy.

Go to La Grenée,[30] and ask him for a picture of *Painting;* he will think he has done what you want when he has put on his canvas a woman before an easel with her thumb through a palette and a brush in her hand. Ask him for *Philosophy;* he will think he has given it you by producing a woman in careless attire resting her elbow on a desk by lamplight, dishevelled and thoughtful, reading or meditating. Ask him for *Poetry;* he will paint the same woman with a laurel-wreath round her brows and a roll of manuscript in her hand. For *Music,* you shall see the same woman with a lyre instead of the roll. Ask him for *Beauty;* ask the same from a cleverer man than him; and, unless I am much mistaken, he will be persuaded that all you want from his art is a picture of a handsome woman. The same fault is common to your actor and to this painter; and I would say to them, 'Your picture, your acting, are mere portraits of individuals far below the general idea traced by the poet and the ideal type of which I hoped to have a representation. This lady of yours is as handsome as you like; but she is not Beauty. There is the same difference between your work and your model as between your model and the type.'

The Second. But, after all, this ideal type may be a phantom!

The First. No.

The Second. But since it is ideal it is not real; and you cannot understand a thing that is impalpable.

The First. True. But let us take an art, say sculpture, at its beginning. It copied the first model that came to hand. Then it saw that there were better models, and took them for choice. Then it corrected first their obvious, then their less obvious fault, until by dint of long study it arrived at a figure which was no longer nature.

The Second. Why, pray?

The First. Because the development of a machine so complex as the human body cannot be regular. Go to the Tuileries or the Champs Elysées on a fête-day; look at all the women in the walks, and you will not find one in whom the

---

[30] A fashionable painter of the time, whose history, curious as it was, need not here be enlarged upon.

two corners of the mouth are exactly alike. Titian's Danaë
is a portrait; the Love at the foot of the couch is an ideal.
In a picture of Raphael's, which went from M. de Thiers'
collection to Catherine the Second's, St. Joseph is a com-
mon-place man; the Virgin is a real and a beautiful woman;
the infant Christ is an ideal. But if you would like to know
more as to these speculative principles of art I will send
you my *Salons*.

The Second. I have heard the work praised by a man of
fine taste and keen discernment.

The First. M. Suard.

The Second. And by a woman who combines an angel's
purity with the finest taste.

The First. Madame Necker.

The Second. Let us go back to our subject.

The First. By all means; though I would rather sing the
praises of virtue than discuss somewhat idle questions.

The Second. Quinault-Dufresne, a boaster by nature,
played the Boaster[31] splendidly.

The First. You are right; but how do you know that he
was playing his own self? And why should not Nature
have made a boaster very near the line between the fine real
and the fine ideal, the line on which the different schools find
their exercise-ground?

The Second. I do not understand you.

The First. I have explained myself more fully in my
Salons, in which I commend to your notice the passage on
Beauty in general. Meanwhile tell me this: Is Quinault-
Dufresne Orosmanes? No. However, who has taken his
place, or ever will take his place, in this part? Was he the
man for the *Préjugé à la Mode*? No. Yet with how much
truth he played it!

The Second. According to you the great actor is everything and nothing.

The First. Perhaps it is just because he is nothing that he
is before all everything. His own special shape never interferes with the shapes he assumes.

Among all those who have practised the fine and valuable
profession of actors or lay preachers, one of the most sterling
characters, one who showed it the most in his physiognomy,

[31] Le Glorieux.

his tone, his bearing, the brother of the *Diable Boiteux* of Gil Blas, of the *Bachelier de Salamanque,* Montmesnil [32]. . . .

The Second. Son of Le Sage, the father of the illustrious family you have named.

The First. . . . played, with equal success, Aristides in the *Pupille,* Tartufe in the comedy so named, Mascarille in the *Fourberies de Scapin,* the lawyer, or M. Guillaume, in the farce of *Patelin.*

The Second. I have seen him.

The First. And to your astonishment, for all these different parts he had a fitting visage. This did not come by Nature, for Nature had given him but one, his own; the others he drew from Art.

Is there such a thing as artificial sensibility? Consider, sensibility, whether acquired or inborn, is not in place in all characters. What, then, is the quality acquired which makes an actor great in *l'Avare, le Joueur, le Flatteur, le Grondeur, le Médecin malgré lui* (the least sensitive or moral personage yet devised by a poet), *le Bourgeois Gentilhomme, le Malade Imaginaire, le Cœur Imaginaire*—in Nero, in Mithridates, in Atreus, in Phocas, in Sertorius, and in a host of other characters, tragic and comic, where sensibility is diametrically opposed to the spirit of the part? It is the faculty of knowing and imitating all natures. Believe me, we need not multiply causes when one cause accounts for all appearances.

Sometimes the poet feels more deeply than the actor; sometimes, and perhaps oftener, the actor's conception is stronger than the poet's; and there is nothing truer than Voltaire's exclamation, when he heard Clairon in a piece of his, *'Did I really write that?'* Does Clairon know more about it than Voltaire? Anyhow, at that moment the ideal type in the speaking of the part went well beyond the poet's ideal type in the writing of it. But this ideal type was not

---

[32] Montménil, son of the celebrated Le Sage, made his first appearance at the Français in May 1726, as Mascarille in *L'Etourdi.* He gained some success, but his fellow-actors counselled him to work in the provinces. This he did, reappearing in Paris in 1728 as Hector in *Le Joueur.* Thenceforward his success was not doubtful. Montménil, Le Mazurier says, played capitally *L'Avocat Patelin, Turcaret,* the Valet in *Les Bourgeoises à la Mode,* M. Delorme in *Les Trois Cousines,* 'et en général tous les paysans [and uncultivated characters generally].' He died suddenly in September 1743.

Clairon. Where, then, lay her talent? In imagining a mighty shape, and in copying it with genius. She imitated the movement, the action, the gesture, the whole embodiment of a being far greater than herself. She had learnt that Æschines, repeating a speech of Demosthenes, could never reproduce 'the roar of the brute.' He said to his disciples, 'If this touches you, or nearly, what would have been the effect *si audivissetis bestiam mugientem* [had you heard the roaring beast]?' The poet had engendered the monster, Clairon made it roar.

It would be a strange abuse of language to give the name of sensibility to this faculty of reproducing all natures, even ferocious natures. Sensibility, according to the only acceptation yet given of the term, is, as it seems to me, that disposition which accompanies organic weakness, which follows on easy affection of the diaphragm, on vivacity of imagination, on delicacy of nerves, which inclines one to being compassionate, to being horrified, to admiration, to fear, to being upset, to tears, to faintings, to rescues, to flights, to exclamations, to loss of self-control, to being contemptuous, disdainful, to having no clear notion of what is true, good, and fine, to being unjust, to going mad. Multiply souls of sensibility, and you will multiply in the same proportion good and bad actions of every kind, extravagant praise and extravagant blame.

Work, poets, for a nation given to vapours, and sensitive; content yourselves with the tender, harmonious, and touching elegies of Racine; this nation would flee the butcheries of Shakespeare; its feeble spirit cannot stand violent shocks; beware of offering it too vigorous a picture; rehearse to it, if you will,

> 'Le fils tout dégouttant du meurtre de son père,
> Et sa tête à la main, demandant son salaire.'
> [The son all bloodied from the murder of his sire,
> Bearing the severed head and clamant for his hire.]

But go no further. If you dared to say with Homer, 'Whither goest thou, unhappy one? Thou know'st not, then, that it is to me Heaven sends the children of ill-fated fathers; thou wilt not receive thy mother's last embraces; e'en now I see thee stretched on the earth; the birds of prey, grouped round thy corpse, tear out thine eyes, flapping their wings with delight'—If you said this all the women, turning away their heads, would cry, 'Oh! horrible!' . . . And it would be all the worse if this speech, delivered by a great actor, had all the strength of truthful accent.

The Second. I am tempted to interrupt you to ask what you think of the bowl presented to Gabrielle de Vergy,[33] who saw in it her lover's bleeding heart.

The First. I shall answer you that we must be consistent, and if we are revolted at this spectacle neither must we permit Œdipus to show himself with his eyes torn out, while we must drive Philoctetes, tormented by his wound, and expressing his pain with inarticulate cries, off the stage. The ancients had, as I think, an idea of tragedy different from ours; and these ancients—that is the Greeks, that is the Athenians, this fine people, who have left us models in every direction of art unequalled by other nations—Æschylus, I say, Sophocles, Euripides, were not at work for years together to produce the trifling passing impressions which disappear in the gaiety of a supper-party. It was their object to rouse a deep grief for the lot of the ill-fated; it was their object not only to amuse their fellow-citizens but also to make them better. Were they wrong? Were they right? To produce their effect they made the Eumenides rush on the scene, tracking the parricide and guided by the scent of blood in their nostrils. They had too much taste to approve the imbroglios, the jugglings with daggers, which are fit only for children. A tragedy is, to my thinking, nothing but a fine page of history divided into a certain number of marked periods. Thus, we are waiting for the sheriff.[34] He arrives. He questions the squire of the village. He proposes apostasy to him. The other refuses. He condemns him to death. He sends him to prison. The daughter implores mercy for her father. The sheriff will grant it; but on a revolting condition. The squire is put to death. The inhabitants rush on the sheriff. He flies before them. The lover of

[33] The troubadour story of Gabrielle de Vergy is told, with the lady's name given as Margaret de Roussillon, in chap. xxix. of Scott's *Anne of Geierstein.*

[34] All this talk about *Le Shérif* refers directly to one of Diderot's *scenarios* for plays which he never actually wrote. The *scenario* of *Le Shérif* is published in the eighth volume of M. Assézat's edition of the *Œuvres complètes de Diderot* (Garnier, Paris). It would, so far as I can see, have made a curiously bad play.

the squire's daughter strikes him dead with one dagger thrust, and the abominable fanatic dies cursed by all around him. A poet does not need much more material for a great work. Suppose the daughter goes to her mother's tomb to learn her duty to the author of her being; suppose that she is in doubt about the sacrifice of honour demanded from her; that in this doubt she keeps her lover aloof, and will not hear the language of his passion; that she obtains leave to visit her father in prison; that her father wishes to marry her and her lover, and she refuses; that she does sacrifice her honour, and her father is put to death the while; that you are unaware of her fate until her lover, when she is distracted with grief at her father's death, learns what she has done to save him; that then the sheriff comes in hunted by the mob and is struck down by the lover. There you have part of the details of such a work.

The Second. Part?

The First. Yes, part. Will not the young lovers propose flight to the squire? Will not the villagers propose to him to exterminate the sheriff and his satellites? Will there not be a priest who preaches toleration? And in the midst of this terrible day will the lover be idle? And cannot one suppose certain ties between these characters, and make something out of such ties? Why should not the sheriff have been a suitor of the squire's daughter? Why should he not return with vengeance in his heart against the squire, who has turned him out of the place, and the daughter, who has scorned his suit? What important incidents one can get out of the simplest subject if one has patience to think it over! What colour one can give them if one is eloquent! And you cannot be a dramatic poet without being eloquent. And do you suppose I shan't have a fine stage effect? The sheriff's interrogatory, for instance, will be given with all the pomp of circumstance. No, leave the staging to me, and so an end to this digression.

I take thee to witness, Roscius of England, celebrated Garrick; thee, who by the unanimous consent of all existing nations art held for the greatest actor they have known! Now render homage to truth. Hast thou not told me that, despite thy depth of feeling, thy action would be weak if, whatever passion or character thou hadst to render, thou couldst not raise thyself by the power of thought to the grandeur of a Homeric shape with which thou soughtest to identify thyself? When I replied that it was not then from thine own type thou didst play, confess thine answer. Didst not avow avoiding this with care, and say that thy playing was astounding only because thou didst constantly exhibit a creature of the imagination which was not thyself?

The Second. A great actor's soul is formed of the subtle element with which a certain philosopher filled space, an element neither cold nor hot, heavy nor light, which affects no definite shape, and, capable of assuming all, keeps none.

The First. A great actor is neither a pianoforte, nor a harp, nor a spinnet, nor a violin, nor a violoncello; he has no key peculiar to him; he takes the key and the tone fit for his part of the score, and he can take up any. I put a high value on the talent of a great actor; he is a rare being—as rare as, and perhaps greater than, a poet.

He who in society makes it his object, and unluckily has the skill, to please every one, is nothing, has nothing that belongs to him, nothing to distinguish him, to delight some and weary others. He is always talking, and always talking well; he is an adulator by profession, he is a great courtier, he is a great actor.

The Second. A great courtier, accustomed since he first drew breath to play the part of a most ingenious puppet,[35] takes every kind of shape at the pull of the string in his master's hands.

The First. A great actor is also a most ingenious puppet, and his strings are held by the poet, who at each line indicates the true form he must take.

The Second. So then a courtier, an actor, who can take only one form, however beautiful, however attractive it may be, are a couple of wretched pasteboard figures?

The First. I have no thought of calumniating a profession I like and esteem—I mean, the actor's. I should be in despair if a misunderstanding of my observations cast a shade of contempt on men of a rare talent and a true usefulness, on the scourges of absurdity and vice, on the most eloquent preachers of honesty and virtue, on the rod which the man

---

[35] *Pantin.* A figure cut out in card, with strings attached to it. I have used the word puppet to avoid roundabout expression.

of genius wields to chastise knaves and fools. But look around you, and you will see that people of never-failing gaiety have neither great faults nor great merits; that as a rule people who lay themselves out to be agreeable are frivolous people, without any sound principle; and that those who, like certain persons who mix in our society, have no character, excel in playing all.

Has not the actor a father, a mother, a wife, children, brothers, sisters, acquaintances, friends, a mistress? If he were endowed with that exquisite sensibility which people regard as the thing principally needed for his profession, harassed and struck like us with an infinity of troubles in quick succession, which sometimes wither and sometimes tear our hearts, how many days would he have left to devote to our amusement? Mighty few. The Groom of the Chambers would vainly interpose his sovereignty, the actor's state would often make him answer, 'My lord, I cannot laugh to-day,' or, 'It is over cares other than Agamemnon's that I would weep.' It is not known, however, that the troubles of life, common to actors as to us, and far more opposed to the free exercise of their calling, often interrupt them.

In society, unless they are buffoons, I find them polished, caustic, and cold; proud, light of behaviour, spendthrifts, self-interested; struck rather by our absurdities than touched by our misfortunes; masters of themselves at the spectacle of an untoward incident or the recital of a pathetic story; isolated, vagabonds, at the command of the great; little conduct, no friends, scarce any of those holy and tender ties which associate us in the pains and pleasures of another, who in turn shares our own. I have often seen an actor laugh off the stage; I do not remember to have ever seen one weep. What do they, then, with this sensibility that they arrogate and that people grant them? Do they leave it on the stage at their exit, to take it up again at their next entrance?

What makes them slip on the sock or the buskin? Want of education, poverty, a libertine spirit. The stage is a resource, never a choice. Never did actor become so from love of virtue, from desire to be useful in the world, or to serve his country or family; never from any of the honourable motives which might incline a right mind, a feeling heart, a sensitive soul, to so fine a profession.

I myself, in my young days, hesitated between the Sorbonne and the stage. In the bitterest depth of winter I used to go and recite aloud parts in Molière and in Corneille in the solitary alleys of the Luxembourg. What was my project? To gain applause? Perhaps. To mix on intimate terms with actresses whom I found charming, and who I knew were not straitlaced? Certainly. I know not what I would not have done to please Gaussin, who was then making her first appearance, and was beauty itself; or Dangeville,[36] who on the stage was so full of charm.

It has been said that actors have no character, because in playing all characters they lose that which Nature gave them, and they become false just as the doctor, the surgeon, and the butcher, become hardened. I fancy that here cause is confounded with effect, and that they are fit to play all characters because they have none.

The Second. A person does not become cruel because he is an executioner; but an executioner because he is cruel.

The First. It is all very well for me to look into these persons' characters; I see nothing in them to distinguish them from their fellow-citizens except a vanity which might be termed insolence, a jealousy which fills their company with trouble and hatred. Perhaps of all associations there is not one where the associates' common interest and that of the public is more constantly and more clearly sacrificed to wretched little pretensions. Envy is worse among them than among authors: this is saying a good deal, but it is true. One poet more easily forgives another the success of a piece than one actress forgives another the applause which marks her out for some illustrious or rich debauchee. You find them great on the stage because, as you say, they have soul; I find them little and mean in society because they have none: with the words and the tone of Camille or the elder Horace

36 Mlle. Dangeville was born in Paris in 1714. Daughter of a ballet-master and an actress, she made her first appearance at the Français at the age of seven and a half. Her official first appearance was made in 1730, as Lisette in Destouches's *Médisant*. She was admitted two months afterwards, remained on the stage till 1763, and died in 1796. The editor of the *Mémoires Secrets*, echoing public opinion, wrote of her: 'You alone, inimitable Dangeville, never grow old. So fresh, so novel are you, that each time we see you we take to be the first time. Nature has showered her gifts on you, as though Art had refused to endow you; and Art has hastened to enrich you with her perfection as though Nature had granted you nought.' Her first appearances were so successful that it was said of her at the time that she began where great actresses left off.

they have ever the conduct of Frosine or Sganarelle. Now, to estimate what is at the bottom of their hearts, must I rely on the borrowed reports that are so admirably tricked out, or on the nature of actors and the tenor of their life?

The Second. But of old Molière, the Quinaults, Mont-mesnil, and to-day Brisart[37] and Caillot,[38] who is equally at home in great and little company, to whose keeping you would fearlessly confide your secrets and your purse, to whom you would trust your wife's honour and your daughter's innocence, with much more security than you would to this or that great gentleman of the Court or this or that venerated priest of our altar . . .

The First. The praise is not overcharged. What annoys me is, that I do not hear you cite a greater number of actors who deserve or have deserved it. What annoys me is, that among all these possessors *ex-officio* of one quality, which is the valuable and fruitful source of so many others, an actor who is a man of honour, an actress who is a woman of virtue, are such rare phenomena.

Let us conclude from this that it is untrue that they have an exclusive claim to this quality, and that the sensibility which would overcome them in private life as on the stage, if they were endowed with it, is neither the basis of their character nor the cause of their success; that it belongs to them neither more nor less than to any other class of people; and one sees so few great actors because parents do not bring up their children for the stage; because people do not prepare for it by an education begun in youth; and a company of actors is not—as it would have to be among a people who attached the due importance, honour, and recom-pense to the function of speaking to assembled multitudes who come to be taught, amused, and corrected—a corpo-ration formed like other commonwealths, of persons chosen from every kind of good family, and led to the stage as to

[37] Brizard was born in April 1721, and began his career as an actor by playing in comedy in the provinces. He made his first appearance at the Français in July 1757, as Alphonse in La Motte's tragedy, *Inès de Castro*. He was admitted in the following year, left the stage in 1786, and died in 1791. The *Mémoires Secrets* describe him thus: 'He has the majesty of the king, the sublimity of the pontiff, the tenderness or sternness of the father. He is a very great actor, who combines force with pathos, fire with feeling.'
[38] An account of the great actor Caillot will be found later on in a note on a passage referring to him in greater detail.

the services, the law, or the church, by taste or choice, and with the approval of their natural guardians.

The Second. The degradation of modern actors is, it seems to me, an unlucky heritage from the old actors.

The First. I think so.

The Second. If plays had been invented in these days, when people have more sensible notions, perhaps . . . But you are not listening: what are you thinking of?

The First. I am following up my first idea, and thinking of the influence plays might have on good taste and morals if players were people of position and their profession an honoured one. Where is the poet would dare propose to men of birth to publicly repeat coarse or stupid speeches?— to women, of character not much lighter than the women we know, to impudently utter before a quantity of listeners such things as they would blush to hear in private at their fireside? If the conditions were altered our playwriters would soon attain to a purity, a delicacy, a grace, that they are further from than perhaps they think. Can you doubt that it would re-act upon the national tone?

The Second. One might perhaps object that the pieces, old and new, which your well-behaved players would exclude from their repertory, are the very ones we play in private theatricals.

The First. And what difference does it make if our fellow-citizens lower themselves to the level of the most wretched players? Would it be the less useful, the less desirable, that our actors should raise themselves to the level of the best citizens?

The Second. The change is not easy.

The First. When I gave the *Père de Famille,* the magistrate of police exhorted me to follow the career.

The Second. Why did you not?

The First. Because, not having achieved the success which I had promised myself with it, and not flattering myself that I could do much better, I grew disgusted with a calling for which I thought I had not enough talent.

The Second. And why did this piece, which nowadays fills the house before half-past four, and which the players always put up when they want a thousand crowns, have so lukewarm a welcome at first?

The First. Some said that our habits were too factitious to suit themselves to a style so simple; too corrupt to taste a style so virtuous.

The Second. That was not without a show of truth.

The First. But experience has shown that it was not true, for we have grown no better. Besides, the true, the honest has such an ascendency over us, that if a poet's work includes two characters in this kind, and if he has genius, his success will be only the more assured. It is, above all, when all is false that we love the true; it is, above all, when all is corrupt that the stage becomes purest. The citizen who presents himself at the door of a theatre leaves his vices there, and only takes them up again as he goes out. There he is just, impartial, a good friend, a lover of virtue; and I have often seen by my side bad fellows deeply indignant at actions which they would not have failed to commit had they found themselves in the same circumstances in which the poet had placed the personage they abhorred. If I did not succeed at first it was because the style was new to audience and actors; because there was a strong prejudice, still existing, against what people call tearful comedy; because I had a crowd of enemies at court, in town, among magistrates, among Churchmen, among men of letters.

The Second. And how did you incur so much enmity?

The First. Upon my word I don't know, for I have not written satires on great or small, and I have crossed no man on the path of fortune and dignities. It is true that I was one of the people called Philosophers, who were then viewed as dangerous citizens, and on whom the Government let loose two or three wretched subalterns without virtue, without insight, and, what is worse, without talent. But enough of that.

The Second. To say nothing of the fact that these philosophers had made things more difficult for poets and men of letters in general, it was no longer possible to make oneself distinguished by knowing how to turn out a madrigal or a nasty couplet.

The First. That may be. A young rake, instead of sedulously haunting the studio of the painter, the sculptor, the artist who has adopted him, has wasted the best years of his life, and at twenty he has no resources and no talent. What is he to become? A soldier or an actor. You find him, then, enrolled in a country company. He strolls it until he can promise himself an appearance in the capital. An unhappy creature has wallowed in gutter debauchery; tired of the most abject of conditions, that of a low courtesan, she learns a few parts by heart; she goes one morning to Clairon, as the slave of old used to go to the ædile or the prætor. Clairon takes her by the hand, makes her turn round, touches her with her wand, and says to her, 'Go and make the gaping crowd laugh or cry.'

They are excommunicated. The public, which cannot do without them, despises them. They are slaves, constantly dreading the rod of another slave. Think you that the marks of so continual a degradation can fail to have effect, and that under the burden of shame the soul can be strong enough to reach the heights of Corneille?

The despotism that people practise to them they practise in turn to authors, and I know not which is the meaner, the insolent actor or the author who endures him.

The Second. People like to have their plays acted.

The First. On whatever condition. Give your money at the door, and they will weary of your presence and your applause. Well enough off with the small boxes, they have been on the point of deciding either that the author should give up his profits or that his piece should not be accepted.

The Second. But this project involved nothing less than the extinction of the dramatic author's career.

The First. What does that matter to them?

The Second. You have, I think, but little more to say.

The First. You are mistaken. I must now take you by the hand and lead you to the presence of Clairon, that incomparable enchantress.

The Second. She, at least, was proud of her calling.

The First. As will be all who excel in it. The stage is despised by those actors only who have been hissed off the boards. I must show you Clairon in the real transports of anger. If in them she happened to preserve the bearing, the accent, the action of the stage, with all its artifice and emphasis, would you not hold your sides? could you contain your laughter? What, then, would you tell me? Do you not roundly assert that true sensibility and assumed sensibility are two very different things? You laugh at what you would have admired on the stage; and why, pray? The fact is, that Clairon's real anger resembles simulated anger, and you are able to distinguish between the personality and the passion which that personality assumes. The likeness of passion on the stage is not then its true likeness; it is but extravagant portraiture, caricature on a grand scale, subject to conventional rules. Well, interrogate yourself, ask yourself what artist will confine himself most strictly within the limits of these rules? What kind of actor will most successfully lay hold on this regulated bombast—the man dominated by his own character, or the man born without character, or the man who strips himself of his own to put on another greater, more noble, more fiery, more elevated? One is one's self by nature; one becomes some one else by imitation; the heart one is supposed to have is not the heart one has. What, then, is the true talent? That of knowing well the outward symptoms of the soul we borrow, of addressing ourselves to the sensations of those who hear and see us, of deceiving them by the imitation of these symptoms, by an imitation which aggrandises everything in their imagination, and which becomes the measure of their judgment; for it is impossible otherwise to appreciate that which passes inside us. And after all, what does it matter to us whether they feel or do not feel, so long as we know nothing about it?

He, then, who best knows and best renders, after the best conceived ideal type, these outward signs, is the greatest actor.

The Second. He, then, who leaves least to the imagination of the great actor is the greatest poet.

The First. I was just going to say so. When by long stage habit one keeps a stage accent in private life, and brings into it Brutus, Cinna, Mithridates, Cornelius, Merope, Pompey, do you know what he does? He couples with a soul small or great, exactly as Nature has cut its measure, the outward signs of an exalted and gigantic soul that is not his own. The result of this is ridicule.

The Second. What a cruel satire is this, innocent or of malice prepense, on actors and authors!

The First. How so?

The Second. Any one, I imagine, may have a great and

strong soul; any one, I imagine, may have the bearing, the manner, the action, appropriate to his soul; and I do not think that the expression of true grandeur can ever be ridiculous.

The First. What follows then?

The Second. Ah, you rogue! you dare not say it, and I shall have to incur the general indignation on your behalf. It follows that true tragedy is yet to seek, and that, with all their faults, the ancients came nearer to it than we do.

The First. It is true that it delights me to hear Philoctetes say with such simple strength to Neoptolemus, who brings him back the arrows of Hercules, which he stole at Ulysses's instigation,—'See what a deed you had done! Without knowing it, you had condemned an unhappy wretch to perish of grief and hunger. Your crime is another's, your repentance your own. No; never would you have thought of doing a deed so shameful had you been left to yourself. See then, my child, how important is it for your time of life to keep only honest company. This is what you got by associating with a rascal. And why have aught to do with a man of this character? Would your father have chosen him for your companion and friend? Your good father, who never let any but the first men in the army come near him, what would he say if he saw you with a Ulysses?'

Is there anything in this discourse which you might not address to my son, or I to yours?

The Second. No.

The First. Yet it is finely said.

The Second. Certainly.

The First. And would the tone in which this discourse would be given on the stage differ from the tone in which one would give it in society?

The Second. I do not think so.

The First. And would this tone be ridiculous in private life?

The Second. Not at all.

The First. The stronger the action, the simpler the language, the more I admire it. I am much afraid that for a hundred years on end we have taken the rodomontade of Madrid for the heroism of Rome, and mixed up the tone of the Tragic with that of the Epic Muse.

The Second. Our Alexandrine verse is too harmonious, and is too noble for dialogue.

The First. And our verse of ten syllables too futile and too light. However this may be, I would like you never to go to a performance of one of Corneille's Roman pieces, but when you are fresh from reading Cicero's letters to Atticus. How bombastic our dramatic authors seem to me, how repulsive are their declamations, when I recall the simplicity and strength of Regulus's discourse dissuading the Senate and the Roman people from an exchange of prisoners! Thus he expresses himself in an ode, a poem which includes a good deal more of fire, spirit, and exaltation, than a tragic monologue,— He says:—

'I have seen our ensigns hanging in the temples of Carthage. I have seen Roman soldiers stripped of their arms, unstained with one drop of blood. I have seen liberty forgotten, citizens with their arms bound behind their backs. I have seen the town gates wide open, and the harvest thick on the fields we ravaged. And you think that, brought back, they will return braver. You add loss to shame. Virtue once driven from a degraded soul never returns. Hope nothing from him who might have died and has let himself be strangled. O Carthage, how great and proud thou art in our shame!'

Such was his discourse, such his conduct. He refuses the embraces of his wife and children; he feels himself unworthy of them, like a vile slave. He keeps his eyes moodily fixed on the ground, and scorns the tears of his friends until he has brought the senators to a determination he alone could have proposed, and until he is allowed to go back to his exile.

The Second. That is simple and splendid, but the really heroic moment was afterwards.

The First. You are right.

The Second. He knew well the torture the savage foe was preparing for him. However, recovering his serenity, he disengages himself from his kinsmen, who seek to put off his return, as easily as in former times he disengaged himself from the crowd of his clients to go and shake off the fatigue of business in his fields at Venafrum or his campaign at Tarentum.

The First. Very good. Now lay your hand on your heart
and tell me if our poets contain many passages of a tone
proper for so grand yet so domestic a virtue, and how from
such lips as Regulus's would sound either our tender jere-
miades or most of our brave words in Corneille's manner.
How many things do I not dare to confide to you! I should
be stoned in the streets were I known to be guilty of such
blasphemy; and I am not anxious for any kind of a martyr's
crown. If the day comes when a man of genius dare give
his characters the simple tone of antique heroism, the actor's
art will assume a new difficulty, for declamation will cease to
be a kind of sing-song.[39]

For the rest, in saying that sensibility was the mark of a
good heart and a middling genius I made no common confession; for if Nature ever moulded a sensitive soul that soul
is mine. The man of sensibility is too much at the mercy of
his diaphragm to be a great king, a great politician, a great
magistrate, a just man, or a close observer, and, consequently, an admirable imitator of Nature—unless, indeed, he
can forget himself, distract himself from himself, and, with
the aid of a strong imagination, make for himself certain
shapes which serve him for types, and on which he keeps his
attention fixed, with the aid of a tenacious memory. Only
then it is not his own self that is concerned; it is another's
mind and will that master him.

Here I should stop; but you will more readily forgive me
the misplacing than the omission of an observation. This
phenomenon must surely sometimes have struck you. A
budding actor, or let us say a budding actress, asks you to
come and see her quietly to form an opinion of her talent.
You grant that she has soul, sensibility, passion. You cover
her with praises, and leave her when you depart in hope of
the greatest success. But what happens? She appears, she is
hissed, and you acknowledge that the hisses are deserved.
Why is this? Has she lost her soul, her sensibility, her passion, between the morning and the evening? No; but in her
ground-floor room you were both on the same low level; you

---

[39] It did, in fact, so cease with Le Kain; at least one gathers as much from all
that can be learnt of his method in other authors. This is so much the case that
it is at first sight startling to find in one part of Diderot's work a full reference to
Le Kain, and in another an implication that no actor had yet ventured to vary
the conventional sing-song. But Diderot was as capable of making a slip as Homer.

listened to her regardless of convention; she was face-to-face with you; between you there was no model for purposes of comparison; you were satisfied with her voice, her gesture, her expression, her bearing; all was in proportion to the audience and the space; there was nothing that called for exaltation. On the boards all the conditions were changed: there a different impersonation was needed, since all the surroundings were enlarged.

In private theatricals, in a drawing-room, where the spectator is almost on a level with the actor, the true dramatic impersonation would have struck you as being on an enormous, a gigantic scale, and at the end of the performance you would have said confidentially to a friend, 'She will not succeed; she is too extravagant'; and her success on the stage would have astonished you. Let me repeat it, whether for good or ill, the actor says nothing and does nothing in private life in the same way as on the stage: it is a different world.

But there is a decisive fact, which was told me by an accurate person of an original and attractive turn of mind, the Abbé Galiani, and which I have since heard confirmed by another accurate person, also of an original and attractive turn of mind, the Marquis de Caraccioli, ambassador of Naples at Paris. This is, that at Naples, the native place of both, there is a dramatic poet whose chief care is not given to composing his piece.

The Second. Yours, the *Père de Famille,* had a great success there.

The First. Four representations running were given before the King. This was contrary to court etiquette, which lays down that there shall be as many plays as days of performance. The people were delighted. However, the Neapolitan poet's care is to find in society persons of the age, face, voice, and character fitted to fill his parts. People dare not refuse him, because the Sovereign's amusement is concerned. And when, think you, do the company begin really to act, to understand each other, to advance towards the point of perfection he demands? It is when the actors are worn out with constant rehearsals, are what we call 'used up.' From this moment their progress is surprising; each identifies himself with his part; and it is at the end of this

hard work that the performances begin and go on for six
months on end, while the Sovereign and his subjects enjoy
the highest pleasure that can be obtained from a stage illusion. And can this illusion, as strong, as perfect at the last
as at the first performance, be due in your opinion to sensibility? For the rest, the question I am diving into was once
before started between a middling man of letters, Rémond
de Sainte-Albine,[40] and a great actor, Riccoboni.[41] The man
of letters pleaded the cause of sensibility; the actor took up
my case. The story is one which has only just come to my
knowledge.

I have spoken, you have heard me, and now I ask you
what you think of it.

The Second. I think that that arrogant, decided, dry, hard
little man, to whom one would attribute a large allowance
of contemptuousness if he had only a quarter as much as
prodigal Nature has given him of self-sufficiency, would
have been a little more reserved in his judgment if you had
had the condescension to put your arguments before him
and he the patience to listen to you. Unluckily he knows
everything, and as a man of universal genius he thinks himself absolved from listening.

The First. Well, the public pays him out for it. Do you
know Madame Riccoboni? [42]

The Second. Who does not know the author of a great
number of charming works, full of intelligence, of purity, of
delicacy, and grace?

The First. Would you call her a woman of sensibility?

The Second. She has proved it, not only by her works, but
by her conduct. There was an incident in her life which led
her to the brink of the tomb. After an interval of twenty

---

[40] Author of *Le Comédien.* 1747.

[41] Riccoboni was born at Mantua in 1707, and came to France with his parents
in 1716. In 1726 he made his first appearance, with success, at the Comédie
Italienne, as the lover in Marivaux's *Surprise de l'Amour.* He twice left and
twice rejoined the company. In 1749 he made what seemed a third and definitive
retreat; but in 1759 he reappeared again as a member of the Troupe Italienne. He
died in 1772. Baron Grimm describes him as a cold and pretentious actor. He
was the author of various pieces, alone and in collaboration, and published a work
called *Pensées sur la Déclamation.*

[42] Mme. Riccoboni, wife of the actor at the Comédie Italienne, made her first appearance on that stage in August 1734. She went on acting for forty-six years, and
was, according to all accounts, a very clever and interesting woman, and a bad
actress. She left the stage in 1760 and died in 1792.

years she has not ceased to weep; the source of her tears is not yet dry.

The First. Well, this woman, one of the most sensitive that Nature ever made, was one of the worst actresses that ever appeared on the stage. No one talks better on dramatic art; no one plays worse.

The Second. Let me add that she is aware of it, and that she has never complained of being unjustly hissed.

The First. And why with this exquisite sensibility, which, according to you, is the actor's chief requirement, is Mme. Riccoboni so bad?

The Second. It must be that other requirements fail her to such an extent that the chief one cannot make up for their absence.

The First. But she is not ill-looking; she has her wits about her; she has a tolerable bearing; her voice has nothing discordant about it. She possesses all the good qualities that education can give. In society there is no repellent point about her. You see her with no feeling of pain; you listen to her with the greatest pleasure.

The Second. I don't understand it at all; all I know is, that the public has never been able to make up its quarrel with her, and that for twenty years on end she has been the victim of her calling.

The First. And of her sensibility, out of which she could never raise herself; and it is because she has always remained herself that the public has consistently rejected her.

The Second. Now come, do you not know Caillot?

The First. Very well.

The Second. Have you ever talked with him of this?

The First. No.

The Second. In your place I should be glad to have his opinion.

The First. I have it.

The Second. What is it?

The First. Your own and your friend's.

The Second. There is a tremendous authority against you.

The First. I admit it.

The Second. And how did you know Caillot's opinion?

The First. Through a woman full of intellect and keenness, the Princess de Galitzin. Caillot was playing the De-

serter,[43] and was still on the spot where he had just gone
through the agonies which she, close by, had shared, of an
unhappy man resigned to lose his mistress and his life.
Caillot draws near the Princess's box, and with the smile
you know on his face makes some lively, well-bred, and
courteous remarks. The Princess, astonished, says to him,
'What! You are not dead? I, who was only a spectator of
your anguish, have only just come to myself.' 'No, Madam,
I am not dead. My lot would be indeed pitiable if I died so
often.' 'Then you feel nothing?' 'Ah, pardon me.' And
so they engaged in a discussion which ended as this of ours
will end—I shall keep to my opinion and you to yours. The
Princess could not remember Caillot's arguments, but she had
noticed that this great imitator of Nature at the very moment of his agony, when he was on the point of being
dragged to execution, seeing that the chair on which he
would have to lay down the fainting Louise was badly
placed, rearranged it as he cried in a moribund voice, *Louise
comes not, and my hour is nigh!* [44]

The Second. I am going to propose a compromise; to keep
for the actor's natural sensibility those rare moments in
which he forgets himself, in which he no longer sees the
play, in which he forgets that he is on a stage, in which he

[43] *Le Déserteur*, a pretty and interesting 'melodrama,' in the old sense of the word,
by Sedaine.
[44] Caillot was born in 1733 in Paris, in the Rue St. Honoré, where his father
carried on a jeweller's business. In 1743 he was admitted under the name of
Dupuis to the king's private band of musicians. In 1752 he took to acting in the
provinces, and in 1760 he made his first appearance with the Troupe Italienne as
Colas, in Favart's *Ninette à la Cour*. His success was instant, and increased as his
career went on. He was admirable both as a singer and as an actor. Among his
greatest successes was Blaise in *Lucile* (Marmontel's words to Grétry's music). In
this it was thought unusual daring on his part to appear on the stage in a real
peasant's dress, with really dusty boots, and with a really bald head. Grimm wrote
of this performance: 'Caillot's playing of the part of Blaise is, I believe, one of
the most interesting things that can be seen on any stage. This charming actor
puts into his performance so much fineness, so much perfection, that it is impossible to imagine anything better. I defy Garrick, the great Garrick, to play
the part better. . . . Caillot in all his parts carries truth in nature and in costume
very far. I do not know how he has managed to have just the bald head that
Blaise should have.' As a matter of fact, Caillot in Blaise, like Charles Mathews
in Affable Hawk, appeared for the first time with his own bald head uncovered
by a wig. Of his presence of mind on the stage there is a story parallel to
Diderot's. In *Sylvain* he had to fall at his father's feet and catch him by the
knees. The other actor, misunderstanding the movement, drew back, so that
Caillot fell face forwards on the stage; but he managed the fall so cleverly that
it was taken for a fine stroke of art. He left the stage in 1772, but occasionally returned to fill the place of a sick comrade.

is at Argos, or at Mycenæ, in which he is the very character he plays. He weeps . . .

The First. In proper time?

The Second. Yes. He exclaims . . .

The First. With proper intonation?

The Second. Yes. He is tormented, indignant, desperate; he presents to my eyes the real image, and conveys to my ears and heart the true accents of the passion which shakes him, so that he carries me away and I forget myself, and it is no longer Brizart or Le Kain, but Agamemnon or Nero that I hear. All other moments of the part I give up to art. I think it is perhaps then with Nature as with the slave who learns to move freely despite his chain. The habit of carrying it takes from it its weight and constraint.

The First. An actor of sensibility may perhaps have in his part one or two of these impulses of illusion; and the finer their effect the more they will be out of keeping with the rest. But tell me, when this happens does not the play cease to give you pleasure and become a cause of suffering?

The Second. Oh, no!

The First. And will not this figment of suffering have a more powerful effect than the every-day and real spectacle of a family in tears around the death-bed of a loved father or an adored mother?

The Second. Oh, no!

The First. Then you and the actor have not so completely forgotten yourselves?

The Second. You have already pushed me hard, and I doubt not you could push me yet harder; but I think I could shake you if you would let me enlist an ally. It is half-past four; they play *Dido;* let us go and see Mademoiselle Raucourt: she can answer you better than I can.

The First. I wish it may be so, but I scarce hope it. Do you think she can do what neither Lecouvreur,[45] nor Duclos,

---

[45] Mlle. Le Couvreur, born at Fismes (Marne) in 1690, made her first appearance at the Français in May 1717, as Electra in Crébillon's tragedy. She was admitted the same month. She died in 1730, and the fact that she was refused Christian burial in Paris in the same year in which Mrs. Oldfield was buried with all pomp in Westminster Abbey is well known. Le Mazurier, who gives the outlines of the story concerning her on which the play of *Adrienne Lecouvreur* was founded, has also a full and most interesting account of her acting, from which some brief extracts may here be given. She was of a medium height, with sparkling eyes, fine features, and much distinction of manner. Her voice had naturally few tones, but

nor Deseine,[46] nor Balincourt,[47] nor Clairon, nor Dumesnil has accomplished? I dare tell you this, that if our young beginner is still far from perfect, it is because she is too much of a novice to avoid feeling;[48] and I predict that if she continues to feel, to remain herself, and to prefer the narrow instinct of nature to the limitless study of art, she will never rise to the height of the actresses I have named. She will have fine moments, but she will not be fine. It will be with her as with Gaussin and many others, who all their lives have been mannered, weak, and monotonous, only because they have never got out of the narrow limits which their natural sensibility imposed upon them. You are still bent on marshalling Mademoiselle Raucourt against me?

The Second. Certainly.

The First. As we go I will tell you a thing which has a close enough connexion with the subject of our talk. I knew Pigalle;[49] his house was open to me. One morning I go

she had learnt to give them infinite variety. Her diction was extremely natural, and this told greatly in her favour, as all her predecessors, except Floridor and Baron, had adopted a stilted enunciation. She and Baron were said to be the most loyal members of the company. They both avoided the practice of 'starring' in the provinces, a practice which of late years has given rise to much disturbance at the Français. The excellence of her acting in scenes where she had to listen instead of speaking was especially remarkable. In all scenes her acting was full of nature and fire. She had every merit that Clairon had, with an amount of feeling that Clairon never possessed. She played many parts in comedy and played them well, but it was as a tragedian that she was unrivalled. Her death was felt as a public misfortune.

[46] Mlle. Deseine, who afterwards married Quinault-Dufresne, made her first appearance at Fontainebleau before Louis XV. as Hermione in *Andromaque*. Her success was so marked that the king made her a present of a magnificent Roman dress, and she was at once admitted by special ordinance. She appeared as Hermione at the Français in 1725, left the stage in 1732, returned to it in 1733, and quitted it definitely in 1736. She died in 1759. That she was a great actress would be evident, if from nothing else, from the unreserved praise which Clairon bestows on her in her *Memoirs*.

[47] Mlle. Balicourt (so Le Mazurier spells it) made her first appearance at the Français in 1727 as Cléopâtre in *Rodogune*. A month later she was admitted. Her great success was in parts demanding a queenly presence. All that was against her in these was her youth, and this Le Mazurier says, with a peculiarly French touch, the pit forgave her with more readiness than it forgave Duclos for remaining on the boards when she was sixty. She left the stage in 1738 and died in 1743.

[48] A very distinguished English actor of our own day says of a part in which he has won much well-deserved fame, and which is full of feeling, that his great difficulty was to get over the feeling with which it naturally impressed him. He had to learn the words like a parrot before he could trust himself to give any meaning to them. When he first played it he was still a little liable to be carried away by its emotion, and he notes that 'whenever I began really to cry the audience left off crying.'

[49] Pigalle was born in 1714 and died in 1785. Voltaire called him the French Phidias, and in return Pigalle executed perhaps, the worst statue of Voltaire extant. His *Mercury* gained him his election to the Academy, and led to his visit

there; I knock; the artist opens the door with his roughing-chisel in his hand; then stopping me on the threshold of the studio he says, 'Before I let you pass, assure me you will not be alarmed at a beautiful woman without a rag of clothes on.' I smiled and walked in. He was working at his monument to Marshal Saxe, and a very handsome model was standing to him for the figure of France. But how do you suppose she struck me among the colossal figures around her? She seemed poor, small, mean—a kind of frog; she was overwhelmed by them, and I should have had to take the artist's word for it that the frog was a beautiful woman, if I had not waited for the end of the sitting and seen her on the same level with myself, my back turned to the gigantic figures which reduced her to nothingness. I leave it to you to apply this curious experience to Gaussin, to Riccoboni, to all actresses who have been unable to attain to greatness on the stage.

If by some impossible chance an actress were endowed with a sensibility comparable in degree to that which the most finished art can simulate, the stage offers so many different characters for imitation, one leading part brings in so many opposite situations that this rare and tearful creature, incapable of playing two different parts well, would at best excel in certain passages of one part; she would be the most unequal, the narrowest, the least apt actress you can imagine. If it happened that she attempted a great flight, her predominant sensibility would soon bring her down to mediocrity. She would be less like a strong steed at the gallop than a poor hack taking the bit in its teeth. Then one instant of energy, momentary, sudden, without gradation or preparation, would strike you as an attack of madness.

Sensibility being after all the mate of Sorrow and Weakness, tell me if a gentle, weak, sensitive creature is fit to conceive and express the self-possession of Léontine, the jealous transports of Hermione, the fury of Camilla, the maternal tenderness of Merope, the delirium and remorse of Phædra, the tyrannical pride of Agrippina, the violence of

---

to Frederick the Great. He presented himself at the Palace at Berlin as *l'auteur du Mercure,* and was told that His Majesty would give him twenty-four hours to leave the kingdom. Frederick's poems had been maltreated in the *Mercure de France,* and he took Pigalle for the critic.

Clytemnestra? Leave your ever tearful one to one of our elegiac arts, and do not take her out of it.

The fact is, that to have sensibility is one thing, to feel is another. One is a matter of soul, the other of judgment. One may feel strongly and be unable to express it; one may alone, or in private life, at the fireside, give expression, in reading or acting, adequate for a few listeners, and give none of any account on the stage. On the stage, with what we call sensibility, soul, passion, one may give one or two tirades well and miss the rest. To take in the whole extent of a great part, to arrange its light and shade, its forts and feebles; to maintain an equal merit in the quiet and in the violent passages; to have variety both in harmonious detail and in the broad effect; to establish a system of declamation which shall succeed in carrying off every freak of the poet's— this is matter for a cool head, a profound judgment, an exquisite taste,—a matter for hard work, for long experience, for an uncommon tenacity of memory. The rule, *Qualis ab incepto processerit et sibi constet* [Let it continue as it began, harmonious with itself], rigorous enough for the poet, is fixed down to the minutest point for the actor. He who comes out from the wing without having his whole scheme of acting in his head, his whole part marked out, will all his life play the part of a beginner. Or if endowed with intrepidity, self-sufficiency, and spirit, he relies on his quickness of wit and the habit of his calling, he will bear you down with his fire and the intoxication of his emotions, and you will applaud him as an expert of painting might smile at a free sketch, where all was indicated and nothing marked. This is the kind of prodigy which may be seen sometimes at a fair or at Nicolet's.[50] Perhaps such people do well to remain as they are—mere roughed-out actors. More study would not give them what they want, and might take from them what they have. Take them for what they are worth, but do not compare them to a finished picture.

The Second. I have only one more question to ask you.

---

[50] Nicolet was, as may be judged from the context, one of the greatest managers of the *Théâtres de Foire*. He combated desperately, and had not a little to do with upsetting the exclusive rights claimed by the *Comédiens du Roi*, which rights were so skilfully eluded by Piron in his *Arlequin Deucalion*. The whole story, which is given in M. Bonnassies's *Spectacles Forains* (Paris: Dentu), affords a curious parallel to the similar struggle in England.

The First. Ask it.

The Second. Have you ever seen a whole piece played to perfection?

The First. On my word I can't remember it. Stop a bit— yes, sometimes—a middling piece by middling actors.

Our two talkers went to the playhouse, but as there were no places to be had they turned off to the Tuileries. They walked for some time in silence. They seemed to have forgotten that they were together, and each talked to himself as if he were alone, the one out loud, the other so low that he could not be heard, only at intervals letting out words, isolated but distinct, from which it was easy to guess that he did not hold himself defeated.

The thoughts of the man with the paradox are the only ones of which I can give an account, and here they are, disconnected as they must be when one omits in a soliloquy the intermediate parts which serve to hang it together. He said: Put an actor of sensibility in his place, and see how he will get out of the mess. What did this man do, however? He puts his foot on the balustrade, refastens his garter, and answers the courtier he despises with his head turned on his shoulder; and thus an incident which would have disconcerted any one but this cold and great actor is suddenly adapted to the surroundings and becomes a trait of genius.[51]

[He spoke, I think, of Baron, in the tragedy of the *Comte d'Essex*. He added with a smile:]

Yes; he will tell you she feels when, her head in her confidante's bosom, almost at the point of death, her eyes turned to the third tier of boxes, she suddenly sees an old Justice, who is dissolved in tears, and whose grief expresses itself in ludicrous grimaces, when she exclaims, 'Look up there! there's a fine face for you!' muttering the words under her breath, like the end of some inarticulate moan. Tell me no such stuff!

If I remember right, this was Gaussin in *Zaïre*.

[51] The same story of the accidental unfastening of a garter being turned to excellent account by an actor of great presence of mind has in later days been referred, probably by confusion with Diderot's story, to the scene in *Ruy Blas*, in which Don Salluste, disguised as a lackey, gives his commands to Ruy Blas disguised as Prime Minister.

And this third, whose end was so tragic. I knew him; I knew his father, who asked me sometimes to talk to him through his ear-trumpet.

[Here we are evidently dealing with the excellent Montmesnil.]

He was candour and honour itself. What was there in common between his character and that of Tartufe, which he played so well? Nothing. Where did he find the stiff neck, the strange roll of the eyes, the honeyed tone, and all the other fine touches in the hypocrite's part? Take care how you answer; I have you.

In a profound imitation of Nature.

In a profound imitation of Nature?

And you will note that the inward signs which chiefly mark the simplicity of the soul are not so much to be seen in Nature as the outward signs of hypocrisy. You cannot study them there, and an actor of great talent will find more difficulty in seizing on and examining the one than the other. And if I maintained that of all the qualities of the soul sensibility is the easiest to counterfeit, since there is scarce a man alive so cruel, so inhuman, that there is no germ of it in his heart, and that he has never felt it—a thing which cannot be safely said of all the other passions, such as avarice, distrust? But an excellent instrument . . . ?

Ah, I understand you. Between him who counterfeits sensibility and him who feels there will always be the difference between an imitation and a reality.

And so much the better; so much the better, I tell you. In the first case the actor has no trouble about separating himself from himself; he will arrive at one blow, at one bound, at the height of his ideal type . . .

At one blow, at one bound!

You are pettifogging over an expression. I mean that, never being brought back to the little type before him, he will be as great, as astonishing, as perfect an imitator of sensibility as of avarice, hypocrisy, duplicity—of every character that is not his own, of every passion that he does not feel. What the person of natural sensibility shows me will be little; the other's imitation will be strong; or, if the copies should be of equal strength, which I by no means grant you, the one, master of himself, playing entirely by study and judgment, will be, as daily experience shows us, more of a piece than the one who plays part from nature, part from study, part from a type, part from himself. However cleverly the two imitations may be fused together, a keen spectator will discriminate between them even more easily than a great artist will discern in a statue the line which marks off either two different styles or a front taken from one model and a back from another. . . . Let a consummate actor leave off playing from his head, let him forget himself, let his heart be involved, let sensibility possess him, let him give himself up to it . . .

He will intoxicate us.

Perhaps.

He will transport us with admiration.

It is not impossible; but it will be on condition of not breaking through his system of declamation; of not injuring the unity of the performance; otherwise you will say that he has gone mad. Yes, on this supposition you will, I admit, have a fine moment; but would you rather have a fine moment than a fine part? If that is your choice it is not mine.

Here the man with the paradox was silent. He walked with long strides, not seeing where he went; he would have knocked up against those who met him right and left if they had not got out of his way. Then, suddenly stopping, and catching his antagonist tight by the arm, he said, with a dogmatic and quiet tone, 'My friend, there are three types— Nature's man, the poet's man, the actor's man. Nature's is less great than the poet's, the poet's less great than the great actor's, which is the most exalted of all. This last climbs on the shoulders of the one before him and shuts himself up inside a great basket-work figure of which he is the soul. He moves this figure so as to terrify even the poet, who no longer recognises himself; and he terrifies us, as you have very well put it, just as children frighten each other by tucking up their little skirts and putting them over their heads, shaking themselves about, and imitating as best they can the croaking lugubrious accents of the spectre that they counterfeit. Have you not seen engravings of children's sports?[52]

[52] For special instances of such plates M. Assézat refers us to *Les Jeux des Anciens,* by M. Becq de Fouquières (in 8vo. Reinwald, 1869).

Have you not observed an urchin coming forward under a hideous old man's mask, which hides him from head to foot? Behind this mask he laughs at his little companions, who fly in terror before him. This urchin is the true symbol of the actor; his comrades are the symbol of the audience. If the actor has but middling sensibility, and if that is his only merit, will you not call him a middling man? Take care, for this is another trap I am laying for you. And if he is endowed with extreme sensibility what will come of it?—What will come of it? That he will either play no more, or play ludicrously ill; yes, ludicrously; and to prove it you can see the same thing in me when you like. If I have a recital of some pathos to give, a strange trouble arises in my heart and head; my tongue trips, my voice changes, my ideas wander, my speech hangs fire. I babble; I perceive it; tears course down my cheeks; I am silent. But with this I make an effect —in private life; on the stage I should be hooted.

Why?

Because people come not to see tears, but to hear speeches that draw tears; because this truth of nature is out of tune with the truth of convention. Let me explain myself: I mean that neither the dramatic system, nor the action, nor the poet's speeches, would fit themselves to my stifled, broken, sobbing declamation. You see that it is not allowable to imitate Nature, even at her best, or Truth too closely; there are limits within which we must restrict ourselves.

And who has laid down those limits?

Good sense, which will not play off one talent at the expense of another. The actor must sometimes sacrifice himself to the poet.

But if the poet's composition lent itself to that style?

Then you would have a sort of tragedy very different from what you have here.

And where would be the harm?

I do not know what you would gain, but I know very well what you would lose.

Here the man with the paradox came near his antagonist for the second or third time, and said to him,—

The saying is gross, but it is amusing, and it was said by an actress as to whose talent there are no two opinions. It is a pendant to the speech and situation of Gaussin: she, too, has her head on the breast of Pillot-Pollux; she is dying, at least I think so, and she says to him in a low tone, *'Ah, Pillot, que tu pues!'* ['Oh, Pillot, how you do stink!'] This was Arnould playing Télaïre. At this moment was Arnould really Télaïre? No; she was Arnould, consistently Arnould.[53] You will never bring me to praise the intermediate degrees of a quality which, if it were carried to its fullest extent, and the actor were mastered by it, would spoil all. But let me suppose that the poet has written a scene to be declaimed on the stage as I should recite it in private life, who would play such a scene? No one: no, no one; not even an actor most completely master of his actions; for once that he came well out of it he would miss it a thousand times. Success, then, hangs on so little! This last argument strikes you as not very cogent? So be it, but not the less shall I deduct from it a little bursting of some bubbles, a lowering of some stilts by a few notches, and the leaving things pretty much as they are. For one poet of genius who attained this prodigious truth to nature there would be a vast number of flat and insipid imitators. It is not allowable, under pain of becoming insipid, awkward, and detestable, to go one line below the simplicity of Nature. Don't you think so?

The Second. I don't think anything. I did not hear what you said.

The First. What? We have not been continuing our dispute?

The Second. No.

The First. Then what the deuce were you doing? And of what were you dreaming?

The Second. That an English actor, called, I think, Macklin (I was at the playhouse that day), having to make his excuses to the pit for his temerity in playing I know not what part in Shakespeare's *Macbeth* after Garrick, said, amongst other things, that the impressions which subjugated actors and submitted them to the poet's genius and inspira-

[53] Sophie Arnould, the most famous singer of her day, was born in 1740 and died in 1802. She first attracted notice by singing, when little more than a child, before Mme. de Pompadour, and she made her first appearance at the Opera at the age of seventeen. Mlle. Fel taught her singing, Clairon taught her acting. For details concerning her romantic history readers may be referred to MM. de Goncourt's compilation, *Sophie Arnould d'après sa Correspondance* (Paris, Dentu). The scene related by Diderot took place in the opera of *Castor et Pollux*.

tion were very hurtful to them. I do not remember the reasons he gave for it, but they were very good, and they were felt and applauded. For the rest, if you are curious about it you will find them in a letter inserted in the *St. James's Chronicle,* over the signature of 'Quintilian.' [54]

The First. So, then, I have been talking all alone all this long time?

The Second. Very likely—just as long as I have been dreaming all alone. You know that of old actors played women's parts?

The First. I know it.

The Second. Aulus Gellius recounts in his *Attic Nights* that a certain Paulus, robed in the lugubrious trappings of Electra, instead of presenting himself on the stage with the urn of Orestes, appeared holding in his arms the urn containing the ashes of his own son whom he had just lost; and then it was no vain representation, no petty sorrow of the stage: but the house rang with real shrieks and groans.

The First. And you believe that Paulus at this moment spoke on the stage as he would have spoken at his fireside? No, no. This prodigious effect, as to which I entertain no doubt, depended neither on Euripides's verse nor on the declamation of the actor, but on the spectacle of a desolate father who bathed with his tears the urn holding his own son's ashes. This Paulus was perhaps only a middling actor; no better than that Æsopus of whom Plutarch reports, that, 'playing one day to a full house the part of Atreus, deliberating with himself how he shall avenge himself on his

[54] On this remarkable passage the usually irrefragable M. Assézat has a note which is perhaps equally remarkable, and of which I append a translation. The Italics are my own. 'The fact here recorded is another assistance to fixing approximately the date of Diderot's work. The quarrel between Macklin and Garrick lasted several years, but it was not till 1773 that Macklin took up Garrick's parts, notably that of Macbeth. As he had formerly been the moving spirit of a cabal against Garrick, which, despite his talent, went the length of rotten apples and bad eggs, so now, it is said, Garrick fostered a cabal against Macklin. Less lucky than his compeer, *or, unlike him, being unprovided with a sufficing gang of bruisers,* Macklin had to give up the boards. It was before he played Macbeth for the first time that he made a speech, in accordance with English stage custom, bespeaking the indulgence of the audience.'

Diderot has made a hopeless confusion between Garrick's quarrel with Macklin (as to which Macklin published a pamphlet in 1743) and the riotous proceedings which took place on Macklin's third performance of Macbeth at Covent Garden in 1773. These were due to Coleman's simultaneous engagement of William Smith and Macklin, both of whom claimed an exclusive right to acting certain characters, Macbeth amongst them. Full particulars will be found in Kirkman's *Life of Macklin.*

brother Thyestes, there was one of the servants who wished to run suddenly past him, and he (Æsopus) being beside himself with the vehement emotion and the ardour he threw into representing to the life the furious passion of King Atreus, gave him such a blow on the head with the sceptre he held in his hand that he killed him on the spot.' He was a madman, and the tribune ought to have sent him straight off to the Tarpeian rock.

The Second. Probably he did.

The First. I doubt it. The Romans attached so much importance to the life of a great actor, and so little to the life of a slave.

But they say an actor is all the better for being excited, for being angry. I deny it. He is best when he imitates anger. Actors impress the public not when they are furious, but when they play fury well. In tribunals, in assemblies, everywhere where a man wishes to make himself master of others' minds, he feigns now anger, now fear, now pity, now love, to bring others into these divers states of feeling. What passion itself fails to do, passion well imitated accomplishes.

Do not people talk in society of a man being a great actor? They do not mean by that that he feels, but that he excels in simulating, though he feels nothing—a part much more difficult than that of the actor; for the man of the world has to find dialogue besides, and to fulfil two functions, the poet's and the actor's. The poet on the stage may be more clever than the actor of private life, but is it to be believed that an actor on the stage can be deeper, cleverer in feigning joy, sadness, sensibility, admiration, hate, tenderness, than an old courtier?

But it is late. Let us go sup.

MASKS OR FACES?

Chapter I

INTRODUCTORY

To THE AVERAGE intellect, nothing is so alluring as a paradox. The reason is simple: in accepting a paradox, the average intellect feels that it has risen above the average. Any fool can believe what is possible and probable, but it demands no ordinary gifts, whether mental or spiritual, to believe what is absurd. How 'many an old philosophy' has been based, like an inverted pyramid, on an almost imperceptible point of paradox! How many a world-embracing creed has sprung from a tiny contradiction in terms! What is a miracle, indeed, but a paradox in action? He who has seen a table dancing a hornpipe, or an elderly gentleman reclining on the ceiling instead of on the sofa, naturally feels a certain superiority over the humdrum folk who have seen no miracles save those of Mr. Maskelyne. And if it seems a distinguished thing to believe a paradox, what must it be to invent one? Surely the summit of human ambition.

The paradoxes of philosophy generally prove, on analysis, to be contradictions in terms; those of art, on the other hand, are more often truisms turned inside out. This I believe to be a fair description of Diderot's celebrated *Paradoxe sur le Comédien*. It undoubtedly contains a great deal of truth; but in so far as it is true it is not paradoxical. The paradox is brought in, sometimes in the shape of sheer overstatement, more often by means of a little nimble jugglery with ambiguous terms and misleading analogies. In his arguments from analogy, Diderot does not rise to the fine frenzy of some of his fellow-theorists. 'We no more think feeling a necessary ingredient in acting,' cries one,[1] 'than we should deem it

[1] Oxberry, i. p. 223.

expedient for a painter, after he had finished a likeness upon the canvas, to represent the heart, liver, brains, and the internal formation, on the back of it.' Another—this time an American—executes a still more surprising feat of logical legerdemain. 'Did Rosa Bonheur,' he asks, with withering emphasis,[2] 'feel like a horse-fair when she painted her great picture on that subject? Or did Longfellow feel like "footprints on the sands of time" when he wrote that line of the *Psalm of Life*?' Diderot would no doubt admit that the zeal of these disciples outruns their discretion; yet they merely burlesque some of his own arguments.

Not even the firmest believer in Diderot—not even M. Coquelin, who says,[3] 'Je tiens que ce paradoxe est la vérité même' [I maintain that this paradox is absolutely true]—will deny that the philosopher founded his doctrine on slender evidence. A few anecdotes, of doubtful interpretation, are all that he advances in support of it, and Grimm expressly tells us that for years before he formulated his theory he had gone but rarely to the theatre. 'Able as he was,' a distinguished actress writes to me, 'Diderot, both in his *Paradoxe* and elsewhere, spoke without that intimate knowledge which only actors of the highest order can possess.' For a fruitful discussion of the points at issue, the interlocutors should be, not, as in Diderot's dialogue, a dogmatic 'First' and a docile 'Second,' but a trained psychologist and an experienced and versatile actor. Mr. H. D. Traill, in his *New Lucian,* has given imaginary effect to this idea in a suggestive dialogue between George Henry Lewes and David Garrick. Had these two men ever met in the flesh, with a stenographer behind the screen, their colloquy would certainly have been luminous, if not conclusive. Yet the evidence of one actor, though it were Garrick himself, is obviously insufficient. There are exceptional temperaments as well as exceptional talents, and no one man is entitled to make a dogma of his own experiences and methods. We want to arrive at the laws which govern the average or typical mimetic temperament; and to this end we must study as large a circle as possible of individual cases. Imagine David Hume in the green-room of Garrick's Drury Lane, with a royal commission to cross-

---

[2] *The Voice*, x. No. 3.
[3] *L'Art et le Comédien*, p. 24.

examine His Majesty's Servants severally and collectively, and you have a nearer approach to the ideal conditions of inquiry.

The discussion is not of the first importance; but since it has been started, and has led (in my judgment) to much false logic and empty paradox-mongering, I have long thought that, in the interests of 'lucidity,' a careful investigation should be attempted. I am but an amateur psychologist, and the reasonings contained in the following pages may often stand in need of revision; but at least I have brought together a far larger body of evidence than has hitherto been presented.

My endeavour has been to collect, both from biographical records and from the communications of living artists, the views and experiences of 'actors of the highest order.' I believe, however, that not only 'actors of the highest order,' but every intelligent artist who studies himself and others, has a right to be heard upon the questions at issue. I have therefore drawn no invidious distinction between the greater and the lesser lights of the theatrical firmament, but have accepted for what it is worth every ray of illumination that has reached me. Diderot might object that his theory applies only to the greatest actors; that he does not deny that second-rate actors feel and depend on feeling; nay, that he expressly affirms it. If we define the great actor as 'he who does not feel,' all controversy is of course at an end, for Diderot is safe in the inexpugnable fortress of a circular argument. But if we define the great actor as 'he who powerfully affects his audiences'; if we learn that many of the greatest actors (in this sense) confess to feeling acutely, and are observed by themselves and others to exhibit many symptoms of acute feeling, some of which are quite involuntary, and are of no direct use in heightening the illusion; if we discover that in all grades of the art the majority of players find by experience that they tend to produce a better effect when they play from the heart than when they play from the head alone; if we can find, in certain laws of mental and physical action and reaction, a rational explanation of this tendency; and if we can ascertain with tolerable clearness the artistic checks and limitations to which it must be subjected—then, surely, we shall have made a considerable breach even in the ir-

regular and baffling bastions of Diderot's position. To this
end we should hear not only Hamlet but the Player King,
not only Romeo and Juliet but Friar Laurence and the Fiery
Tybalt.

In setting about the investigation, my first effort was, of
course, to get rid of ambiguities. To ask, 'Do you feel in
acting?' or 'Do you identify yourself with the characters you
represent?' or 'Do you find sensibility an advantage or a disadvantage?' would only be to obscure the issue. It would
have required a whole treatise to define, with anything like
precision, the meaning I proposed to attach to these phrases,
and I could not reasonably expect my obliging informants
to study a disquisition on psychology. Moreover, even if I
had succeeded in defining my terms, it would have been folly
to expect in the general run of actors such habits of minute
and accurate introspection as would enable them to give a
lucid and trustworthy account of their experience. How,
then, could I hope to arrive at practical results? Clearly, by
confining my queries to outward symptoms, while reserving
to myself the task of interpretation. A tear, a blush, or a
tremor is an external, visible, sensible fact; an instance of
presence or absence of mind is a subject for ordinary testimony; a device or process for gaining a particular artistic
end can be observed and described like any other action or
series of actions. It was to these external details that I directed my informants' attention. I neither expected nor desired, of course, that they should refrain from stating their
own inferences and interpretations, but it was the facts themselves with which I was chiefly concerned. These once collected in sufficient numbers, I trusted that by comparing,
classifying, and interpreting them I might throw some light
on the mental processes involved in mimetic art.

The interrogatory which I originally issued will be found
embedded herein. Subsequent experience showed that it was
not so aptly worded and arranged as it might have been;
nevertheless it served its purpose. My own criticisms on it
were implied in the alterations I made when preparing the
French version (not reproduced here); but the sum of the
differences was not great enough to affect the general result.

How comes it, the reader may ask, since the questions were translated into French, that the experiences of living French actors are so meagrely represented? In explaining this, I shall be able to answer incidentally one or two objections to my method of inquiry.

As I could scarcely expect the leading artists of France to be at the pains of answering an interrogatory issued by an unknown Englishman, I forwarded to M. Francisque Sarcey a proof of my pamphlet, expressing a hope that he would call attention to it in his feuilleton in *Le Temps*. M. Sarcey, to whom my name was not quite unknown, met this request with a polite but firm refusal. 'Je regarde le procédé,' he wrote, 'qui est américain, comme fâcheux à la critique et à l'art.' [I regard this approach—which is American—as prejudicial to criticism and to art.] I made no attempt, of course, to alter M. Sarcey's determination, but I respectfully laid before him my own view of the 'procédé.' It was this: The inquiry has no bearing whatever on criticism, which is concerned with the effect produced, not with the phenomena accompanying its production. If an actor can convincingly represent emotion, the critic, as a critic, need not inquire whether he experiences or mechanically simulates it. But criticism is one thing, the psychology of art another; and to this the question at issue belongs. It is more curious than important, granted; but several eminent men, from Diderot to Mr. Irving, have held it worth discussion, so that an attempt to inquire into it systematically can scarcely be altogether idle. Nor is it quite without practical importance. Sensibility can be cultivated or it can be crushed, like any other gift of nature. It is quite conceivable that a young actor may help or hinder the due development of his powers by starting with a right or with a wrong theory as to the artistic value of real emotion. Idiosyncrasy, indeed, will generally determine his theory, but sheer intellectual conviction may not be without its effect.

It is true—and this may have been in M. Sarcey's mind—that by concentrating attention on individual symptoms of emotion the spectator may become insensible to the whole emotional impression of a performance. He 'cannot see the wood for trees.' While in the thick of my inquiry,

I was conscious that this preoccupation displaced my point
of view, so to speak, and interfered with my normal re-
ceptiveness. In my own case, the effect has already quite
worn off; and I can scarcely fear (or hope) that the reader of
the following pages will find his mental attitude towards the
stage seriously or permanently affected by the considerations
they suggest. If this book were in the hands of every playgoer, if the questions it discusses were vividly present to the
minds of any large percentage of an average audience, then
indeed my inquiry might be 'fâcheux à la critique et à l'art.'
Such a disaster, I own, would have its consolations for me,
if not for M. Sarcey. The fear of it, at any rate, does not
disturb my sleep o'nights.

Repulsed by M. Sarcey, I applied to another distinguished
Parisian critic, but he too declined to assist me. I do not mention his name, because the reasons he gave were more frank
than flattering to the artists whose work he criticises. He did
not believe, he said, that my inquiry would lead to any trustworthy result, because few actors had the intelligence, and
none the sincerity, to answer my questions aright. This objection has been urged in more than one quarter; indeed
Diderot himself advances it. 'You may prove my theory to
demonstration,' he says,[4] 'and a great actor will decline to
acknowledge it; it is his secret. A middling actor or a novice
is sure to contradict you flatly.' The experience of actors
gained in the course of my investigation leads me to dissent
entirely from Diderot and my Parisian correspondent. My
questions were answered, whether verbally or in writing,
always, I believe, with perfect sincerity, and generally, I
am sure, with perfect intelligence. When it happened that a
question was misunderstood, the fault, as a rule, was mine
rather than my informant's. Some, of course, answered with
more insight, more precision, in short more ability, than
others; but I seldom received a reply that was altogether beside the mark. Many artists to whom I sent my 'catechism'
lacked time or inclination to respond; but of those who
favoured me with their experience not one proved deficient
either in intelligence or in earnestness. On the latter point, of
course, my opinion must be taken for what it is worth, sincerity being, in the nature of things, incapable of proof. I

[4] Pollock, p. 18.

had now and then to allow for the 'personal equation,' but of wilful insincerity I discovered no trace. Where, indeed, is the motive for it? Once upon a time there might have been a tacit conspiracy among actors to keep what Diderot calls 'their secret' and prevent the outside public from suspecting the hollowness of their emotional displays. If this trick of the trade was ever practised, it has obviously broken down. Great actors—a few, but a very respectable few—proclaim the 'secret' to the four winds of heaven; middling actors, so far from 'flatly contradicting' Diderot, are found to swear by him. Diderot himself has made insensibility honourable. It is an unmistakable distinction to belong to the intellectual few who act from the brain alone. If there is any motive for insincerity, it now operates in Diderot's favour; but, though constantly on my guard, I discovered no trace of wilful deception in either sense. My informants even resisted the temptations to levity which, I admit, were offered them.

The attitude of M. Sarcey and his colleague convinced me that there was little hope of obtaining answers from the leading artists of Paris. Accordingly I did not issue my French interrogatory. Only one or two stray copies of it found their way across the Channel.

As loose quotation too often introduces confusion and error into arguments of this nature, I have in almost all cases given exact references to my authorities. I have also done my best to trace anecdotes to their sources, and to avoid the more or less garbled forms which they are apt, in course of time, to assume. In this I have not always succeeded. Anecdote-tracking is a difficult sport, and those who have most experience of it will most readily excuse an occasional failure to follow up the true scent. I do not pretend to have ransacked thoroughly the theatrical literature even of England and France for evidence upon the points under discussion. A complete collection of the documents in the case would fill ten volumes rather than one. All I can hope to have accomplished is a fairly representative selection of anecdotes and opinions. Where no reference is given, the reader will please understand me to draw upon manuscript authorities in my own possession—either notes of interviews or written answers to my printed questions. In quoting from the *Paradoxe* I have always referred to Mr. Walter Herries Pollock's useful translation,[5] but I have in some cases given my own rendering of Diderot's text, for the sake either of brevity or of literalness. I am further indebted to Mr. Pollock for allowing me to make use of his copy of Sticotti's very rare booklet, the peg on which the *Paradoxe* is hung.

After a careful search for less cumbrous expressions, I have been forced to fall back upon the terms 'emotionalist' and 'anti-emotionalist' to indicate the contending parties in this dispute. They are painfully clumsy; but the choice seemed to lie between them and still clumsier circumlocutions.

Chapter II

HISTORICAL

THE CONTROVERSY is entirely modern. The ancients, so far as I can discover, had no Diderot. They have left us a few anecdotes and remarks (to be quoted hereafter) all tending to show that the emotional theory held the field unquestioned. Far more explicit and weighty are the utterances of Shakespeare, who, as it seems to me, went to the root of this matter and has said what might well have been the last words upon it. But in his time there was no controversy. The emotional theory, under due restrictions, was accepted as self-evident. It was in France, about the middle of last century, that the present dispute arose.

In 1747, Remond (or Rémond) de Sainte-Albine, one of the editors of the *Mercure de France,* published a treatise called *Le Comédien.* It discussed in a rambling and unsystematic fashion the qualifications necessary for an actor, together with certain questions of technique. M. Remond was an emotionalist, thorough-going and unashamed. He writes as though the need for 'sensibility' had never been called in question. His effort is to determine the precise admixture of 'understanding,' 'sensibility,' and 'fire' requisite for the perfect actor; but the idea of altogether banishing sensibility

[5] London: Chatto & Windus, 1883.

never enters his head. The following extract from his table of contents is sufficient to show that he carried his emotionalism to the verge of absurdity:

Livre II.: *Section I.*

Chapitre I.—La gaieté est absolument nécessaire aux Comédiens, dont l'emploi est de nous faire rire.

Chap. II.—Quiconque n'a point l'âme élevée, représente mal un héros.

Chap. III.—Si toutes les personnes de Théâtre ont besoin de *sentiment,* celles qui se proposent de nous faire répandre des larmes, ont plus besoin que les autres de la partie du sentiment, désignée communément sous le nom d'*entrailles.*

Chap. IV.—Les personnes nées pour aimer devroient avoir seules le privilège de jouer les rôles d'Amans.

[Chapter I. Cheerfulness of spirit is indispensable to the actor, and its function is to make us laugh.

Chapter II. Anyone devoid of nobility will give but a distorted representation of a great man.

Chapter III. Everyone on the stage needs sensibility, but he who undertakes to make us weep has greater need than any other of the species of sensibility known as bowels of compassion.

Chapter IV. Only those with a natural aptitude for love have any business to be playing lovers' rôles.]

Such propositions as these appear to me, I confess, not only to touch, but to overshoot, the verge of absurdity; yet I hesitate to dismiss contemptuously a book which Lessing mentions[1] with respect.

Near the close of his *Paradoxe,* Diderot remarks:[2] 'For the rest, the question I am diving into was once before started between a middling man of letters, Remond de Sainte-Albine, and a great actor, Riccoboni. The man of letters pleaded the cause of sensibility; the actor took up my case. The story is one which has only just come to my knowledge.' It is evident that Diderot speaks from hearsay, not having himself seen the documents; and I think he confounds

[1] *Hamburgische Dramaturgie,* June 23, 1767.
[2] Pollock, p. 58.

Luigi Riccoboni the father with François Riccoboni the son.
The father, who alone could be called a great actor, was an
uncompromising emotionalist. He published in London, in
1725, a poem entitled *Dell' Arte Rappresentativa: Capitoli
Sei,* dedicated 'A Sua Eccellenza My Lord Chesterfield.'
He was too intent on his triple rhymes to make his doctrine
very clear or exhaustive; but on the question of sensibility
the following passage[3] is perfectly explicit:

> Per seguitare il naturale instinto
>   E moversi senz' Arte or che s' ha a fare
>   Scordare i quatro membri, e forse il quinto,
> Che è la Testa; ma si ben cercare
>   Di sentire la cosa, che ci esponi,
>   Che si creda esser tuo l' altrui affare.
> D' Amor, di Sdegno, o Gelosia li sproni
>   Se al Cor tu provi, o s' anco pur sarai
>   Qual Orreste invasato da Demoni;
> E l'Amore, e lo Sdegno sentirai,
>   E Gelosia, e Belzebu germani,
>   Senz' Arte braccia, e gambe moverai.
> Ed io scommetterei, e piedi, e mani,
>   Che un sol non troverai, che ti censuri
>   Fra tutti quanti li fidei Christiani
> Se con il Cuore i tuoi moti misuri.

[Act by raw instinct? Go through the motions heedless
    Of conscious art? Forget your feet and hands
    And treat to boot that fifth, the head, as needless?
So be it, but perpend: the question stands,
    Not how yourself to feel the part you're playing,
    But how make others feel what it demands.
Say love, say scorn, say jealousy are preying
    Upon your vitals; say you are devil-hounded,
    A new Orestes: there is no gainsaying
You *feel* this love, this scorn, this rage unbounded;
    All Satan's imps have made your breast their seat—
    But will your limbs do acting that is rounded?
For my part, I will bet *my* hands and feet
    You'll comb the cosmos and not meet the notion
    That in the actor it is indiscreet
To mix his gestures with some true emotion.]

---

[3] *Capitolo Secondo.*

Again, in his *Pensées sur la Déclamation,*[4] Riccoboni warns the orator not to work up tears, but to make no effort to repress them if they arise naturally. *'Sentir ce que l'on dit,'* he says emphatically, *'voilà les tons de l'âme.'* [To feel the words uttered—that is the inflection of the soul itself.] François Riccoboni, on the other hand, after due protestations of perfect filial respect, takes the liberty of flatly contradicting his father. In his book called *L'Art du Théâtre*[5] he maintains the necessity of absolutely repressing the physical symptoms of emotion. He gives two reasons: the difficulty of governing the voice, and the impossibility of passing from one passion to another with the rapidity required under the artificial conditions of the stage. 'S'il tombe une seule larme de vos yeux,' he says, 'des sanglots involontaires vous embarrasseront le gosier, et il vous sera impossible de proférer un seul mot sans des hocquets ridicules. Si vous devez alors passer subitement à la plus grande colère, cela vous sera-t-il possible? Non, sans doute.' [Let one tear fall from your eyes, and involuntary sobs will constrict your throat, so that you will be unable to get out a word without a ludicrous hiccoughing; and if the next moment you are supposed to simulate extreme anger, can you do it? By no possibility.] In these arguments Diderot is clearly, though incompletely, anticipated. It appears that Riccoboni's work was written before Sainte-Albine's, though published later; otherwise he might have gone into the question more fully. He seems to have published a second treatise on the same subject some years later, but I have not been able to procure it. As Diderot professes to have no personal knowledge of Riccoboni's productions, they do not enter into the genealogy of his ideas.

Paradox begets paradox; and we could scarcely have a wilder paradox than the assertion that none but a magnanimous man can act magnanimity, and that lovers alone can do justice to a love-scene. Sainte-Albine's budget of paradoxes was the direct progenitor of Diderot's, though there are two intermediate stages in the pedigree. Three years after *Le Comédien* appeared in Paris, an anonymous Englishman published an adaptation of it under the title of *The*

---

[4] Paris, 1738.
[5] Paris, 1750.

Actor: a Treatise on the Art of Playing.[6] The book has
generally been attributed to Aaron Hill, the adaptor of Voltaire's *Zaïre, Alzire,* and *Mérope;* but as the sequel, published in 1755, is expressly stated [7] to be 'written by the
Author of the former,' and contains allusions to events which
occurred after Aaron Hill's death,[8] this attribution must be
incorrect. Whoever the author may have been, he made as
little as possible of his obligations to Sainte-Albine, men-
tioning them in such ambiguous terms that their true nature
seems to have escaped notice from that day to this. As a
matter of fact, the whole theoretical portion of *The Actor* is
simply translated from *Le Comédien.* For example, the
chapter-headings quoted above are literally reproduced, as
well as the arguments they summarise. The adaptation,
however, is, if not an abler, at least a more entertaining book
than the original. Sainte-Albine dealt far more in precept
than in example. Indeed he is curiously chary of anecdote
and illustration. The adaptor, on the other hand, lost no
opportunity of pointing his moral by references to the plays
and actors of his own day—Quin, Garrick, Barry, Mossop,
Macklin; Mrs. Cibber, Mrs. Pritchard, Peg Woffington, and
Kitty Clive. We are indebted to him for some of our clearest
information as to the methods of the 'palmy days.' In 1755,
as I have said, a sequel or second edition was published,
under the same title. It professed to be 'A New Work. . . .
Adapted to the Present State of the Theatres,' but was in
truth a mere recapitulation of the former argument, with
some new anecdotes inserted. Though his use of Sainte-
Albine's work showed a deficiency in psychological acumen
as well as in literary ethics, the nameless writer ('an author
unknown to you, and who shall ever remain so') was certainly no fool. He was well read; he wrote a very fair style;
and, theories apart, he was an excellent critic of acting.

Here the matter may be said to have rested for fourteen
years, until, in 1769, Antonio Fabio Sticotti, who seems to
have been an actor of the Italian company in Paris,[9] bethought him to re-adapt into French the English adaptation of Sainte-Albine's work. Sticotti, however, seems to

6 London, 1750.
7 Lowe, p. 2.
8 Feb. 8, 1749–50.
9 On the Sticotti family, see Campardon, ii. p. 144.

have had no suspicion that *The Actor* was not entirely original. The fact that he makes no mention of Sainte-Albine might possibly be due to an underhand design of giving his book a false air of novelty; but in that case he would certainly have taken some pains to lessen the similarity between the two treatises. As it is, *Garrick, ou les Acteurs Anglois* bears the most evident marks of its descent: a similar design, similar theories, similar arguments. For instance, the four chapter-headings quoted on p. 83 are replaced by the following, unnumbered, but in the same order:[10]

'De la Gaieté nécessaire à l'Acteur Comique.'
'De la Noblesse d'ame nécessaire à l'Acteur Tragique.'
'De la Tendresse.
'Du Penchant à l'Amour.'

[Cheerfulness of spirit indispensable to the player of comedy
Nobility of soul indispensable to the player of tragedy
Concerning the tender emotions
Concerning the aptitude for love]

Sticotti, indeed, gave most of his attention to the anecdotic side of his English original, translating many anecdotes, and (in foot-notes) adding parallel cases from French stage history. Thus Sainte-Albine himself might not at the first glance have recognised in *Garrick* a grandson of his own *Comédien*. Amid all changes, however, his emotional extravagances were faithfully reproduced; and it is to these that we owe the anti-emotional extravagances of Diderot and his followers. In a letter to Mlle. Jodin,[11] dated some years before the appearance of *Garrick,* we find Diderot expressing himself a convinced emotionalist. 'Si, quand vous êtes sur le théâtre,' he writes, 'vous ne croyez pas être seule, tout est perdu. . . . Un acteur qui n'a que du sens et du jugement est froid; celui qui n'a que de la verve et de la sensibilité est fou. C'est un certain tempérament de bon sens et de chaleur qui fait l'homme sublime; et sur la scène et dans le monde, celui qui montre plus qu'il ne sent, fait rire au lieu de toucher.' [If, on the stage, you do not feel that you are alone, the case is hopeless. . . . The actor who has nothing but reason and calculation is frigid; and the one who has nothing

[10] Ed. 1770, pp. 128-146.
[11] Assézat, xix. p. 387.

but excitement and emotionalism is silly. What makes the
human being of supreme excellence is a kind of balance between calculation *and* warmth. Whether on the stage or in
ordinary life, the man who displays more than he feels
evokes ridicule rather than sympathy.] After this, we can
scarcely be wrong in attributing the extreme anti-emotion-
alism of his later position to the reaction begotten by emotionalist excesses.

Sticotti's work became highly popular. At least three
editions were published in three consecutive years, and a German translation appeared in 1771. The German translator
may have been put on the track of the booklet by a somewhat elaborate criticism of its theories contributed by
Diderot, in 1770,[12] to Monsieur Grimm's *Correspondance*.
'Un homme illustre dans les Lettres,[13] says Sticotti in his
preface,[14] 'aimé autant qu'estimé pour sa politesse et l'hu-
manité de ses sentimens, a bien voulu m'avouer que mon
livre lui avoit fait *naître de bonnes idées.* Je conviens que
s'il m'eût été permis de les employer, j'aurois été certain de
réunir tous les suffrages de mes Lecteurs.' [A man eminent
in literature, one equally respected and beloved for his
urbanity and his benevolence, was good enough to declare
to me that my book had suggested to him some good ideas.
I am persuaded that, had he but allowed me to make use
of them, I should assuredly have won the assent of every one
of my readers.] Little did he think that Diderot's 'good
ideas,' which, with polite contempt perhaps, he insisted on
keeping to himself, ran in flat contradiction to the whole
tenor of his book. They made 'good copy,' however, for
Grimm's princely clients, and the essay contributed to the
Correspondance contains the entire gist of the subsequent
Paradoxe.

It was probably in 1773 that Diderot remodelled his essay
in the form of a dialogue, adding new anecdotes and instances, but in no way modifying his theoretical position. An
allusion to a miraculous actress playing, at seventeen, the
heaviest tragic parts, is taken to refer to Mlle. Raucourt,
who made her first appearance September 23, 1772. It has
since been discovered that, like other Infant Phenomena,

---

[12] Assézat, viii. p. 339.
[13] Monsieur Diderot.—[Sticotti's note.]
[14] Ed. 1770, p. xi.

she had remained stationary at sweet seventeen for several years. There are allusions, also, to events which occurred in 1776 and in 1778; so that Diderot must evidently have retouched it, perhaps more than once. As was his habit with many of his writings (*Le Neveu de Rameau* is a notable instance) he took no steps to publish it. The draft of 1770 was first printed as part of Grimm's *Correspondance* between 1812 and 1814. The completed *Paradoxe* did not see the light till 1830.

Chapter III

THE *PARADOXE*

THE DIALOGUE, as a form of exposition, has this disadvantage, that it stimulates the pugnacious, or, more politely speaking, the chivalrous instinct in human nature. One of the disputants invariably goes as a lamb to the slaughter, and his pre-arranged massacre cannot but stir our sympathy. Thus a feeling of antagonism to the writer's argument is aroused by the very form. There is a cat-and-mouse cruelty about the Socratic method against which our sense of justice, nay, of humanity, rebels.

In few expository dialogues—I need not, surely, insist on the distinction between an exposition in form of argument and a merely fanciful or satirical colloquy—in few expository dialogues do we feel the imperfection of the form more keenly than in Diderot's *Paradoxe*. One of its chief paradoxes is that the second speaker is practically dumb. He now and then bleats forth a semi-articulate objection; but he evidently knows that he is there to be slaughtered, and is anxious to get the operation over as soon as possible. Acting upon Grimm's favourite maxim, 'Ne vous expliquez point si vous voulez vous entendre' [If you would be understood, never explain yourself], he never thinks of demanding that unpleasant preliminary to all fruitful debate: a definition of terms. Why, then, does Diderot, who must have known (none better) that Grimm's maxim was a mere pleasantry, ensconce himself behind it in order to enjoy an empty tri-

umph over an imaginary opponent? For the very reason, I
suspect, that he was not satisfied with his own argument.
That he believed himself right in the main is not for a moment doubtful; but re-reading his hasty sketch of 1770, he
felt, I think, the lack of system in his ideas, and chose at
once to disguise and to excuse it by recasting the little treatise
in dialogue form. He says himself,[1] 'I have not yet arranged
my ideas logically.' To have undertaken a systematic psychology of acting would have led him too far afield. He probably did not think the subject worth the trouble. Besides,
he wanted to kill two birds with one stone: to refute the
heresies of Sticotti (or rather of Sainte-Albine) and to hint
at the absurdities of French classic tragedy. That the latter
object was present to his mind no one can doubt who reads
the *Paradoxe* carefully, in connection with Diderot's other
writings on the drama.[2] He was a 'naturalist' (I do not
mean a Zolaist) born out of due time. He foresaw the
modern drama and he believed in it, though his own attempts to realise it were not encouraging. When we find him,
then, as in the *Paradoxe*, assuming throughout that the
personages of the stage must necessarily be 'magnified and
non-natural men,' can we help suspecting him of laughing
in his sleeve? Yet that is the groundwork of his whole
contention, so far as it can be reduced to any sort of unity.
Agamemnon and Orestes, Cleopatra and Agrippina, according to his own illustration,[3] are like the ghosts which children manufacture with the aid of a sheet, a broomstick, and
a gruff voice. These spectres neither move, speak, nor think
like men; why should they weep like men? That is the gist
of the argument, and so far it is logical enough; though it
is not quite clear that a certain thrill of real emotion might
not help the actor to rise to the 'magnified and non-natural'
emotion of his personage. But supposing this thesis absolutely right, what does it amount to? Not a fundamental
principle of art, but a commentary (not to say a satire) upon
French tragedy. And no one, I think, knew this better than
Diderot. How else are we to read such a passage as this? [4]—

[1] Pollock, p. 14.
[2] Morley, i. p. 328.
[3] Pollock, pp. 16-17.
[4] Pollock, p. 21.

'*Le Second.* C'est que peut-être Racine et Corneille, tout grands hommes qu'ils étaient, n'ont rien fait qui vaille.

Le Premier. Quel blasphème! Qui est-ce qui oserait le proférer? qui est-ce qui oserait y applaudir?'

[*The Second.* Perhaps Racine and Corneille, great names as they are, did nothing of account.

The First. Oh, blasphemy! who could dare to say it? Who to endorse it? . . .]

He was sincere in his admiration for Corneille and Racine, but Lessing himself had scarcely a lower opinion of the form in which they worked.

I know not how better to display the multitudinous meanings which Diderot attributes to 'sensibility' than by taking the place of 'The Second' speaker and interjecting a few comments upon the main positions of 'The First.' My quotations shall be accurate so far as they go; if the reader suspects me of doing Diderot injustice in wrenching them from their context, he can satisfy himself by referring to the original.

The First. 'How should Nature without Art make a great actor, since nothing happens on the stage exactly as in nature?'[5]

The Second. Granted; but no one has ever argued that Nature without Art, or sensibility without training, is sufficient to make a great actor, a good actor, or any sort of actor at all. The emotionalists to a man—Sainte-Albine, the nameless Englishman, and Sticotti—insist strongly on the need for technical accomplishment.

The First. 'What I require of a great actor is penetration and no sensibility; the art of imitating everything, or, in other words, the same aptitude for every sort of character and part.'[6]

The Second. No doubt the ideal actor (the unattainable ideal) is the man who has a perfect aptitude for every conceivable character—'a soft mass of sculptor's clay,' as M. Coquelin puts it,[7] 'capable of assuming at will any form.' But what you have to prove is that the lack of sensibility in

[5] Pollock, p. 13.
[6] Pollock, p. 14.
[7] *Harper's Magazine,* lxxiv. p. 894.

himself will assist him in imitating the manifestations of sensibility in his characters, and in affecting the sensibilities of his audience.

The First. 'It is not in the stress of the first burst that characteristic traits present themselves. . . .[8] He who comes upon the stage without having his whole action arranged and marked out will be a beginner all his life. Or if, endowed with intrepidity, confidence, and spirit, he relies on his quickness of wit and the habit of his calling, he will carry you away with his fire and fury, and you will applaud him as an expert in painting may smile at a free sketch where all is indicated and nothing defined.' [9]

The Second. Here we come upon one of the most frequent forms in which 'sensibility' is held to manifest itself—to wit, a tendency to rely on the inspiration of the moment. It is clear that, whether wise or unwise, this is possible only within very narrow limits. In any properly rehearsed play it can apply to nothing but facial expression, gesture, and tones of the voice; or if to positions and 'business,' then only in scenes in which the player has the stage practically to himself. When two or more persons are playing together, their movements can no more be determined on the spur of the moment than can the movements of a watch-wheel. Each is part of a mechanism which the least lack of precision will put out of gear. Only among amateurs, or in the veriest 'scratch' performances, is this rule neglected, and then not from any trust in the virtues of sensibility, but simply from bad stage-management. Diderot admirably states[10] the object of rehearsal to be 'the striking of a balance between the different talents of the actors, so as to establish a general unity in the playing.' This is its final function; but its first and more obvious purpose is merely to put each of the cog-wheels in its proper place. The watch must be pieced together before it can be regulated.

The details which it is possible to leave to inspiration are, doubtless, of vast importance, and, as we shall see, the practice of different actors in admitting or excluding the suggestions of the moment varies very widely. But we shall also

[8] Pollock, p. 17.
[9] Pollock, p. 64.
[10] Pollock, p. 26.

see that absolute preregulation of even the minutest gestures is quite consistent with genuine feeling—that is, with the presence in the actor's own organism of the physical symptoms of the emotion he is seeking to express.

The First. 'These plaintive and sorrowful tones, drawn from the very depth of a mother's heart . . . are these not the result of true feeling? Are these not the very inspiration of despair? Not at all; and the proof is that they are measured, that they form part of a system of declamation, that, raised or lowered by the twentieth part of a quarter of a tone, they ring false.' [11]

The Second. Precisely; but is it not the skilful use of that delicate imaginative mechanism called 'sensibility' which enables the great actress to adjust her vocal cords to this subtle nicety of tone?

The First. At the close of a performance 'The actor is tired, you are sad. He has had exertion without feeling, you feeling without exertion. Were it otherwise, the player's lot would be the most wretched on earth; but he is not the person he represents; he plays it, and plays it so well that you think he is the person; the illusion is all on your side; he knows well enough that he is not the person.' [12]

The Second. Another purely imaginary phase of sensibility —a tendency to become absolutely incarnate in your character, so as to undergo all his emotions in their fullest acuteness. Not even Sainte-Albine has argued that this is either advisable or possible; yet it is one of the absurdities which the anti-emotionalists are fondest of setting up and knocking down again. ' "Are you, sir [Dr. Johnson asked John Philip Kemble], one of those enthusiasts who believe yourself transformed into the very character you represent?" [13] Upon Mr. Kemble's answering that he had never felt so strong a persuasion himself; "To be sure not, sir (said Johnson;) the thing is impossible. And if Garrick really believed himself to be that monster, Richard the Third, he deserved to be hanged every time he performed it." '

Diderot's psychology of the audience is surely as false as his psychology of the actor. Here Johnson was in advance of

[11] Pollock, p. 19.
[12] Pollock, pp. 19-20.
[13] Boswell, iv. p. 243.

him. 'Nay, you know,' he said,[14] 'nobody imagines that he
[the player] is the character he represents. They say "See
Garrick! how he looks to-night! See how he'll clutch the
dagger!" That is the buz of the theatre.' There is no absolute illusion on either side. Salvini knows as well as the
public, and the public knows as well as Salvini, that he is
not Othello. Were it otherwise, we could no more endure
to see the tragedy than he to act it. The emotionalist position
is that both actor and audience should yield themselves up
to the illusion to a certain extent; the anti-emotionalist position is that the actor will more easily and certainly beget
illusion in the audience if he remains entirely free from it
himself. These, I take it, are the opposing theses. To disprove or ridicule a theory which no one has advanced—a
theory which implies an absolute transmigration of soul
from Richard to Garrick, from Othello to Salvini—is to
darken counsel by words without relevance. Salvini, indeed,
uses the word 'transmigration,' but he uses it in a figurative,
not in a literal and, so to speak, supernatural sense.

The First (emphatically). *'Extreme sensibility makes middling actors; middling sensibility makes the ruck of bad
actors; a complete absence of sensibility paves the way for the
sublime actor.'* [15]

The Second. This, at least, is explicit and precise. But beware, Monsieur le Premier! It is rash for a disputant of your
nimbleness to tether himself to a dogma. The chain may
gall you ere long.

The First. 'If this or that actor or actress were as deeply
moved as people imagine, do you suppose one would think
of casting an eye round the boxes, another of smiling to
someone at the wing, and almost all of speaking straight at
the pit? [16] Do you suppose that the call-boy would have to
interrupt a hearty fit of laughter in the green-room, to tell
the laugher that the time has come for him to go on and
stab himself?' [17]

The Second. These, you tell me, are common incidents of
the player's calling? So be it. And they indicate absence of

---

[14] Boswell, v. p. 46.
[15] Pollock, p. 20.
[16] 'Parler au parterre.' I am not sure that this does not refer to the practice of
interrupting the play to address the audience, noticed in so many anecdotes.
[17] Pollock, p. 28.

sensibility? Quite so. Are we to understand, then, that the majority of actors are 'sublime'? Even at the Théâtre-Français in 1770 one would rather expect to find the majority 'middling' along with a fair percentage of the unmistakably 'bad.' Now middling actors, according to the dogma, owe their mediocrity to 'extreme sensibility,' while 'middling sensibility' is the bane of 'the ruck of bad actors.' Hence it ensues that in any given company two or three 'sublime' players at most should be capable of giving the above-mentioned proof of insensibility, while the majority should be subject to those errors and weaknesses which arise from sensibility, whether middling or extreme. In short, the dogma and the argument do not dovetail. One or other must be abandoned; and, for my part, I think the argument the fitter to survive. It is quite true that many actors can recognise their friends in the boxes; quite true that many can indulge in bye-play of all sorts, unnoticed (more or less) by the audience; quite true that many a player has broken off a burst of laughter in the green-room to go and give himself the happy despatch on the stage. But of these truths we have an obvious explanation, involving no paradox. It is simply that the ruck of middling and bad actors perform their parts mechanically, not feeling, not even understanding them; while, on the other hand, there is no reason why actors who feel, be they good, bad, or indifferent, should not at the same time have all their wits about them.

We shall find hereafter that many of the greatest actors remain intent on their character throughout the whole of a performance, even when absent from the stage, and though not, of course, unconscious of their audience, are neither able nor willing to distinguish individuals in front of the house. Sarah Siddons was one of these concentrated players; Tommaso Salvini is another. According to the dogma, then, Siddons and Salvini should be, not the greatest in their respective spheres, but at best a pair of mediocrities. Is the dogma false? Or is the world deluded?

The First. 'When *Inès de Castro* was first performed, the pit burst out laughing at the point where the children appear. Mlle. Duclos, who played Inès, apostrophised the laughers indignantly: "Ris donc, sot parterre, au plus bel endroit de la pièce. . . ." ['Go on and laugh, you silly groundlings, at the finest part of the play!'] [18] Quinault-Dufresne plays the part of Severus in *Polyeucte*. Sent by the Emperor Decius to persecute the Christians, he confides to a friend his real feelings with regard to that calumniated sect. Common sense requires that this confidence . . . should be uttered in a low tone. The pit calls to him, "Plus haut!'" ["Louder!"] He replies to the pit, "Et vous, messieurs, plus bas!" . . . ["And you, sirs, not so loud!"] Caillot is playing *Le Déserteur*. . . . At the very moment of his agony, when he is on the point of being dragged to execution, he notices that the chair on which he will have to lay down the fainting Louise is badly placed, and he rearranges it while singing in a moribund voice, "Mes yeux vont se fermer sans avoir vu Louise." ["Mine eyes shall close ere they have seen Louise."] [19] . . . Lekain, as Ninias, enters his father's tomb, and there cuts his mother's throat. He comes forth with blood-stained hands, horror-stricken, wild-eyed, quivering. . . . Yet seeing a diamond drop which has fallen from an actress's ear, he pushes it with his foot towards the wing. And these actors feel? Impossible!' [20]

The Second. Concerning the first two anecdotes: is a sudden revulsion of feeling a phenomenon undreamt of in your psychology? Even supposing that to 'feel' a part necessarily implied a somnambulistic absorption in it (a quite gratuitous supposition), can we not conceive Duclos and Quinault to have been wakened from their trance by the interruptions of the pit, and to have vented the irritability of 'the sleeper awakened' in the first phrases that sprang to their lips? Their very audacity indicates that they were not acting in cold blood, but were in a measure beside themselves. As for Caillot and Lekain, their actions afford simple instances of the manifold activity of consciousness at any given moment. Why should stage emotion be supposed to absorb all a man's faculties, when the most poignant emotion in real life does nothing of the sort? On the contrary, it will often sharpen our senses in every direction, producing, not anæsthesia, but hyperæsthesia. We all know how memory registers the smallest details of any scene which has wit-

[18] Pollock, pp. 37-38.
[19] Misquoted in the original. Pollock, p. 60.
[20] Pollock, p. 38.

nessed a crisis in our lives, as Fagin, in the dock, 'counted the iron spikes before him, and wondered how the head of one had been broken off, and whether they would mend it or leave it as it was.' We know how, even under the first shock of a great catastrophe, men are often found to attend with mechanical punctiliousness to the minutest trifles of everyday existence. The man who has determined to jump off Waterloo Bridge at midnight will wind up his watch as usual at eleven o'clock; and if he chance to see a sixpenny-piece on the pavement of Wellington Street, he will, in all probability, stoop and pick it up. The actual Ninias, had he found a jewel lying in his path, would probably have picked it up and put it in his pocket. Men led to execution have been known to be very particular about details of their dress, or to borrow an umbrella from the sheriff lest they should catch cold. Sir Thomas More jested with the headsman. Charles II., with the death-rattle in his throat, apologised to his courtiers for taking such an unconscionable time to die. All these persons may be presumed to have felt their situation deeply, and no situation can be more absorbing than that of a man in the jaws of death. We shall find many instances in the sequel of divided mental activity. In the meantime, I submit that Lekain's adroitness in saving the jewel does not prove him to have been insensible to the terror of the situation, any more than William Tell's dexterity in splitting the apple proves him to have been indifferent to the fate of his son.

No array of examples of presence of mind will practically further the anti-emotionalists' case. They should rather bring forward instances in which an actor's total absorption in his part has placed him at the mercy of accidents, and has thus injured the desired effect. These, unfortunately, are not so easily discovered.

The First. 'A sure way to play in a petty, mean style, is to play your own character. Suppose you are a tartuffe, a miser, a misanthrope; you may play the part well enough, but you will not come near the poet's creation; for that is *the* Tartuffe, *the* Miser, *the* Misanthrope.'[21]

The Second. What has this to do with sensibility, in any conceivable sense of the term? Sensibility comes into play

[21] Pollock, p. 39.

through imaginative sympathy; and no one, however great a hypocrite or miser, can have any sort of sympathy with Tartuffe or Harpagon. Egoism is of the essence of evil. The hypocrite lives upon the uprightness of others, the miser upon their generosity; and every additional hypocrite and miser is a victim the less and a competitor the more. They are not even influenced by the motives which induce felons to form offensive and defensive alliances. Each would like nothing better than to have a monopoly of his own vice. They are the Ishmaels of the social system. Vices of sensuality establish a freemasonry among their devotees, but hypocrisy and avarice serve only to isolate and harden.

A conscious hypocrite, even if it were possible that the triumphs and defeats of his patron saint should touch his 'sensibility,' would be the last to reveal the mysteries of his craft and of his soul by playing Tartuffe. To do so would be, not to assume, but to throw away, a mask; and his mask is his stock-in-trade. An unconscious hypocrite, if naturally unctuous in manner (which by no means follows), might have a peculiar facility for entering into the skin of Tartuffe. John Palmer, the first and perhaps the greatest Joseph Surface, was commonly known as 'Plausible Jack.' In a dispute with Sheridan, he began in his oily and rotund manner, 'If you could but see my heart, Mr. Sheridan!' when the playwright-manager cut him short with the remark, 'Why, Jack, you forget that I wrote it!' [22] But Palmer's success in Joseph Surface had nothing to do with 'sensibility.' No one thinks of engaging a murderer to play Macbeth, not because his sensibility would lead him to act 'in a petty, mean style,' but because the very idea is an absurdity. To argue that Mr. Willard is not necessarily a villain because he plays the villain so well, or that his 'Spider' would not be so good as it is were he himself a swell-mobsman, is simply to insult our intelligence. Only in the lowest stages of dramatic culture does anyone think of confounding the actor's ethics with those of his personage. There is a legend of a backwoodsman becoming so incensed with the villainy of Iago that he drew his revolver and shot, or shot at, the actor. It is said, too, that Provost, who played Napoleon's gaoler, Sir Hudson Lowe, at the Porte Saint-Martin, had to be es-

[22] Doran, iii. p. 142.

corted home from the theatre lest the infuriated gods should
fall upon him and lynch him.[23] These savages of the back-
woods or the boulevards are the persons who require to
have it proved to them that a hypocrite will not make the
best Tartuffe or a miser the best Harpagon. The old lady
who left Edmund Kean a handsome legacy on seeing his
Othello, and revoked it after his performance of the con-
temptible Luke in Massinger's *City Madam*,[24] might also
have learnt something from Diderot's argument.

Whether a lover will make the best Romeo is another and
somewhat more rational question, to be considered hereafter.

I shall not dispute Diderot's demonstration of the incon-
veniences of too much sensibility in private life. It is scarcely
to the purpose; for the idiosyncrasy which makes a man
stammer and hesitate in improvising a declaration of love
on his own account, may be the very thing to aid him in
lending fervour and conviction to a mimic declaration, the
words of which are supplied by Shakespeare or Alfred de
Musset. Neither do I insist upon the fact, which Diderot's
actor-disciples should lay to heart, that his theory is based
upon a hearty contempt for their calling. 'In society,' he
says,[25] 'unless they are buffoons, I find actors polished, caustic,
cold, proud, dissipated, profuse, selfish, alive to our absurdities rather than touched by our misfortunes; unmoved
at the sight of a melancholy incident or at the recital of a
pathetic story; pariahs, vagabonds, slaves of the great; without conduct, without friends, without any of the holy and
tender ties which associate us in the pains and pleasures of
another, who in turn shares our own. I have often seen an
actor laugh off the stage, I do not remember to have seen
one weep. What do they do, then, with the sensibility they
arrogate, and are supposed to possess? Do they leave it on
the stage at their exit to take it up again at their next entrance?' Here we have again the contradiction pointed out
above. If this be a fair description of actors in general, what
comes of the dogma that extreme sensibility makes middling
actors and middling sensibility the ruck of bad actors? We

[23] *Coquelin*, p. 30.
[24] Hawkins, i. p. 259.
[25] Pollock, p. 47.

are now assured that actors as a class are devoid of sensibility; how comes it, then, that actors as a class are not
'sublime'? This, however, is not essential. Diderot's theory
may be right though his arguments are inconsistent. What
I have sought to show is that his reasoning breaks down, or
at least straggles off and loses itself, for lack of a definition
of terms. He does not know clearly either what he himself is
maintaining, or what he is arguing against. He is proving,
half the time, that sensibility is mischievous, while the other
half he devotes to showing that it does not exist.

We have seen that he attributes to sensibility four leading
phases:

i. A tendency to do without study and to rely on momentary inspiration.

ii. A tendency to become incarnate in your personage, to
live in it and in it alone, to feel all its emotions and endure
all its agonies.

iii. A tendency to somnambulistic absorption in the business of the scene, making consciousness for the moment one
and indivisible.

iv. A tendency to express your own moral nature, instead
of assuming and exhibiting the character created by the
playwright.

At last, however, in a rash moment, Diderot is actually
betrayed into defining 'sensibility,' and at once the debate
is practically at an end. 'Sensibility,' so the definition runs,[26]
'. . . is that disposition which accompanies organic weakness, mobility of the diaphragm, vivacity of the imagination,
delicacy of the nerves, which inclines one to . . . loss of
self-control, to exaggeration, to contempt, to disdain, to ob-
tuseness to the true, the good, and the beautiful, to injustice,
to madness.' Sensibility, then, is a morbid habit of mind and
body, which must interfere, not with acting alone, but with
all healthy art whatsoever. This is self-evident. Any criticism
of such a conclusion is futile. But how about the definition?
Supposing such a multitude of effects—I have only quoted
half of them—to arise from one cause, can we fairly call
that cause sensibility? Hysteria, surely, is a much apter name
for the disease. Substituting this term, then, we read

[26] Pollock, p. 43.

Diderot's thesis as follows: 'The great actor must not be hysterical.' Agreed. But where is the paradox?

'Ne lui demandez pas,' says M. Paul Janet of Diderot,[27] 'des œuvres méditées, composées avec art, écrites avec goût, liées dans toutes leurs parties. . . . Ce ne sont jamais que des fragments, des lueurs éclatantes, mais passagères, d'admirables improvisations: mais tout ce qui est raisonnement suivi, liaison d'idées, enchaînement systématique de propositions, enfin construction régulière et équilibrée, est chose inconnue pour cet esprit fumeux où tout est sans cesse à l'état de bouillonnement et de fermentation.' [Do not look to him for writings closely reasoned, subtly framed, gracefully expressed, unified throughout. . . . His works are never other than fragmentary—made up of brilliant but fitful flashes, sudden inspirations. Whatever is rigorously logical—sequence of thoughts, organized concatenation of ideas; in short, balanced design, conformable to rule—is utterly foreign to this turbulent mind, a mind given up entire to seething and to ferment.]

Chapter IV

'SUNT LACRYMÆ RERUM'

THE FIRST two sections of my interrogatory are, I think, the most essential. They take us to the very kernel of the matter.

There are certain simple emotions which tend to express themselves directly and unmistakably in changes of the physical organs. The chief of these are grief and joy (with all their subdivisions), rage, terror, and shame. The more complex emotions have no such proper and instant symptoms. Love and hatred, jealousy and envy, for example, are rather attitudes of mind than individual emotions. They may have their appropriate facial expressions, but a very slight effort of will suffices to smooth even these away; whereas we all know how hard it is to repress the physical manifestations of grief or terror. The complex and, so to speak, ha-

27 *Nineteenth Century,* ix. p. 695.

bitual emotions utter themselves from time to time through
the medium of the simple emotions. Love, it is needless to
say, will run the whole gamut of grief and joy; hatred, in
the presence of the hated object, will burst forth in the form
of rage. Thus the physical effects of the simple emotions may
be regarded as the raw material of expression; whence it
follows that the reproduction of these physical effects must
be the very groundwork of the actor's art. And of the simple
emotions, grief in all its phases is, to the actor, by far the
most important. I do not mean that life is a vale of tears,
and that the stage, in holding as 'twere the mirror up to
nature, must therefore be more intimately concerned with
weeping than with laughter. Something might be said for
this view of the matter, but I do not intend to say it. What
I mean is that, with the exception of terror, which is of
comparatively rare occurrence, no emotion manifests itself
so directly, so inevitably, and so peculiarly as grief. Joy is
much more easily repressed, and much more various in its
symptoms; therefore it calls for less absolute fidelity of imitation. We take it for granted much more readily than grief.
Great joy, indeed, will often borrow its expression from
grief, but not so grief from joy, unless it passes over into
positive madness. To look at the matter from another point
of view, do we not see that from the days of Thespis downwards the gift of pathos has been regarded as the actor's
highest endowment, the representation of pity, sorrow, and
despair as his worthiest task? It is often said that every low
comedian aspires to play Macbeth; in other words, everyone
instinctively recognises that it is a much simpler and more
trivial task to make the unskilful laugh than to make the
judicious grieve. Some years ago, on the occasion of one of
Mr. Toole's numerous appearances in the witness-box, the
judge, intending a compliment, maladroitly remarked that
he was sure no one had ever wept while Mr. Toole was on
the stage. 'I am very sorry to hear it, my lord,' was the
comedian's reply; and indeed his lordship's pleasantry
showed a strange ignorance not only of human nature in
general but of Mr. Toole's art in particular. To sum the
matter up, then, the rendering of grief and its kindred
shades of emotion is universally accepted as the highest
problem of the actor's craft; and the question, 'How may

this rendering be best effected?' is the central point of the whole discussion.

There is no doubt that the imagination can in some cases so act on the physical organism as to produce in a more or less acute degree the characteristic symptoms of grief; while, on the other hand, these symptoms may to some extent be imitated by the direct action of the will upon the muscles, with little or no aid from the imagination. Which method is the better calculated to work on the sympathies of a theatrical audience? 'The latter,' say Diderot and his adherents; 'The former,' his adversaries retort. I have tried, therefore, to ascertain, first, whether the tendency of the imagination to act on the lachrymal glands and the muscles of the throat is general or exceptional; secondly, whether the actors in whom this tendency exists have found it help or hinder their efforts to speak to the hearts of their hearers. For this, I need scarcely say, is the one ultimate test. Whatever may be the case with the other arts, its immediate effect upon the average audience is the be-all and end-all of acting. Nothing is absolutely right or wrong, artistic or inartistic. If real tears help to move the average audience, they are right and artistic; if they tend to cast a damp over the house, they are inartistic and wrong.

My first question, then, was this:

In moving situations, do tears come to your eyes? Do they come unbidden? Can you call them up and repress them at will? In delivering pathetic speeches does your voice break of its own accord? Or do you deliberately simulate a broken voice? Supposing that, in the same situation, you on one night shed real tears and speak with a genuine 'lump in your throat,' and on the next night simulate these affections without physically experiencing them: on which occasion should you expect to produce the greater effect upon your audience?

All testimony, old and new, agrees in asserting that, whatever their artistic value, real tears are habitually and copiously shed upon the stage. The ancients are at one both as to their reality and as to their artistic value. Hackneyed though it be, the inevitable passage from Horace[1] must lead the way:

[1] *Ars Poetica*, l. 101-103.

> Ut ridentibus adrident, ita flentibus adsunt[2]
> Humani vultus. Si vis me flere, dolendum est
> Primum ipsi tibi; tunc tua me infortunia lædent.

> Smiles are contagious; so are tears; to see
> Another sobbing, brings a sob from me.
> No, no, good Peleus; set the example, pray,
> And weep yourself, then weep perhaps I may.[3]

Some critics have maintained that the maxim is not addressed to actors but to tragic poets. If so, Horace has certainly expressed himself with less than Horatian lucidity; and there can be little doubt that even if he had not the stage actually in his mind, he would without hesitation have extended the principle to mimetic art.

The orators are still more emphatic; and oratory is sufficiently analogous to acting to give their opinions great weight. Judging by mere antecedent probability, one would not be surprised to find them in the anti-emotionalist camp. However important self-control may be to the actor, it must be doubly so to the forensic orator. If, then, the symptoms of emotion, physically experienced, are inconsistent with perfect self-control, one would expect to find Cicero and Quintilian insisting on absolute insensibility. The fact that their precepts take the opposite direction seems to show that the clouding of the eyes does not necessarily involve the clouding of the brain.

First let us hear Cicero: 'Nor is it possible,' he says,[4] 'for the hearer to grieve, or hate, or fear, or to be moved to commiseration and tears, unless the emotions which the speaker wishes to communicate are deeply impressed upon himself, and stamped on his own bosom in characters of fire. . . . Never, I assure you, have I endeavoured to excite in the judges the emotions of grief, commiseration, envy or hatred, without becoming sensibly touched myself with the passions I wished to communicate to them. . . . And do not suppose it something extraordinary and wonderful for the speaker to be so often subjected to the violent excitement of grief, and anger, and every other passion of the mind, especially in the interests of strangers; for there is an emotional power

[2] Or 'adflent.'
[3] Conington's translation (1870).
[4] De Oratore, ii. 45, 46 (Calvert's translation).

in the sentiments and topics themselves which supersedes the necessity of all simulation and falsehood. . . . What can be more unreal than poetry, than fable, than the creations of the drama? Yet often in this fictitious scene I have marked the eyes of the actor flashing fire through his mask when declaiming these lines:

> What! did you then dare to spurn him from you?
> Or to enter Salamis without him?
> Did you not dread the aspect of his father?

. . . Then subduing his voice to the tone of commiseration, he proceeded mournfully, and in seeming tears:

> Whom, in extremest age and penury,
> You cruelly have lacerated, robbed
> Of children, and of life, regardless of
> Your brother's death, regardless of the child,
> The little child committed to your charge.

If the actor who had to declaim these verses daily could not do so effectually without an emotion of sorrow, can you suppose that Pacuvius himself, when composing them, was in an indifferent and listless state of mind?' The phrase 'flens et lugens dicere videbatur,' here translated 'he proceeded mournfully and in seeming tears,' does not appear to me to bear quite that interpretation. The word 'seeming' conflicts with the general tenor of the passage; better Latinists than I must determine whether the inconsistency is due to Cicero or to his translator.

Quintilian, again, is very explicit on the subject of stage tears, while he speaks with no less conviction than Cicero of the rhetorical value of emotion physically experienced: 'The great secret . . . for moving the passions is to be moved ourselves; for the imitation of grief, anger, indignation, will often be ridiculous, if our words and countenance alone conform to the emotion, not our heart. . . . Wherefore, when we wish to attain verisimilitude in emotion, let us put ourselves in the place of those who really suffer; and let our speech proceed from the very state of mind which we wish to induce in the judge. Will he grieve who hears me declaim unmoved? . . . Will he weep who sees me dry-eyed? . . . But how shall we be affected, our emotions not being at our

command? This, too, I shall try to explain. What the
Greeks call φαντασίας, we call *visiones;* whereby the images
of things absent are so represented to the mind, that we seem
to see them with our eyes, and to have them present before
us. Whoever shall have conceived these thoroughly, will have
complete power over his emotions. . . . I have often seen
histrions and actors, on laying aside their masks after some
mournful scene, continue to shed tears. If, then, the mere
pronouncing of another's words can thus beget unreal emotions, what should not we effect, who ought to think our own
words, and to be moved on behalf of our clients? . . . I
have often been moved, not only to tears, but to pallor and
every symptom of grief.' [5]

The often-cited anecdotes of Polus and Æsopus will come
in at a later stage of our inquiry. For the present, I need only
note that these passages from Cicero and Quintilian seem to
represent the general opinion of the antique world upon
mimetic tears and their value. I do not pretend to have ransacked the classics for utterances on the subject, but we are
justified in supposing, I think, that if any Greek or Roman
had anticipated Diderot, the anti-emotionalists would not
have failed, long ere this, to appeal in triumph to his authority. For my part, I lay no great stress on the evidence of
antiquity. The conditions of acting, and even of oratory,
have altered too much to justify us in accepting as infallible
the maxims of classic theorists. The passages quoted above
prove that real tears were habitually shed on the antique
scene, and that Cicero and Quintilian believed in their
artistic value. I do not allege that their authority is conclusive. We cannot receive with blind humility the doctrines
in vogue in a city where the theatre was overtowered by the
amphitheatre.

Shakespeare's utterances on the subject of mimetic emotion[6] are familiar to everyone. As I have said before, they
seem to me to sum up the subject, and as my argument
proceeds I shall have to quote them for the ten-thousandth
time. For the present, I need only mention them to recall
their purport, at any rate, to the reader's memory.

The records of the stage, it may almost be said, are tear-

[5] *De Institutione Oratoria,* vi. 2.
[6] *Hamlet,* ii. 2, and iii. 2.

stained on every page. We have ample and unquestionable
evidence that many of the greatest artists frequently, if not
habitually, wept in pathetic situations. To go at once to the
greatest of all, we read in Tom Davies,[7] who had the best
opportunities for observation, that 'In some very affecting
scenes, Garrick and Mrs. Cibber have worked themselves up
to the shedding of tears, especially in the parts of Lear and
Cordelia.' Garrick's most formidable rival was Spranger
Barry, and the part in which their rivalry culminated was Romeo. Here is the account of Barry's death-scene given by that
excellent critic the anonymous author of *The Actor*:[8] 'His
sensibility gets the better of his articulation; his grief takes
effect upon the organs of his voice; and the very tone of it
is altered: it is broken, hoarse, and indistinct. We give the
applause to this consummate piece of playing that it deserves: we see nature triumphing over what art would direct; and we give it a praise which art, without this strong
appearance of nature, never could deserve.' Charles Reade,
if we may believe the same writer, was justified in making
the famous tear roll down Peg Woffington's cheek. 'Mrs.
Woffington,' he says,[9] 'has great sensibility; and she has,
more than most players of either sex, given a loose to nature
in the expressing it; to this she owed the greatest part of her
fame as an actress; and in this she always excelled, when her
private passions did not interfere.' Garrick's famous criticism[10] of Mrs. Pritchard, whose commanding genius is at-
tested by Churchill and Johnson, among a host of lesser critics,
shows that she not only wept, but wept immoderately. 'Her
scenes of grief were tiresomely blubbering,' he said to Tate
Wilkinson. As for Mrs. Siddons, though she belonged to a
school we should not have been surprised to find dry-eyed, we
have her own testimony to the 'bitter tears of rage, disappointment, betrayed confidence, and baffled ambition' which
'gushed into her eyes' in the part of Constance—one of her
very greatest. Fanny Kelly, in her 'Dramatic Recollections'
(a sort of lecture which she used to deliver), related[11] that
when, as a child, she played Arthur in *King John*, 'her collar

[7] *Davies*, iii. p. 75.
[8] Ed. 1755, p. 56.
[9] P. 105.
[10] Wilkinson, i. p. 140.
[11] Crabb Robinson, iii, p. 19.

was wet with Mrs. Siddons' tears.' Mr. Siddons, it may be added, took an irreverently prosaic view of his wife's emotion. 'Do you know,' he said to the Rev. Dr. Mackenzie, minister of Portpatrick, 'that small beer is good for crying? The day that my wife drinks small beer, she cries amazingly; she is really pitiful. But if I was to give her porter, or any stronger liquor, she would not be worth a farthing.'[12] It is to be feared that Mr. Siddons was indulging in a joke at the expense of his clerical friend.

Fanny Kemble, if not so great an actress as her aunt, was a keen observer. She bears witness to the reality of her own tears in a passage to be quoted in another place. Still more interesting is her account of the emotional idiosyncrasy of Miss O'Neill, that living embodiment of womanly pathos, who, according to Talma, drew tears from Frenchmen who knew no English by the mere magic of her voice.[13] 'She had a rare endowment for her especial range of characters,' says Fanny Kemble,[14] 'in an easily excited superficial sensibility, which caused her to cry, as she once said to me, "buckets full," and enabled her to exercise the (to most men) irresistible influence of a beautiful woman in tears. The power (or weakness) of abundant weeping without disfigurement is an attribute of deficient rather than excessive feeling. In such persons the tears are poured from their crystal cups without muscular distortion of the rest of the face. In proportion to the violence or depth of emotion, and the acute or profound sensibility of the temperament, is the disturbance of the countenance. In sensitive organisations, the muscles round the nostrils and lips quiver and are distorted, the throat and temples swell, and a grimace, which but for its miserable significance would be grotesque, convulses the whole face. . . . Women of the temperament I have alluded to above, have fountains of lovely tears behind their lovely eyes, and their weeping, which is indescribably beautiful, is comparatively painless, and yet pathetic enough to challenge tender compassion.' In this very curious analysis there is no doubt a great deal of justice. It is particularly interesting in its bearing upon the quantitative relation (so to speak) of mimetic to real emotion.

[12] Dibdin, p. 190.
[13] *Réflexions sur Lekain*, p. 56.
[14] *Record of a Girlhood*, ii, p. 20.

In French dramatic records there is sometimes a difficulty
in distinguishing between the figurative and the literal use
of the word 'larmes.' A critic will often talk of an actor's
'larmes' when he is evidently thinking merely of his pathetic
power in general, and does not mean expressly to affirm
that at any given moment he shed actual tears. I have come
across many instances, however, in which there is no am-
biguity. Of the great actress, for example, who was trained
by Racine to create the chief of his heroines, Lemazurier
writes as follows:[15] 'Il n'était pas nécessaire de répéter à
Mad. Champmeslé ce précepte de Boileau,

> Il faut dans la douleur, que vous vous abaissiez;
> Pour m'arracher des pleurs, il faut que vous pleuriez.

Sa sensibilité était naturelle et vraie; quelque force d'esprit
que l'on eût, quelque violence que l'on se fît, il fallait parta-
ger sa douleur, et pleurer avec elle.' [There was no need to
remind Mlle. Champmeslé of Boileau's admonition,

> To make pain felt, thyself in pain plunge deep:
> Weep first thyself if thou wouldst have me weep.

Her feeling was spontaneous and genuine; regardless of one's
strength of mind or degree of resistance, one could but
share her sorrows and weep when she did.] Lemazurier, it is
true, could not speak as an eye-witness, but he was a careful
writer who would not have expressed himself thus explicitly
without good authority. Dorat, on the other hand, wrote as
an eye-witness of Duclos, Adrienne Lecouvreur's chief rival:
'Ses larmes étoient belles, sa douleur touchante, sa figure
vraiment tragique: elle pleuroit à tort et à travers; mais enfin
elle pleuroit, et c'en étoit assez pour émouvoir le Spectateur.' [16] [Her tears were lovely to see; her grief was moving,
her expression truly tragic. She wept without rhyme or reason, but anyway she wept, and that was enough to carry
away the audience.] Sticotti, in a note to his *Garrick*, declares[17] that *'Dufrêne, la Gaussin, Mlle. Q[uinault]* jouant la
sœur du *Glorieux*, versoient des pleurs; notre ame reconnois-
sante se plaît encore à s'en retracer les charmes.' [Dufrêne, la
Gaussin, and Mlle. Quinault all wept in playing the Boast-

[15] Lemazurier, ii. p. 72.
[16] Dorat, Préface, p. 17.
[17] Ed. 1770, p. 149.

er's sister, and I still treasure grateful and beguiling memories of it.] Quinault-Dufresne was the greatest actor of his time, the French Quin; Mlle. Gaussin was the original Zaïre; and Mlle. Quinault was one of the most famous members of a famous family. Rachel, I suspect, was apt to have more fire than moisture in her eyes. It is related that on her deathbed she told her sister Sarah that she had been thinking over and trying to elaborate the part of Pauline in *Polyeucte,* adding pathetically, 'Pour étudier il faut penser et pleurer, mais je ne vois plus que des fantômes qui fuient.' [18] [Studying a part calls for thinking and weeping until I can see nothing but blurred shadows.] This is sufficient to prove that she was by no means the emotionless creature who, according to Diderot, has alone the right to be 'sublime'; but tears shed in study or rehearsal are not the same thing as tears shed in the moment of the performance. Frédérick Lemaître, with all his faults, was undoubtedly one of the greatest of great actors, and of him Victor Hugo wrote, in a note on *Ruy Blas*: 'Et puis, partout, à travers les éclairs éblouissants de son jeu, M. Frédérick a des larmes, de ces vraies larmes que font pleurer les autres, de ces larmes dont parle Horace:

> Si vis me flere, dolendum est
> Primum ipsi tibi';

[Moreover, intermingled with the dazzlingly brilliant strokes of his acting M. Frédérick sheds tears—those genuine tears that make others weep; the tears to which Horace refers:

> If you would have me weep,
> You must first know grief yourself;]

and Frédérick himself mentions, among the great qualities of his comrade Madame Dorval, 'ses larmes qui débordaient réellement du cœur.' [19] [. . . her tears, truly an overflow from the heart itself.]

Adelaide Neilson, I am assured by several observers, used to weep profusely both at rehearsal and during performance. Charlotte Cushman was not a woman one would suppose inclined to the melting mood; yet her biographer, Mrs. Clement, says of her performance of Mrs. Haller in *The*

[18] Houssaye, p. 335.
[19] *Souvenirs,* p. 99.

Stranger, 'So much did Miss Cushman herself enter into the spirit of the part, that I have, on more than one occasion, seen

Cadent tears fret channels in her cheeks.' [20]

Mr. Toole in his *Reminiscences* says of Benjamin Webster, the creator of Triplet: 'His Luke Fielding in *The Willow Copse* was full of his peculiar genius for domestic drama. It had one scene that was pathetic in the extreme. I have cried at it myself, and I never knew him play it without the tears streaming down his cheeks. It is the scene where the supposed dishonour of his daughter is made manifest to him. "Come with me, we have no longer a place among the honest and the good," were, I think, the words which take him off from among the neighbours and friends before whom the disgrace of his child had been pronounced.'

I pass now to the observations and experiences of living artists. Among those who are in the habit of playing pathetic parts the proclivity to tears is almost universal. As to their precise artistic value, opinions are a good deal divided; but I find no one in whom they tend to arise asserting that they should be altogether repressed. It is upon the question how far they may safely be indulged without endangering self-control that authorities differ. Almost everyone admits that at the commencement of his stage career (the stiff frigidity of the amateur being once overcome) the emotion of a part has often tended to run away with him; but I can find no case in which this has been corrected by a deliberate effort to eradicate the habit of feeling. It has simply been left to experience and practice to establish that due balance of the faculties which begets a temperance in the very torrent, tempest, and whirlwind of passion.

As I gave precedence to David Garrick among the actors of the past, no one will wonder to find me place Tommaso Salvini in the post of honour among living artists. To attempt any 'order of merit' among my other informants would be invidious and absurd; but Salvini's world-wide reputation entitles him to a priority which will scarcely be contested.

He delivers himself with no less emphasis than authority.

'If you do not weep in the agony of grief,' he writes, 'if you do not blush with shame, if you do not glow with love, if you do not tremble with terror, if your eyes do not become bloodshot with rage, if, in short, you yourself do not intimately experience whatever befits the diverse characters and passions you represent, you can never thoroughly transfuse into the hearts of your audience the sentiment of the situation.' Such an utterance from such an actor is of itself sufficient to prove that the anti-emotionalist theory, whatever truth it may contain, is not of universal application. The actor who is by constitution or conviction a disciple of Diderot may produce very great effects, but it is certain that some, at least, of the sublimest possibilities of theatrical art can be achieved by an actor who utterly rejects the philosopher's doctrine.

As a corollary to Salvini's dictum, let me quote an anecdote which he related to me during his last visit to London (February 1884). It occurred in the course of a conversation on the subject of the *Paradoxe*. 'See, I shall tell you a story,' he said. 'In *La Morte Civile* I always weep, and greatly. Now, there is in Rio Janeiro a newspaper editor, Senhor de Castro, a big, bearded man, with gold spectacles—proprio un' uomo serio!—who is famous for his lack of feeling. They say he buried his wife without a tear—I do not know, but they say so. He saw *La Morte Civile,* and after the curtain fell he came upon the stage. Behold! on each side of his nose there was a great wet furrow, and as he laid his hand upon my shoulder I could feel that it was twitching and trembling. And next day every one in Rio Janeiro went about saying: "He has made De Castro weep! What a triumph!"' Then Salvini added: 'As to French tragedy, however, I can understand Diderot's theory. I now rarely appear in it. Orosmane is as a ghost after Othello.'

'The performance of a moving situation,' Mrs. Bancroft writes, 'without the true ring of sensibility in the actor, must fail to affect any one. . . . An emotional break in the voice must be brought about naturally, and by a true appreciation of the sentiment, or what does it become? I can only compare it to a bell with a wooden tongue—it makes a sound, but there it ends. I cannot simulate suffering without an honest sympathy with it. . . . I hold that without great nervous sensibility no one can act pathos. . . . It is impossible to feel the sentiments one has to utter, and but half the author's meaning can be conveyed. It is a casket with the jewel absent. . . . The voice in emotion must be prompted by the heart; and if that is "out of tune and harsh," why, then, indeed, the voice is "like sweet bells jangled." Art *should* help nature, but nature *must* help art. They are twin sisters, and should go hand in hand, but nature must be the firstborn. I was once much impressed by a small child's criticism. He watched for a long time silently and attentively a scene of great emotional interest between two people. When asked what he thought of it, he answered, "I like that one best." "Why?" "She speaks like telling the truth, and the other speaks like telling lies." What criticism can be finer than this? One was acting straight from the heart, the other from not even next door but one to it.' To give this anecdote its full value we should of course have positive evidence that the one was in tears, the other dry-eyed and unmoved. For obvious reasons such evidence is unattainable; but Mrs. Bancroft, watching the scene doubtless from close at hand, and certainly with the keen eye of a mistress of the craft, is a scarcely less trustworthy witness than the artists themselves. Mr. Bancroft fully agrees with his accomplished wife as to the advantage possessed by an actor whose nerves and muscles sensitively respond to the touch of his imagination; and no one who has seen Mr. Bancroft's irresistibly pathetic performance of Triplet will hesitate to admit that he speaks with authority. He adds that any counter-irritant which tends to dissipate the energy of the imagination is certain to interfere with the effect. For instance, he avows that amid the excitement of his farewell performance at the Haymarket he could not enter so thoroughly into the part of Triplet as to do himself full justice.

Mr. and Mrs. Kendal are strongly of opinion that the emotional effect they produce upon their audience varies in accordance with the greater or less emotional effect experienced by them in their own persons. The difference between parts they like and parts they do not like is that in the former they fall easily and naturally under the sway of the appropriate emotion, while in the latter they have to work themselves up to it. 'We should all be great artists,' says Mrs. Kendal, 'if we could choose each night the part we feel in a humour for.' Could anything contradict more flatly the theory of the musical-box actor who, having once wound himself up, can switch on at will any tune in his whole repertory, and reel it off without missing the twang of a single note? Mrs. Kendal confesses herself very prone to tears on the stage, even to the detriment of her make-up. She mentions as an instance of the kind of speech which she can never utter without real tears and a very real break in the voice, that saying of Kate Verity in *The Squire,* where she burns the relics of Thorndyke's courtship, and holds her hands to the flame: 'A lucky thing that Christie made such a bright fire for me—(*shivering*)—and yet it's cold. Ah, I suppose heat never comes from burnt love-letters.' No one who remembers this play will contend that Mrs. Kendal's emotion failed to move the audience.

This is perhaps the fittest place in which to quote some suggestive remarks on the value of stage-tears by a critic I greatly esteem: 'An obtrusively lachrymose performance,' he writes, 'tends to shock rather than to move me, and I think most people would say the same. It is such emotion as is not expressed by tears and sobs—shame, despair, pity— or even the exquisite expression of a quite opposite order of emotion—wonder, love pure and simple, or even joy—that brings tears to my eyes and sends cold shivers down my spine. For example, in the second act of *The Squire* there was much emotion that could be expressed only by sobs and tears, and was so expressed by Mrs. Kendal, most admirably; yet the two moments of the play that have remained in my memory and will always remain there are (1) Kate Verity's confession to Thorndyke in the first act' [the confession which causes Thorndyke, when left alone on the stage, to drink 'Baby's health!'—in milk] 'and (2) her sinking into a chair in Act III. exclaiming "All the troubles of all the world upon one little head"—in neither of which is the emotion one that could possibly be expressed by the signs you choose.' There is much truth in this criticism. I am inclined to think that the actual shedding of tears is not, in itself, particularly effective, and that we Anglo-Saxons of this generation are perhaps less apt than our ancestors and ancestresses—less apt, too, than some of our continental neighbours—to be moved by the 'summer tempest' of sorrow. My correspondent goes too far in arguing that mere sobs and tears are never moving. In a naturally pathetic situation which, in Bottom's phrase, 'asks some tears in the true performing of it,' a woman's weeping, even though it be of the convulsive kind described by Fanny Kemble, will always give the sorrow its crown of sorrow. If my correspondent was unmoved by Mrs. Kendal's tears in the third act of *The Squire,* that may have been owing to what I take to be the essential falsity of much of the sentiment in that particular scene. As a general rule, however, unrestrained weeping is a mark of passivity, whereas it is activity in one form or another that most deeply interests and moves us. One of the most touching of all phases of activity is the successful repression of tears. Triplet's exit speech, for example, in the first act of *Masks and Faces* would be ruined by the overflow of even a single teardrop. 'Madam,' he says, 'you have inspired a son of Thespis with dreams of eloquence; you have tuned to a higher key a poet's lyre; you have tinged a painter's existence with brighter colours; and—and——God in heaven bless you, Margaret Woffington.' This should clearly be spoken with a tremor of the voice and a quiver of the lip, showing that tears are near the surface and are only restrained by the poor fellow's sense of manly dignity. Similar cases could be cited in hundreds. They swarm in Shakespeare. The best instance of all, perhaps, is that wonderful snatch of dialogue in the fourth act of *Julius Cæsar:*

Cassius. Of your philosophy you make no use,
If you give place to accidental evils.
Brutus. No man bears sorrow better:—Portia is dead.
Cassius. Ha! Portia!
Brutus. She is dead.
Cassius. How 'scaped I killing when I crossed you so? . . .
Brutus. . . . With this she fell distract,
And, her attendants absent, swallowed fire.
Cassius. And died so?
Brutus. Even so.
Cassius. O ye immortal gods!

Here, of course, the effort of repression can be simulated in cold-blood; but, if my observation does not mislead me, it is precisely in such passages that the ear most quickly detects and rejects even the most delicate art of the mechanical performer.

Again, there is a distinction to be drawn between emotion belonging strictly to the character and emotion which comes, as it were, from outside. The player is both a participator in the action and a spectator. He looks before and after; he cannot divest his mind of a knowledge of the past and future; the irony of things, which is, by hypothesis, concealed from the personage he represents, is patent to him. Thus many speeches which, to the character uttering them, seem unemotional and even insignificant, are in the eyes of the audience and of the player charged with pathetic meaning. There is a famous instance in Racine's *Iphigénie en Aulide*,[21] where Iphigénie, little dreaming of her doom, questions her father as to the pompous sacrifice which Calchas is preparing:

> *Iphigénie.* Verra-t-on à l'autel votre heureuse famille?
> *Agamemnon.* Hélas!
> *Iphigénie.*　　　　　Vous vous taisez!
> *Agamemnon.*　　　　　　　　　Vous y serez, ma fille.

> [*Iphigenia* . . . shall thy glad family
> Surround the altar?
> *Agamemnon.* Ah!—
> *Iphigenia.*　　　　Why art thou silent?
> *Agamemnon.*　　　　　　　Thou shalt be there, my daughter!
> Translation by Robert Bruce Boswell, *op. cit.*]

Nay more, the mere literary perfection of a speech may give it, for some natures, a moving quality. For example, there are many passages in Chaucer, Wordsworth, Tennyson, and other poets—passages of no particular emotional significance —which I, for my part, would not undertake to read aloud without a tremor of the voice and an unwonted moisture of the eye. Actors as a class, I suspect, are not keenly susceptible to this form of emotional influence, but there must be cases in which it makes itself felt. In the part of Minnie Gilfillian in *Sweet Lavender* Mr. Pinero has placed several of those speeches which seem to me to acquire an emotional quality from their mere verbal charm. For example:

[21] Act ii. 2.

Minnie. But, Clem dear, I wish you'd do something to please me.

Clement (seizing her hands). I'll do anything.

Minnie. Anything but marry me. *(Seriously)* Well, don't wait for Uncle Geoffrey's return, but write to him, to Paris, and tell him how you adore—my hated rival. Uncle Geoff is a bachelor, but married men and bachelors are manufactured by the same process—Love, Clem—and he'll understand. Tell him all, and say that the girl you have lost your treacherous heart to has won one staunch friend—Minnie Gilfillian.

Another instance, to compare great things with small, is Gretchen's soliloquy in *Faust:*

> Du lieber Gott! was so ein Mann
> Nicht alles, alles denken kann!
> Beschämt nur steh' ich vor ihm da,
> Und sag' zu allen Sachen ja.
> Bin doch ein arm unwissend Kind,
> Begreife nicht was er an mir find't.

> [Dear God! However is it such
> A man can think and know so much?
> I stand ashamed and in amaze
> And answer 'Yes' to all he says,
> A poor, unknowing child! and he—
> I can't think what he finds in me!
>
> (Bayard Taylor's translation)]

It would clearly be wrong for Iphigénie, or Minnie Gilfillian, or Gretchen to bedew these speeches with tears; but I conceive that sensitiveness to such extraneous emotional stirrings would have to be quite abnormal before it could injuriously affect an artist's performance. In many declamatory passages it might impart a vibration to the voice, the effect of which could only be for good.

Much more might be said of this distinction between what may be called intrinsic and extrinsic feeling—the feeling to which an actor is subject in so far as he is identified with his character, and the feeling to which he is subject precisely because such identification is necessarily incomplete. One form of extrinsic feeling which must of course be overcome is the awe with which great actors have been known to inspire their fellow-performers, to such a pitch as to destroy

their self-mastery. Charles Young,[22] Macready,[23] and even
the great John Philip himself,[24] confess to having been so
overcome by the acting of Mrs. Siddons as to be unable for
the moment to carry on the business of the scene. 'Would you
not, Sir,' said Boswell to Johnson, 'start as Mr. Garrick does,
if you saw a ghost?' 'I hope not,' replied Johnson; 'if I did, I
should frighten the ghost.' [25] If the majesty of buried Den-
mark was ever 'frighted from his propriety' by the acting of
his son, that emotion was evidently not only extrinsic but
very much out of place. I fear, however, that the players of
to-day are but little exposed to this danger.

'I shed tears on the stage every night when my "personage" weeps,' says Madame Sarah Bernhardt.[26] 'Tears always come to my eyes,' writes Miss Geneviève Ward, 'in a
moving situation, but seldom run over. Sometimes they are
unbidden, and sometimes I work up to them. I have been
obliged when studying a part (Constance in *King John,* for
instance) to stop owing to the tears and sobs, and would not
have attempted to play it until I could control my feelings.
I find that I feel much more when alone than before my
audience—then I must make them feel—control myself to
control them. I have not found that it made any difference
with my audience whether I actually shed tears or not—
very few *see* the real tear—they *feel* the pathos of the situation, and do good part of the acting themselves.' Miss
Mary Anderson's experience tallies curiously with this.
While quite a young girl, and before she had any intention
of going on the stage, Miss Anderson made the acquaintance
of a lady of morbidly lachrymose temperament, who induced
in her a horror of this Mrs. Gummidge-like weakness. She
therefore deliberately schooled herself in the repression of
tears, without any thought of their good or evil effect in
acting. The consequence is that neither on nor off the stage
do her tears flow very copiously; but they none the less rise
to her eyes and make themselves felt in her voice. I have
myself seen Miss Anderson's eyes very distinctly suffused

[22] Campbell, i. p. 205.
[23] *Reminiscences*, i. p. 54.
[24] Boswell, iv. p. 243.
[25] Boswell, v. p. 38.
[26] *The Star*, July 14, 1888.

at the point in *The Winter's Tale* where Perdita bids Florizel farewell:

> This dream of mine
> Being now awake, I'll queen it no inch further,
> But milk my ewes and weep;

and I may add that the thrill of voice with which she spoke these lines (on this particular occasion, at any rate) seemed to me singularly just. Miss Anderson, however, like Miss Ward, feels a part more acutely when not in presence of the audience. 'In my own room at night,' she says, 'when all the house is quiet, I weep and laugh with the character I happen to be studying.' M. Coquelin related to me an anecdote of Mlle. Mars, to the effect that she was one day found by a friend bathed in tears, and being asked the reason, answered, 'Je juge de mes larmes' ['I am criticising my tears']. We find Rachel, too, writing to her instructor, Samson, 'J'ai étudié mes sanglots (dans le quatrième acte de *Phèdre*), je n'ose pas me vanter pour la seconde représentation, mais je suis sûre qu'ils me viennent.' [27] ['I have practised my sobs (in Act IV of *Phædra*); I daren't plume myself on the second performance, but I am sure they will come to me.'] Miss Anderson will scarcely admit that in her midnight vigils with Juliet or Hermione she is testing her tears and selecting her sobs. Miss Alma Murray tells me that in reading aloud at home or before a private audience she is very apt to break down under stress of emotion, but that on the stage, though tears come to her eyes and her voice breaks, she has never felt any danger of losing her self-control. Thus Miss Ward, Miss Anderson, and Miss Murray agree in holding that the mere sight of the footlights tends to beget that 'temperance' on which Hamlet insists. Miss Janet Achurch expresses herself very much to the same effect. 'I have often cried bitterly while rehearsing a part,' she writes, 'and yet been dry-eyed on the first performance. Over-nervousness, I suppose, as in playing the part afterwards the tears have come back.'

Here let me cite the testimony of Miss Clara Morris, an American actress who is declared by excellent judges to possess, along with some unfortunate mannerisms, a rare

[27] *D'Heylli*, p. 26.

and individual genius of the emotional order. Miss Morris has never appeared in England, but several English critics who have seen her have concurred in, and even outdone, the eulogies of her countrymen. 'You must feel,' she writes,[28] 'or all the pretty and pathetic language in the world won't make other people feel. I never go on the stage but that about four o'clock in the afternoon I begin to suffer. My hands get cold as ice, my face gets hot, and I am in a nervous tremor, because I am afraid I won't cry in the play. I do everything to get my feelings thoroughly aroused. Then I only have to look out for the other danger and keep from being overcome myself. All the tremolo and false sobs in the world will never take the place of real emotion. Of course, after such an emotional effort I cannot throw the whole effect off, and my poor nerves suffer.' Miss Morris's theory of art evidently differs from that of Talma, who, according to Samson,[29] 'se déclarait mécontent d'un succès qui lui avait coûté trop de fatigue [pronounced himself dissatisfied with a performance that left him too exhausted].' It appears that Miss Morris has permanently endangered her health by acting at too high pressure, and this, no doubt, shows either a morbid temperament or deficient technical training. At the same time the thrilling effects she produces are beyond question, however extravagant the price she pays for them.

'Yes,' writes Mr. Wilson Barrett, 'tears come to my eyes unbidden when I am acting at my best. With an effort I can repress them, but if I am not sufficiently in my part for them to come uncalled, no power of mine can bring them. If one night I have to simulate what I felt the night before, I should certainly expect the effect to be lessened. . . . But mere feeling unguided by art is seldom, if ever, effective. Art without feeling is better than that, but feeling with art is better than both. The most sensitive organisation, coupled with the highest art, makes the greatest actor. In America you will hear the remark, "Yes, he's a fine artist, but he has no magnetism." In London you will hear people say, "Yes, he's a capital actor, but somehow he never touches me." The meaning is the same; the fine artist is watched and admired,

[28] *The Voice*, x. No. 3.
[29] *L'Art Théâtral*, p. 176.

and often he will get the most praise. He has not stirred the emotions of his audience, and they have had ample time to watch his art. But the actor who feels deeply and guides his emotions by his art will draw to see him hundreds to the other's units.'

'Whether tears do or do not readily come to the eyes,' writes Mr. Beerbohm Tree, 'will depend upon the mere physical development of the individual. Some people have sensitive lachrymal glands, which may be affected by the simple test of the onion—apply the vegetable and the tears will flow. Others, again, have not this physical sensitiveness. It is, therefore, only possible to speak from personal experience. Tears do undoubtedly rise to my eyes in moving situations, perhaps less readily on the stage than in private contemplation. I do not believe that any emotion can be satisfactorily portrayed outside unless the inside emotion exists also; and I think that the effect upon an audience will generally be in proportion to the power of self-excitation possessed by the actor—given, of course, equal advantages in the way of physique, voice, &c.' Mr. Tree then goes on to remark that the use of acquired knowledge, technique, training, canons of art, and so forth, is simply to enable the imagination to work without let or hindrance—to adjust and oil the machinery through which it must give itself utterance.

Mr. John Clayton,[30] whose Hugh Trevor in *All for Her* is remembered as one of the most pathetic creations of our time, assures me that if tears do not rise spontaneously to his eyes the effect of his acting is distinctly diminished. There are passages in *All for Her* which he has never been able to play without profound emotion—lines which he can scarcely quote in ordinary talk without a tremor in his voice; and in these passages (as many playgoers well remember) he used to produce upon his audience that highest emotional effect which is expressed, not in immediate applause, but in

---

[30] Mr. Clayton was the first actor (with one exception) who responded to my request for aid in this investigation, and my talk with him in his dressing-room at Toole's Theatre (where he was then playing) was one of the pleasantest and most instructive of many pleasant and instructive interviews. When the above lines first appeared he was yet among us, and we had every reason to hope that the best part of his career, as a manager if not as an actor, lay before him. I cannot place him among actors of the past. He will live for many a day to come in the kindly recollection of thousands.

absorbed, breathless, tearful silence. Mr. Hermann Vezin is equally decided in his opinion. Tears come readily to his eyes in pathetic situations, and when they fail to come he is conscious of a diminished hold upon his audience. He adds that Charles Kean, with whom he was long and intimately connected, used to paraphrase Churchill's couplet, and say, 'You must feel yourself, or you'll never make your audience feel.' Mr. Vezin remarks, however, that the natural breaking of the voice sometimes occurs apart from tears. He mentions an actress of great pathetic power who can produce the most moving tones with perfectly dry eyes; but this he regards as an exception to the rule.

'I have often shed tears in sympathetic situations,' writes Mr. Henry Howe, an excellent actor, and one of the last survivors of a great school, 'especially when aided by the sensibility of the artist who is acting with me. For instance, in the last scene of *Charles I.,* when Huntley leads the children to their mother, I invariably shed tears at the point where Miss Terry, also with tears in her eyes, asks Huntley if the children know of their father's fate. Again, when the King takes leave of Huntley, previous to going to execution, Mr. Irving copiously sheds tears. . . . I have often been told by those who have witnessed the scene that there was scarcely a dry eye in the house.' No one who was near the stage on the first night of *The Amber Heart* can doubt the reality of Miss Ellen Terry's tears. In the second act they literally streamed down her cheeks, while her whole frame was shaken with weeping. Her emotion was not, of course, uncontrollable, but for the moment it was uncontrolled; and I may add that the effect upon the audience was instant and intense.

'In moving situations,' writes Miss Bateman (Mrs. Crowe), 'if real tears do not come to my eyes I do not truly feel what I am acting, nor can I impress my audience to the same extent when I feign emotion as when I really feel it. I have acted the part of Leah for twenty-four years, and the tears always come to my eyes when the little child says "My name is Leah."' Miss Isabel Bateman expresses herself to the same effect.

Mr. Lionel Brough, who, though best known as a comic actor, has every claim to be heard on the question of pathos, writes as follows: 'In moving situations I always cry. I can't help it. My voice goes of its own accord. In a certain pathetic scene of a melodrama, which I played in Liverpool with Miss Phillis Hill, we used every night to agree "not to make fools of ourselves," as we called it; and every night there would be mutual recriminations at the end of the scene, as, "I thought you promised me you wouldn't cry?" Answer, in the same tearful voice (with all the make-up washed off): "So did you, stupid." But neither of us ever regretted the tears, or the way in which the scene went with the audience. If ever I play a pathetic scene with a child (and in most cases with a woman) I am sure to cry. With men, not so; as in any domestic trouble of my own I should endeavour to restrain my tears in telling my sorrows to a man, but should give them free vent in the presence of the other sex. I don't think an actor *ever* can be said to play pathos properly unless he feels it.' Those who have seen Mr. Brough's admirable performance of the old cab-owner in *Retiring* will realise the value of his observations.

Several of my informants are undecided in their evidence, and of these I may take Mr. Forbes Robertson as a typical example. 'Tears come to my eyes,' he writes, 'but not unbidden. Neither would I let my voice break of its own accord. I feel all emotional scenes, under favourable conditions, very strongly, but I never dare let myself go. Nevertheless I like to persuade myself that I am, for the time being, the person I am playing; to surrender myself to the passion of the moment, and only to know myself, as it were, sufficiently to prevent breaking down. . . . Phelps often shed tears. On one occasion when I was playing with him in an emotional scene, being young and much affected at his acting and my own emotions, I got beyond my own control. Phelps afterwards warned me, and admitted that he might easily be carried away by an affecting scene did he not keep a strict watch on himself.' On the whole, I think, Mr. Forbes Robertson may be said to take the emotional side, though he dwells more than some of his comrades on the necessity for keeping a tight rein on the feelings. One of the few decided disbelievers in emotion is Mr. Frank Harvey, who writes as follows: 'The late Mademoiselle Beatrice, with whom I was long associated, moved her audience to tears to a painful degree; but she felt little emotion herself. On the other hand, when acting with the late Miss Neilson, I have seen real tears streaming down her cheeks, but I don't think she moved her audience any more.' Miss Neilson's extreme susceptibility to emotion seems to have been quite incommensurate with her power of producing pathetic effect. But then no one supposes that an actress's command over her audience is proportionate to the mere quantity of her tears.

The most resolute upholder of the non-emotional theory with whom I have come in contact is Mr. A. W. Pinero, whose keen intelligence and wide knowledge of the stage, both as actor and author, must give his opinions exceptional weight. He does not deny that tears are shed, but he argues that they are not a true sign of feeling, and that actors deceive themselves in supposing that they are. With a week's practice, he says, anyone can learn to produce tears at will. You have only to 'breathe, not through the nose, but through the closed throat'—that is, as I understand it, to produce mechanically the *globus hystericus*. That thoughtful young actor Mr. Bernard Gould makes a similar assertion. 'I have frequently,' he writes, 'found it possible at a moment's notice, and without any (even simulated) affecting surroundings, to force tears into the eyes by merely speaking in a mechanically-produced broken voice.' This is a curious testimony to the intimate connection between the muscles of the throat and lachrymal glands. Mr. Pinero proceeds to maintain that in many actors the habit of thus 'pumping up' tears becomes a second nature, and almost a disease. He mentions a well-known actress who could read you a comic poem, weeping copiously all the time; and a popular actor who, even in private life, could scarcely relate an ordinary incident, such as having seen a horse fall in the street, without being bathed in tears. Miss Wallis, who studied acting under the late John Ryder, gives me a curious case in point. She once expressed to her instructor her wonder at the way in which an actress much in vogue at the time managed to turn on tears wherever there was the slightest excuse for them. 'Look at me, my dear,' Mr. Ryder replied; and instantly she saw a tear gather in his eye and roll slowly down his cheek!

Another strong argument of Mr. Pinero's is that, in a part

with which he is quite familiar, an actor will often produce a powerful effect upon his audience in total unconsciousness of what he is doing; just as some people will read aloud whole pages of a book, intelligently enough to all appearance, and will suddenly wake up to the fact that their thoughts have been absent, and that they do not know a single word they have been reading. Of this Miss Mary Anderson relates a curious instance. After the fourth act of *Romeo and Juliet,* one night, her maid began to unfasten her dress in order to put on the white draperies of the Tomb scene. 'Don't do that,' said Miss Anderson; 'I have to play the Potion scene yet'; and it took some time to convince her that she had not only just played it, but had played (as her comrades assured her, and as the applause of the audience showed) with unusual effect. I could adduce several similar cases. It is said that Mr. and Mrs. Alfred Wigan, having made some mistake in a cue at the end of an important scene, actually played the whole scene over again in blissful unconsciousness of their blunder. John Ireland relates[31] how poor Reddish, when his faculties were failing, played Posthumus for his benefit under the full conviction that he was playing Romeo! 'I congratulated him on his being enough recovered to perform. Yes, sir, replied he, I shall perform, and in the garden scene I shall astonish you!—In the garden scene, Mr. Reddish?—I thought you were to play Posthumus —No, sir, I play Romeo . . . At the time appointed he set out for the Theatre. The gentleman who went with him . . . told me that his mind was so imprest with the character of Romeo, he was reciting it all the way. . . . When the time came for his appearance, they pushed him on the stage, fearing he would begin with a speech of Romeo. With the same expectation I stood in the pit. . . . The instant he came in sight of the audience his recollection seemed to return . . . he made the bow of modest respect, and went through the scene much better than I had ever before seen him. On his return to the green-room the image of Romeo returned to his mind.' We have here a real 'paradox of acting'; but I doubt whether such freaks of consciousness can be regarded as telling either for or against Diderot's argument.

[31] Ireland, p. 58.

'No audience, in my opinion,' says Mr. Toole, 'was ever made to weep unless the actor had wept, or could weep, at what touched the audience. At the same time, an actor must be able to control himself.' That is the real turning-point of the whole discussion. The anti-emotionalists from Diderot, or rather from François Riccoboni, onwards, assume that real emotion is inconsistent with self-control; whereas the emotionalists argue (as I think, justly) that the accomplished actor is he who, in the moment of performance, can freely utilise the subtle action of the imagination upon the organs of expression, without running the least risk of its over-mastering him. The illustration given by Mr. Lawrence Barrett in a recent 'interview' is very much to the point. Mr. Barrett says:[32] 'In my opinion the prime requisites of an actor are sensibility and imagination. But he must have these under perfect control. The moment that they become his masters instead of his servants, he ceases to be an artist. Mr. Booth and I were discussing this point the other day, and he gave this illustration. A friend invites you out to take a drive behind two high-spirited horses, that can go in, say 2.30. He speeds them along at, perhaps, a three-minute gait, and you admire his control of them. Presently the horses get fuller of spirit, their enthusiasm is communicated to the driver. He lets them out, nay, he even urges them on to their fastest pace, but he doesn't lose control over them. If he did they would soon be running away with him. You see the delight in his face, the eagerness to get the best out of his animals, you appreciate and enjoy his excitement, which is communicated to you, but you have confidence that he remains master. So it is with acting. The actor's powers and feelings will sometimes carry him along faster than at others, but he must always keep a strong hand over them.' To the same effect writes Miss Clara Morris.[33] 'As to really losing oneself in a part, that will not do: it is worse to be too sympathetic than to have too much art. I must cry in my emotional *rôles* and feel enough to cry, but I must not allow myself to become so affected as to mumble my words, to redden my nose, or to become hysterical.'

Some actors (a very small percentage) do undoubtedly

[32] *New York Tribune*, December 18, 1887.
[33] Matthews and Hutton, v. p. 224.

suffer from their inability to keep their feelings properly in check. Of Walker, a tragedian of some note, though chiefly remembered as the original Macheath in the *Beggar's Opera,* the author of *The Actor* writes:[34] 'His ruin was that his sensibility continually ran away with him; . . . the blood was in his face before the time, his whole person was disordered, and unless people knew the part, they could not find out for what; for the vehemence of his feeling took away his utterance. *Vox faucibus hæsit,* and he could not speak articulately.' The same writer tells of a Mr. Berry, whose excessive sensibility injured his playing in all parts save that of Adam, in *As You Like It,* where it stood him in good stead. 'I remember a great tragedian, Powell,' says Cape Everard,[35] 'performing the part of Jaffier, and when he said,

I have not wrong'd thee—by these tears I have not,

his feelings were so great that they choaked his utterance, his articulation was lost, his face was drowned in tears.—The audience from these causes, not understanding what he said, the effect was of course lost. When Garrick, in the same part, spoke the same line, every eye in the house dropt a tear! If he did not feel himself he made everybody else feel.'

Servandoni d'Hannetaire, again, who published a book of *Observations sur l'Art du Comédien* in 1776, quotes the younger Riccoboni's remarks on the danger of tears, and then adds, 'Bien des Acteurs, comme nous, ont été obligés d'abandonner le genre pathétique par rapport à cette pente excessive à l'attendrissement et au trop de facilité à répandre des larmes.' [A good many actors, like myself, have had to relinquish the highly emotional style just in the measure of this exaggerated bent for the softer emotions and readiness to shed tears.] Since M. d'Hannetaire avers that this was his own case, we have no reason to doubt him; but it is certainly rarer than he seems to suppose. The exaggeration which we call 'ranting' is, indeed, common enough, but that is due, not to excess of uncontrolled sensibility, but to imperfect technical training and defective taste. Many artists, as we have seen, concur in holding that the mere presence of the audience is sufficient to beget the necessary self-command, and M. d'Hannetaire is the only player I ever heard of who was forced by a too copious flux of tears either to abandon the stage or to confine himself to comic characters.

It is obvious that even a consummate artist may, on occasion, be carried beyond himself to the detriment of the desired effect. An anecdote of Molé, quoted in Assézat's notes to the *Paradoxe*,[36] affords a case in point. Lemercier was so much charmed with Molé's acting one evening that he rushed to congratulate him. Molé replied that he was not pleased with his own performance, and had not affected the audience as much as usual. 'Je me suis trop livré,' he said, 'je n'étais plus maître de moi; j'étais entré si vivement dans la situation que j'étais le personnage même, et que je n'étais plus l'acteur qui le joue; j'ai été vrai comme je le serais chez moi, mais pour l'optique du théâtre, il faut l'être autrement.' ['I let myself go too much; I parted company with my self-control. I felt the dramatic situation so keenly that I was the character himself, instead of an actor playing him. I was real as I should be in my own house, but theatrical illusion demands something other.'] He begged Lemercier to come and see him again when the piece was repeated. Lemercier did so, taking his station at the wing, and as Molé passed him to go on the stage he whispered, 'Je suis bien maître de moi, vous allez voir.' ['I have myself in hand: you'll see.'] Lemercier declares that, as Molé predicted, he produced a much greater effect on the second occasion than on the first. The brothers Mounet, the leading tragedians of the contemporary French stage, both convinced champions of the emotional theory, are subject to occasional failures of self-control. Paul Mounet, of the Odéon, admits[37] that he now and then yields to a delicious 'intoxication' of feeling; but returning sobriety brings with it self-criticism and dissatisfaction. The aforesaid Molé summed up in a single phrase the true artistic principle. 'Au théâtre,' he used to say, 'il fout livrer son cœur et garder sa tête.' ['In the theatre you have to surrender your heart but retain possession of your head.'] M. Albert Lambert père, a highly esteemed actor of

[36] Vol. viii. p. 346.
[37] *Revue d'Art Dramatique*, v. p. 291.

the Odéon, expresses himself in almost identical terms. 'Comme principe général sur mon art,' he writes, 'j'ai celui-ci: *Le cœur chaud, la tête froide*. J'entends par *cœur*: les facultés cérébrales, qui peuvent conserver la sensibilité à l'état ardent, qui savent appeler les larmes par un simple effort de volonté: les suffocations, les angoisses, toutes les affres de la douleur, soit en souvenir des situations semblables vues ou éprouvées dans la vie, soit par l'identification voulue avec le personnage qu'on représente. Par *tête froide*: le pouvoir directeur toujours en éveil, une espèce d'instinct de conservation artistique qui, dans la plus affolée des explosions, sait la diriger selon les lois d'un art appris et médité.' [For a general law of my own acting I hold to this: A warm heart, a cool head. By 'heart' I mean the mental powers that can sustain emotion at a pitch of intensity, that by a mere exertion of the will can summon tears, struggles for breath, torments, all the nuances of anguish, whether by recalling like situations observed or experienced in real life or by deliberately identifying oneself with the character played. By 'a cool head' I mean a superintending faculty that never nods—a kind of instinct of artistic self-preservation that contrives to channel even the most impassioned outburst into conformity with the principles of an art learned and reflected upon.] Finally, let me quote from J. J. Engel's *Ideen zu einer Mimik*,[38] the views of a very penetrating critic of last century, who, though not an actor himself, was for some years a manager, and lived in hourly communion with actors. 'Actors,' he says, 'all speak of *feeling*, and think that they are certain to play excellently if . . . they fill themselves with the enthusiasm of their subject. I can cite only one (but he certainly the greatest) actor I have known, our *Eckhof* to wit, who, neither in regard to declamation nor to action, relied on feeling alone; but rather in the moment of performance kept himself in hand so as not to fall into an excess of feeling, and, from lack of self-command, play with defective truth, expression, harmony, and finish. . . . I know actors who can in a single moment fill their eyes with tears. . . . Happy he who possesses this gift, and knows how to govern it wisely; for a falling tear is often, unquestionably, of excellent effect; but to heat the fancy to such a

[38] Berlin, 1785-86.

degree that its suggestions become as moving as reality itself, seems to me a dangerous course. . . . Real emotions too easily take possession of the whole heart and obstruct or distort the utterance they are designed to intensify.' If this tendency be so potent in any particular case that it must at all costs be eradicated, then, doubtless, the player should school himself to automatism. But to make automatism an imperative ideal for all is like condemning the whole world to total abstinence because one man in ten thousand is a dipsomaniac.

Chapter V

'ET MENTEM MORTALIA TANGUNT'

'TEARS,' say the upholders of Diderot, 'are no trustworthy sign of feeling. An onion or a grain of sand will call them up just as readily as the agony of Alkestis or the woes of Ophelia. The practised actor can produce them mechanically if he thinks it worth while, and with some the habit of producing them for any reason, or no reason, becomes a disease. The Master himself permits his ideal actor to weep, so long as he has arranged beforehand "the precise moment at which to produce his handkerchief, the word, the syllable at which his tears must flow." ' [1] Are there no cases, then, in which we can prove that the actor is really feeling in his own person something similar in kind, if not equal in degree, to the emotion he is representing? It was the object of my second question to elicit evidence on this point. This question, here re-phrased to improve its lucidity, but without essential change, ran as follows:

When Macready played Virginius shortly after the death of a favourite daughter, the thought of her, as he confessed, mingled with, and intensified, his mourning for Virginia. Have you any analogous experience to relate? Has a personal emotion (whether recent or remote) influenced your acting in a situation which tended to revive it? If so, was the influence, in your opinion, for good or ill? And what was the effect upon the audience?

[1] Pollock, p. 19.

Personal emotion may influence acting in two ways. The actor may consciously or unconsciously note the external manifestations of his feeling while it is actually upon him (Talma and Rachel are said to have noted them consciously), and then may voluntarily reproduce or mimic them on the stage without again experiencing the slightest emotion, just as he might mimic the gesture or accent of some totally indifferent person. This process, as a writer in the *Westminster Review* has remarked,[2] 'substantially squares with Wordsworth's canon of poetic composition—that it is emotion recollected in tranquillity.' The next question bears upon this point, not the question now before us. What I here wanted to get at was the direct influence of real and present personal emotion upon acting. I wanted to learn how far, and with what effect, personal sorrow tends to mingle with the imaginary woes of the theatre. If we find that actors who profess to 'feel' recognise no essential distinction, but at most a mere difference of degree, between purely mimetic emotion and personal sorrow revived by the similarity of their mimic to their real situation, then, surely, we shall be justified in concluding that mimetic emotion and personal emotion belong to the same order of mental phenomena, however much they may differ in poignancy and persistency.

The classical case in point is that of the Greek actor Polus, declared by Plutarch[3] to have been unequalled in his craft. Aulus Gellius is our authority for the anecdote. 'Polus, therefore,' he says,[4] 'clad in the mourning habit of Electra, took from the tomb the bones and urn of his son, and as if embracing Orestes, filled the place, not with the image and imitation, but with the sighs and lamentations of unfeigned sorrow. Therefore, when a fable seemed to be represented, real grief was displayed.' This anecdote is often loosely cited with the addition that the actor's unwonted fervour produced an unwonted effect upon the audience. Even Diderot seems to have fallen into this error.[5] Aulus Gellius says nothing whatever about the effect on the audience. The anecdote shows that a protagonist whom the Athenians reckoned

[2] N. S. vol. lxxi. p. 55.
[3] *Demosthenes*, xxviii.
[4] *Noctes Atticæ*, vii. 5.
[5] Pollock, p. 70.

great believed in the good effect of real emotion on the stage, and did not shrink from an extravagant device for securing the genuine article. It proves 'only this and nothing more.'

In Barry Cornwall's *Life of Edmund Kean* we find [6] a strange instance of the deliberate and calculated infusion of personal feeling into a theatrical situation. One of the great little man's most striking successes was achieved in Maturin's tragedy of *Bertram*. 'The benediction "God bless the child," ' says his biographer, 'for which Kean obtained so much applause, had been previously uttered a hundred times over his own son Charles. He repeated it so often, and so fervently, that he became touched by the modulation of his own voice; which, under the before-mentioned circumstances, acquired a tenderness "beyond the reach of art." ' This elaborate working-up and dragging-in of paternal feeling tallies, in a sense, with both emotionalist and anti-emotionalist theory. Diderot would greatly have approved of the hundredfold rehearsal, but would have held the utilisation of 'Charles his son' an unworthy lapse into sensibility. The truly great actor, according to his theory, would have lavished his blessings just as fervently on a chair or a coal-box. And here, I grant, Diderot might have claimed the authority of Garrick, if we may believe one of Cape Everard's anecdotes.[7] Everard, then a boy, was playing Thomas, Duke of Clarence, in the second part of *King Henry IV*. After the first rehearsal, Garrick called him 'into the Great Green Room; Mrs. Pritchard, Mrs. Yates, and many others, the first performers there. He told me that I spoke the part extremely well, only one line he wished me to give with a little more feeling. I said, "Oh yes, sir, I intend to do so at night." He caught at my expression as if lightning had shot athwart him!—"At night!" says he, "why, can you speak or play better at *night* than in the *morning?* . . . Then, sir, you are no actor! I suppose, too, you could give Romeo's, or Jaffier's speech, of

Oh woman, woman, lovely, charming woman!

with more softness and feeling if you addressed it to Mrs. Yates there, than you could to this marble slab?" ' The boy

[6] Vol. ii. p. 159.
[7] Everard, p. 4.

owned the soft impeachment; whereup Garrick continued, 'Then, you are no actor! If you cannot give a speech, or make love to a table, chair, or marble, as well as to the finest woman in the world, you are not, nor ever will be a great actor!'

Macready's daughter Nina died on February 24, 1850. On November 14 he notes: 'Acted Virginius. . . . I kept my mind on the part, and acted it, certainly, never better. The audience was extraordinarily excited. . . . In the second act my thoughts so fixed upon my blessed Nina that my emotion nearly overpowered me.' Again, on January 3, 1851, he writes: 'Acted Virginius, one of the most brilliant and powerful performances of the character I have ever given. I did indeed "gore my own thoughts" to do it, for my own Katie was in my mind, as in one part the tears streamed down my cheeks; and, in another, she who is among the blest, beloved one! Such is a player's mind and heart! Called.' [8] In these cases there can surely be no doubt that Macready did feel. The mimic situation reopened a real and recent wound, and the personal sorrow reinforced the mimic emotion, both together acting potently upon his physical organism. Nor can there be any doubt that he believed the effect upon his acting to be for good, and that the enthusiasm of the audience gave him valid ground for this belief. Note that, on the first occasion, his emotion 'nearly overpowered him.' Nearly, but not quite, for he was a consummate artist; and so long as it did not quite carry him away he had nothing to reproach himself with. On the contrary, 'the audience was extraordinarily excited.'

Miss Helen Faucit (Lady Martin) relates a similar event in her own experience. A few days after learning of the death of her dearly-loved sister, she had to appear at a benefit (sorely against her will) in some scenes from *Romeo and Juliet*. It was represented to her that the charity would suffer by her failure to perform, and she resolved to make the effort. 'I got on very well,' she writes, 'in the scene with the Friar. There was despair in it, but nothing that in any way touched upon my own trial. My great struggle was in Juliet's chamber when left alone. Then her desolation, her loneliness, became mine, and the rushing tears would have

[8] *Reminiscences,* ii. pp. 358, 363.

way. Happily the fearful images presented to Juliet's mind
of what is before her in the tomb soon sent softer feelings
away; but how glad I was when the fancied sight of Tybalt's
ghost allowed the grief that was in my heart to find vent in
a wild cry of anguish as well as horror!' [9] This passage is
particularly interesting because it lays stress on the analogy
between the real and the mimic situation, showing how the
sorrow in Miss Faucit's heart at once rushed into the channel provided for it by Juliet's lonely anguish.

Perhaps the most touching instance on record of the
mingling of personal with mimetic emotion is to be found
in Legouvé's account[10] of a midnight rehearsal of *Adrienne
Lecouvreur,* very shortly before its production. Legouvé
himself, Régnier, Maillard, and Rachel had remained behind
all the rest, when Rachel proposed that they should go over
the fifth act once more. No sooner had she commenced than
Legouvé was struck by the intense and unusual pathos in
Rachel's voice. She played the whole scene with heartrending power, and the three auditors were visibly moved.
After it was over Rachel sat silent in a corner of the green-
room, still weeping and shaken by nervous tremors. Legouvé
went up to her and said: 'Ma chère amie, vous avez joué ce
cinquième acte comme vous ne le jouerez jamais de votre
vie!' 'Je le crois,' she replied, 'et savez-vous pourquoi? . . .
Ce n'est pas sur Adrienne que j'ai pleuré, c'est sur moi! Un
je ne sais quoi m'a dit tout à coup que je mourrais jeune
comme elle; il m'a semblé que j'étais dans ma propre
chambre, à ma dernière heure, que j'assistais à ma propre
mort. Aussi lorsqu'à cette phrase "Adieu triomphes du
théâtre! Adieu ivresses d'un art que j'ai tant aimé" vous
m'avez vu verser des larmes véritables, c'est que j'ai pensé
avec désespoir, que le temps emporterait toute trace de ce
qui aura été mon talent, et que bientôt—il ne resterait plus
rien de celle qui fut Rachel!' ['My dear friend, you played
that fifth act as you never will again.' 'I believe I did, and do
you know why? . . . I was weeping, not for Adrienne, but
for myself. All at once something told me that I was going
to die young, as she did; and it seemed to me as if I were
in my own bedroom, living through my last hour—as if I

[9] *Shakespeare's Female Characters*, p. 130.
[10] *Soixante Ans de Souvenirs*, ii. p. 228.

were a spectator of my own death. And when at that speech "Good-bye to the triumphs of the stage, good-bye to the intoxications of the art that I have so dearly loved" you saw me bathed in actual tears, it was because I was having the dreadful thought that time was going to obliterate every vestige of whatever gift I have had—that there would be nothing left of her who was Rachel.'] This anecdote reminds one of the extreme emotion displayed by the American actor Thomas A. Cooper (the pupil of William Godwin), in acting Wolsey, at a time when his fame and fortune were on the wane. Tears coursed down his cheeks in the scene with Cromwell, and those who knew him best believed that he was overcome by the analogy between Wolsey's situation and his own.[11]

We are indebted to M. Coquelin, curiously enough, for one of the most interesting of the anecdotes bearing on this point. One morning, in the spring of 1849, he says,[12] Régnier was crossing the Pont des Arts with his little daughter. The child ran away from him; he chased her, caught her, lifted her up, and kissed her, 'd'un mouvement admirable de paternité heureuse [in a beautiful gesture of happy fatherhood].' 'Bravo!' said someone behind them, applauding as if in the theatre; and, turning, the comedian recognised Emile Augier. Borrowing the words of Henri IV. when found playing with his children, Régnier said: 'Etes-vous père, Monsieur l'Ambassadeur?' ['Are you a father, Monsieur Ambassador?'] and they passed on laughing. Three months afterwards, Augier stood with Régnier at the little girl's grave. He was then giving the final touches to his *Gabrielle,* and on returning from the cemetery he added to Julien's part in the fifth act, the lines:

> Nous n'existons vraiment que par ces petits êtres
> Qui dans tout notre cœur s'établissent en maîtres,
> Qui prennent notre vie et ne s'en doutent pas,
> Et n'ont qu'à vivre heureux pour n'être point ingrats.

'Et ces vers, si charmants et si vrais, à quelque temps de là, le père lui-même les disait sur la scène, imposant comme artiste silence à ses douleurs, ou plutôt, par une espèce de

[11] Ludlow, p. 371.
[12] *L'Art et le Comédien*, p. 31.

courage propre à notre art, les pétrissant avec celles de son
rôle pour en faire une création admirable.'

> [We are not half alive without these little ones
> Who move into our hearts and lord it over them,
> Who own our lives all unaware and need but be
> Alive and happy to show perfect gratitude.

And there came a day when that father himself was speaking these true and graceful lines on the stage, stifling his
personal sorrows as artists do; or rather, with a kind of
fortitude peculiar to our profession, kneading them together
with the emotions of his rôle to make of both together something new and wonderful.] It seems to me that in admitting
the good effect of this 'kneading together' of real with
imagined feeling, M. Coquelin practically abandons his anti-
emotionalist position.

'Macready's experience,' writes Signor Salvini, 'has also
been mine. One evening, in *Le Marbrier* by Alexandre Dumas
père, I had to play the part of a father who has lost his
daughter. That very evening, my own daughter, three years
old, lay on her death-bed! My tears choked my voice, and
my sobs went so directly to the heart of the audience that
their enthusiasm was intense.' 'Many and many a time,'
writes Salvini's countrywoman and sister-artist Ristori, 'in
sustaining the part of a daughter who loses her parents or of
a mother who sees her sons in the grasp of death, my tears
have blinded me, and I have felt my heart bursting with
sorrow. I have occasionally been so overcome by the analogy
between a fictitious situation and an event in my own life,
that I have had to put forth all my strength in order to
retain my self-control, and have not always entirely succeeded! The effects obtained under such mental conditions
are naturally stronger because they are truer.' Diderot meets
with short shrift at the hands of the great Italians.

Most of my informants, however, who have anything to
say on this point, agree that a too recent sorrow is hurtful.
Mr. John Clayton went from the deathbed of his father to
play in a similar scene, and utterly broke down. In other
cases in which a stage situation has recalled a recent personal
trouble, the effect upon his acting was bad, as he did not
dare to let himself go. It will be remembered that during

the historic run of *Hamlet* at the Lyceum in 1874–75, Mr. H. L. Bateman, the manager, died. His daughter, Miss Isabel Bateman, was playing Ophelia to Mr. Irving's Hamlet, and had to resume the part after a very short intermission. 'The effect of the real experience,' Miss Bateman writes, 'was anything but beneficial to my performance. In my effort for self-control I believe I never acted so badly; it remains in my memory as a terrible nightmare, and I have had a horror of the part ever since.' When we think of such speeches as 'I would give you some violets, but they withered all when my father died,' we can easily conceive what a terrible ordeal this must have been. 'On the other hand,' Miss Bateman continues, 'my acting has been greatly influenced for good by real but more remote sorrows.' 'The death of a beloved female relative,' writes Mr. John Coleman, an actor trained in the school of Macready, 'affected me so much that while playing Hamlet, soon afterwards, I was carried quite beyond myself in the scene of Ophelia's funeral, and overcome by an attack of semi-hysterical emotion. Although I have no personal knowledge or recollection of the effect upon the audience, I was assured that both actors and audience were very much excited by the occurrence.' It is curious that Mr. Coleman and Macready should use the same word, 'excited,' to indicate the effect upon an audience of a performance in which personal sorrow intensified the mimic emotion of the scene. The difference between the two cases is that, whereas Macready himself observes and reports the excitement of the audience, Mr. Coleman confesses that he was too much carried away to observe anything. I take it that Mr. Coleman does not consider the 'excitement' he created an artistically desirable effect. It is certain that where a player (in Macready's phrase) is too obviously 'goring his own thoughts,' the effect cannot but be crudely painful, like that of a bull-fight or of a gladiatorial display. Yet the fact that powerful effects, however undesirable, have been and can be produced under these circumstances, is a sufficient disproof of Diderot's argument that real emotion on the stage is of necessity 'paltry and weak,' meagre and unconvincing.

Two very distinguished actresses have been good enough to communicate to me experiences which exactly illustrate the influence upon acting of recent and of more remote personal sorrow. Even in her early girlhood—from the age of sixteen onwards—Miss Madge Robertson used to play the part of Lady Isabel Carlyle (afterwards Madame Vigne) in a dramatic version of *East Lynne*. She used to mourn over the dying child without knowing what sorrow meant. Then she became Mrs. Kendal; and, in the loss of her first child, she learned to sympathise only too vividly with the distracted mother of the play. *East Lynne* was at this time vastly popular, especially with Saturday-night audiences; and on a Saturday evening, less than a fortnight after her bereavement, Mrs. Kendal had to play Lady Isabel before a crowded audience at Hull. Everything, even to the name of the child, reminded her of her loss; and in the third act her emotion became so heartrending that she was utterly overpowered by it, and the curtain had to be dropped before the end of the act. The effect upon the audience was electrical and thrilling. A woman stood up in the pit and cried, 'No more! no more!' But it was not an effect which, either as a woman or an artist, Mrs. Kendal could bring herself to repeat. She got through the last act as best she might, and from that day to this has never reappeared in *East Lynne*.[13]

This was an instance in which acute and present personal sorrow absorbed rather than reinforced the mimic emotion, and changed the imagined heroine's imagined agony into real torture for the real woman. We come now to a case in which the memory of a more remote sorrow has aided in the production of an effect, the pathos of which must be fresh in the minds of thousands of playgoers. Mrs. Bancroft writes as follows: 'When a circumstance on the stage strikes home, reminding me of a great grief, a domestic sorrow, or a grievous wrong, it must for the time being cause a feeling of pain which of necessity gives an impetus to my acting. I can well sympathise with Macready, and understand how the loss of a loved child would affect his acting in *Virginius*. . . . When I played the Vicar's wife in *The Vicarage,* I had to deliver a particular speech which always affected me deeply: "God gave me a little child; but then, when all was bright

[13] As an instance of that mingling of the grotesque with the tragic which makes such a motley web of life, I may mention that Mrs. Kendal remembers vividly the broad Yorkshire accent of the child who played little Willie. His last words were: 'A cannut see yu or eear your voïce. A can oanly eear the singin' of those voïces in the shinin' gärden. Theear! Theear!'

and beautiful, God took His gift away," &c. The remembrance of the death of my own child was revived in these words. My heart was full of his image, and my tears came in tribute to his memory. I could not have stopped them if I had tried.' No one, surely, will maintain that Mrs. Bancroft deceives herself in supposing that she was feeling with her character—that is to say, was going through in her own person something very like the mental experience (with its physical accompaniments) attributed by the author to Mrs. Haygarth. 'The effect upon my audience,' Mrs. Bancroft continues—and no one who saw *The Vicarage* need be reminded of this—'was that not a heart amongst them did not feel with me. Their silence spoke volumes, and their tears told me of their sympathy.'

Miss Geneviève Ward, though doubtful as to the artistic effect of personal emotion, has no doubt as to its tendency to mingle with the emotion of the scene. 'Many sad experiences in my life,' she writes, 'have helped to intensify my feelings on the stage, even though not strictly analogous; but I have not found that it made any difference in the effect upon my audience. The influence on myself was to make me suffer, not only from the sorrow, but from the effort to control my feelings and keep them within the bounds of the situation. I have seen a young actress, whose pathos rarely touched her audience, perform one night under the influence of the deepest sorrow, tears rolling down her cheeks freely, and sobs breaking her voice. Yet the audience was quite as unmoved as on other occasions in the same situation.' This proves, what is sufficiently obvious, that emotion alone, without the faculty of dramatic expression, will not make itself felt across the footlights; and the proof of this fact is mistaken by some supporters of Diderot for the proof of his theory. Mr. Wilson Barrett mentions several analogous cases to the one just quoted. 'I have seen an emotional novice,' he writes, 'drown herself in tears. Evidently she has been torn with emotion, but, beyond the tears, there has been absolutely no outward and visible sign of this inward and spiritual suffering. I have again and again held a mirror to a young actor, and when he has evidently been feeling deeply, his face, to his astonishment, has borne a peaceful, placid smile.' All this merely shows that the use of inward emotion is to reinforce, not to supplant, outward expression. No one has ever doubted that the actor must be able to express what he feels, or feeling will avail him nothing. The question at issue is whether he ought, or ought not, to feel what he expresses.

Returning to the special subject of personal emotion, I am glad to be able to cite the experience of two actors who (as I can vouch from my own observation) have been most successful in mastering and moving the vast audiences of East End and suburban theatres. In the West End Mr. George Conquest is chiefly known as a pantomimist, but he is also a melodramatic actor of rare intensity. He, like Macready, has had to appear in a situation reminding him of the loss of a beloved daughter; and he, too, felt his personal sorrow mingle with his mimic emotion. 'I think,' he writes, 'the influence may have been good while the situation applied, but afterwards it distracted the mind from the true object of the drama.' Mr. J. H. Clynds, again, gives me his experience as follows: 'I was one night playing Hamlet during a short starring engagement, while my father lay dead at home; and during the whole of the first act the tears were literally streaming down my face. At the line "My father!—methinks I see my father!" it was only with the greatest effort that I could proceed. . . . The audience knew nothing of the (to me) sad event, and what effect was created I was too much engrossed to observe; but it was afterwards conveyed to me that it was a matter of general comment that night, "What wonderful pathos the Hamlet possessed, and what a voice of tears!"' In answer to my first question Mr. Clynds writes, 'It has always made itself felt to me that I produce a greater effect with *real* tears and the *genuine* lump in the throat than when these affections are not physically experienced'; and Mr. Clynds, I repeat, is an actor to whose strong hold upon large popular audiences I can myself bear witness. Now, if real feeling on the stage were, as many anti-emotionalists contend, absolutely and essentially ineffective, it certainly would not tell at the Grecian and the Adelphi any more than at the Lyceum. I would therefore lay stress on the testimony of Mr. Conquest and Mr. Clynds as showing that, whatever its artistic value, real sorrow does mingle with mimic emotion, and (to state the case in the most guarded terms) at least does not annul the desired effect.

The remaining answers to this question must be briefly summarised. Among the artists who assure me that personal sorrows have influenced their acting, and, as they believe, for good, I may mention M. Albert Lambert père, Mr. Wilson Barrett, Mr. Forbes Robertson, Miss Wallis, Miss Maud Milton, Miss Dorothy Dene, Mr. Leonard Boyne, and Mr. Leonard Outram. Mr. Outram writes, 'The public has frequently been agreeably surprised by the sudden accession of pathetic power in an actor or actress who has for the first time in a happy life encountered a domestic affliction.' Mr. Herbert Standing, again, sends me the following note: 'I have been playing Triplet in *Masks and Faces* lately, and in the scene where he speaks of his starving children I could not but think of my motherless little ones. I always got the right feeling and the "lump in the throat," along with the appreciation of the audience.'

Many of my informants, happily, have no experience of the effect of personal sorrow upon art. Others say that their domestic griefs are 'too sacred' to be 'used' on the stage; meaning, I presume, that in a situation recalling any private sorrow, they would make a deliberate effort to forget or ignore the analogy. This implies a curious mental state or faculty, of no importance, however, to our present inquiry.

The purport of this section, let me repeat, is primarily to prove that actual emotion is felt on the stage, and only in the second place to test its artistic value. My object has been to rebut the assertion that what actors describe and think of as 'feeling' is merely a state of nervous excitement not in the least resembling the emotional condition they have to portray. I have shown that the actor does, in some cases, indubitably feel with his character, the imagined emotion happening to coincide with a real emotion in his real life. It is pretty clear, too, I think, from the answers I have quoted, that the effect upon the actor of this mingling of real with imagined emotion differs in degree rather than in kind from the effect of the imagined emotion, pure and simple, to which my first question referred. If so, is there not at least a very strong probability that the artists who say that they 'feel' are not deceiving themselves, and that, in the particu-

lar order of emotions in question, the imagination can, and
does, beget in the actor's mind and body a condition more
or less analogous to that of the character he represents?

Sorrow is not, of course, the only emotion which may
transfuse itself from the real man or woman into the imaginary personage, though for the reasons indicated above
it is by far the most important. Joy will be dealt with in a
later chapter; in the meantime let me say a few words as
to love, hate, and their kindred sentiments.

We have seen how Sainte-Albine, followed by his English
adaptor, and by Sticotti, asserted roundly that 'Les personnes
nées pour aimer devroient avoir seules le privilège de jouer
les rôles d'Amans.' (None but those born to love should
be privileged to enact lovers' roles.) An obvious corollary
to this principle is that only an actor and actress who are
positively in love with each other can do justice to Romeo
and Juliet; the author of *The Actor* even going so far as to
assert,[14] with refreshing cynicism, 'that husband and wife
have seldom been observed to play the lovers well upon
the stage.' Diderot, of course, rebuts the extravagant assumption that stage lovers must be lovers in reality,[15] and
his remarks on the subject led me, in first interrogatory,
to put a question as to the effect of personal 'likes and dis-
likes' upon acting.

The general tenor of the answers was precisely what I
anticipated. Unlike the simple emotions, love and hatred
do not manifest themselves in characteristic and unmistakable external symptoms. They are emotional attitudes rather
than individual emotions. Personal feelings of this sort, then,
can but little help or hinder dramatic expression, any influence they may possibly possess being quite indirect. Dramatic annals, it is true, abound in anecdotes of lovers throwing exceptional fervour into love-scenes, and even of haters
giving treble force to passages of invective. In most of these
cases, however, there is probably a lurking fallacy of observation. Spectators who know, believe, or suspect that a certain personal relation exists between two artists, are apt to
see 'confirmation strong' in trifles light as air, and to make

14 Ed. 1775, p. 196.
15 Pollock, pp. 28-32.

much of differences which are imperceptible to the uninitiated. More than any other members of society (princes, perhaps, excepted), actors and actresses are the favourite playthings of gossip. To see beneath the mask, to discover personal warmth in mimic caresses and personal bitterness in mimic scorn, gives the theatrical busybody a sense of superiority. The wish is so apt to beget the thought that we cannot accept such evidence without suspicion.

One of the most famous instances of lovers excelling in a drama of love is thus quaintly related by the brothers Parfaict: 'Le mercredi premier Juin [1703], les comédiens remirent au Théatre la Tragédie-Ballet de Psyché, de M. Moliere, que eut vingt neuf représentations. . . . Ce qui contribua beaucoup au succès de cette remise, c'est que . . . l'Actrice qui représentoit le personnage de Psyché (Mademoiselle Desmares) et l'Acteur qui jouoit celui de l'Amour (M. Baron, fils) quoiqu' excellens tous deux, se surpasserent encore dans ces deux rôles; on dit qu'ils ressentoient l'un pour l'autre la plus vive tendresse, et que leurs talens supérieurs ne furent employés que pour marquer avec plus de précision les sentimens de leurs cœurs.'[16] [On the first Thursday of June 1703 the company revived M. Molière's ballet tragedy *Psyche,* and it was given twenty-nine performances. . . . A large factor in the success of the revival was the fact that . . . the actress who played Psyche (Mlle. Desmares) and the actor who played Cupid (Baron the younger), both of them always admirable, outdid even themselves in these two parts. One would have thought that what they mutually felt was the most ardent devotion and that they were but using their superlative abilities to give a more definite outward expression to what they felt in their hearts.] It is said [17] that the fervour of Psyche's passion for Cupid was so obvious as to lead to explanations between the actress and her 'amant en titre,' the Duc d'Orléans, which resulted in her giving the prince his dismissal and installing the actor in his stead. A less pleasant anecdote[18] in connection with this play is to the effect that the playing of Cupid and Psyche led to an intrigue between the elder Baron and Mlle. (or,

[16] *Histoire du Théâtre-Français,* xiv. p. 307.
[17] Lemazurier, i. p. 120.
[18] Gueullette, p. 20.

as we should say, Madame) Molière, the wife of his bene-
factor.

Cases in which lovers have played love scenes are, of
course, as plentiful as blackberries in dramatic annals; but
it is less easy to find trustworthy evidence that they played
them either exceptionally well or exceptionally ill. Lekain,
towards the close of his career, fell madly in love with a
lady who was not an actress. Whenever he was to play a
love scene he made her take her stand at the wing, and addressed to her the raptures intended by the poet for his heroine.[19] A popular Juliet has told me that an old lady of
her acquaintance used to say to her, 'Ah, you young people
may be all very well, but I saw Charles Kean and Ellen Tree
play Romeo and Juliet the evening before their marriage,
and I shall never again see the Balcony Scene done as they
did it.' Even supposing the old lady to have been a competent critic, I fear her memory must have deceived her. Mr.
and Mrs. Charles Kean, 'by an odd but accidental coincidence,' says their official biographer,[20] played *The Honey-
moon* the evening after their marriage. Had they played
Romeo and Juliet the evening before, the coincidence would
have been still more quaint, and he could scarcely have
failed to notice it.

Cases are not uncommon in which personal hatred and
emulation have added zest to scenes of recrimination and
invective. The central incident of Scribe and Legouvé's
Adrienne Lecouvreur is, if not historical, at least legendary.
The Duchesse de Bouillon, who was doing her best to supplant Adrienne in the affections of the Maréchal de Saxe,
happened one evening to be seated in a stage box while her
rival was playing Phèdre. The actress saw her, and turning
away from her confidant, hurled at the head of the great
lady the lines:

> Je sais mes perfidies,
> Œnone, et ne suis point de ces femmes hardies,
> Qui, goûtant dans le crime une tranquille paix,
> Ont su se faire un front qui ne rougit jamais.

[19] Talma, p. 73.
[20] Cole, i. p. 334.

[I know my treason, and I lack the boldness
Of those abandoned women who can taste
Tranquillity in crime, and show a forehead
All unabashed. . . .
     (Translation by Robert Bruce Boswell, *op. cit.*)]

The public, it is said, recognised the application, and applauded it.[21] We read of Rachel, too,[22] that in the part of Marie Stuart in Lebrun's tragedy of that name, she played flatly and without inspiration until, in the scene with Elizabeth, she stood face to face with an actress whom a hostile clique were trying to exalt into rivalry with her. Then she suddenly threw off her languor and played the scene with such intensity that the unhappy Elizabeth 'étonnée et confondue, reculait d'épouvante. . . . Ce fut une verve incroyable, une passion qui allait jusqu'au délire [astounded and taken aback, shrank appalled. . . . Here was an ecstasy passing belief, a passion verging on frenzy].' It swept her rival from her path at once and for ever. These cases of hatred touch our argument more nearly than those of love. Hatred, uttering itself in the form of rage, presents far more active and characteristic external symptoms than belong to any form of the tender passion; so that a personal predisposition to anger may very well assist and intensify its mimetic presentation.

Among the artists of to-day I find it generally agreed that an extreme dislike for any fellow-actor might, in spite of themselves, influence their playing for ill, whatever might be the supposed relation of their respective characters. One artist, however, pleads guilty to having entered with peculiar gusto into the nightly task of baffling and finally checkmating a fellow-artist of extremely unsympathetic private character; while, on the other hand, a well-known actor says, 'I never played Claude Melnotte better than to the Pauline of Miss So-and-so, whom I detested.' One or two actresses admit, theoretically, that they would feel constrained and ill at ease in playing Juliet to a Romeo who stood to them in a nearer relation than one of ordinary esteem and courtesy. It would seem like wearing their heart upon their

[21] Lemazurier, ii. p. 292.
[22] Houssaye, p. 151.

sleeve, and making a show of the sanctities of life. But, with a few reservations and exceptions, the general answer to this question is that personal feeling towards a fellow-artist makes but little difference, while the fellow-artist's talent and earnestness make all the difference in the world. I add earnestness, because talent, though the main thing, is not the whole secret. A bad actor, it is said, may sometimes be easy to play to, and a good actor difficult. I have been much struck by a remark of Miss Alma Murray's, to the effect that in playing to an actor who is languid and uninterested one is forced, in order to keep oneself up to the emotion of the scene, mentally to act the other part as well, of course at the cost of great exertion. Diderot's clockwork actor would certainly have the advantage of being exempt from this necessity.

In sum, then, there is no reason to deny that lovers have often played love-scenes well (though according to Diderot, they had no business to do so), and still less can we doubt that real love has often grown out of the mimic passion of the scene. But whereas it is evident that personal sorrow may, and often does, lend exceptional truth and intensity to mimic pathos, there is no convincing proof that personal love ever reinforces, in any perceptible degree, the utterance of stage-love. And the reason is—pardon the reiteration— that love, unlike sorrow, has no simple and characteristic physical expression to which the nerve-centres require to be attuned.

Chapter VI

THE LIFE SCHOOL

LET us now compare with personal emotion revived by the mimic situation, that 'emotion recollected in tranquillity' of which some great artists are known to have made use. Talma is the classic case in point. 'A peine oserai-je dire,' he says, [1] 'que moi-même dans une circonstance de ma vie

[1] *Réflexions sur Lekain*, p. 74.

où j'éprouvai un chagrin profond, la passion du théâtre était telle en moi, qu'accablé d'une douleur bien réelle, au milieu des larmes que je versais, je fis malgré moi une observation rapide et fugitive sur l'altération de ma voix et sur une certaine vibration spasmodique qu'elle contractait dans les pleurs; et, je le dis non sans quelque honte, je pensais machinalement à m'en servir au besoin; et en effet cette expérience sur moi-même m'a souvent été très-utile.' [I hardly dare confess that, in a passage of my life in which I was undergoing a deep distress, my histrionic obsession was so overmastering that, crushed as I was by a genuine enough unhappiness, in the very moment of shedding tears I took involuntarily a quick, fleeting notice of how my voice altered and acquired a kind of spasmodic vibrancy as I wept. And —I set it down not without some shame—I was thinking automatically how I could make use of the fact on occasion; indeed, that experiment on myself has often stood me in good stead.] M. Coquelin states,[2] on I know not what authority, that this 'circumstance' in Talma's life was the death of his father.

In scenes of emotion in real life, whether you are a participant in them (e.g. the death-bed of a relative) or a casual onlooker (e.g. a street accident), do you consciously note effects for subsequent use on the stage? Or can you ever trace an effect used on the stage to some phase of such a real-life experience automatically registered in your memory?

I have been told of Rachel (but have failed to find the authority for the anecdote) that one of her greatest effects in Corneille's *Horace* was studied from life. Overhearing a chance conversation one day, she learned of the unexpected death of a dear friend. She uttered a cry, and staggered half-fainting to a chair; but at the same moment it struck her that this was the very tone and action required for the cry of 'Hélas!' when Camille learns of the death of her lover. She studied and rehearsed the passage in this new light, making it one of her most famous effects.

'I have seen in Mrs. Siddons,' says Boaden,[3] 'hundreds of touches caught by herself from the real world—

[2] *L'Art et le Comédien*, p. 27.
[3] *Life of Mrs. Siddons*, ii. p. 180.

> She is a great observer, and she looks
> Quite through the deeds of men.

It is commonly deemed no slight ordeal to have her steady gaze bent upon you, as she sits, too willingly, silent a long time in society. Nor is this the result of prudence or reserve, for she has a sound understanding, and is well read—it is her choice: to *observe* is her mental discipline.' 'Kean,' writes Alfred Bunn,[4] 'sat up all night in a room opposite the Debtor's Door of the Old Bailey, to catch a full view of the deaths of the Cato Street conspirators; and as he was going on the stage in the evening, he said to me, "I mean to die like Thistlewood to-night; I'll imitate every muscle of that man's countenance." ' Macready told Lady Pollock[5] that he 'once in a dream saw and heard definitely and distinctly a friend lately dead, who came to address to him words of admonition. He woke in extraordinary emotion, and the image of this man filled his mind for long afterwards. Whenever he was to act Hamlet, he summoned up the passion of that dream.' Macready himself relates[6] that the recollection of a prisoner on trial at Carlisle 'vainly attempting to preserve his composure under the consciousness of guilt' greatly aided him in 'giving reality to the emotion of the agonised Mentevole' in Jephson's *Julia, or the Italian Lover*. Studies of madness are very common. Macready, when quite a young man, visited an asylum in Glasgow, and 'took from thence,' he says,[7] 'lessons . . . that in after years added to the truth of my representations.' Again, when preparing to play Lear, he notes in his diary (August 31, 1832), 'Went to Bedlam. . . . Nerves not able to bear it; came away.' [8] Fru Hedvig Winterhjelm, one of the leading actresses of Scandinavia, tells me that she has gone through a systematic study of madness, and has been 'struck by the few and slight touches required to produce the most terrible effects.' Miss Ellen Terry, before her first performance of Ophelia, paid a long visit to Banstead Asylum.

Many actors deny that they ever note the effects upon themselves or others of moments of high excitement. 'I am

---

[4] Bunn, ii. p. 208.
[5] *Macready as I knew him*, p. 11.
[6] *Reminiscences*, i. p. 105.
[7] *Reminiscences*, i. p. 188.
[8] *Reminiscences*, i. p. 344.

not so cold-blooded,' writes Mr. Dion Boucicault; and several other artists answer to the same effect. The majority of my informants, however, admit that the actor's habit of mind prompts him, as he goes through life, to seize upon and treasure up details which may be of use in his art; though this seems often to occur without any distinct act of will. 'A thousand times,' writes Salvini, 'I have availed myself of emotions experienced in real life, adapting them to the personage and situation.' 'Malgré moi,' M. Albert Lambert writes, 'quelle que soit la douleur que j'éprouve, je vois tous, j'entends tout, je note tout, et cela ne diminue pas mon émotion. On n'a pas qu'une case dans le cerveau. Il me semble que cela doit arriver à tout le monde, à moins d'avoir un cerveau incomplet.' [Whatever distress I may be feeling, in spite of myself I watch it all, listen to it all, take note of it all; and doing so does not lessen my emotion. It seems to me that the same thing must happen to everybody, and that its absence would constitute a mental limitation.] 'There have been events,' writes Mrs. Bancroft, 'which have so impressed me that when opportunity offered I have reproduced them.' 'As a casual onlooker,' writes Miss Isabel Bateman, 'I have noted effects of real emotion, and stored them up for possible use.' Mr. Lionel Brough holds that 'all scenes in real life are impressed on the mind of the real actor, and if occasion requires he will try to reproduce them.' Mr. John Drew, the excellent light comedian of Daly's company, writes as follows: 'I have consciously noted facts in real life for future use, but have never yet had opportunity to put them in practice. I have been able, however, to trace effects made to certain incidents automatically registered in my memory, though at the time of using them I fancied them imaginary or invented.' Miss Dorothy Dene is conscious of studying effects of real emotion in which she herself participates; 'but,' she adds, 'it is quite against my will.' Similarly, Miss Janet Achurch writes: 'It is impossible for me to help it. Everything that comes, or ever has come, into my own life, or under my observation, I find myself utilising; and in scenes of real personal suffering I have had an under-consciousness of taking mental notes all the time. It is not a pleasant feeling.' 'I often trace an effect used on the stage,' Miss Maud Milton writes, 'to some real experience of my own auto-

matically registered in my memory. I think,' she adds—and
the remark is most suggestive—'that good works of fiction
by students of human nature have a great influence on our
conception of stage-character and on our methods of expressing emotion.' If this be so (and it seems highly probable) one cannot but wonder whether the faults of some
actors may not be due to false conceptions of life and nature
gathered from bad works of fiction.

Lastly, let me cite a remarkable instance in which a casual
but very impressive real-life experience has been utilised on
the stage—as my informant believes, with good effect. 'In
the streets of Cardiff,' writes Mr. Leonard Boyne, 'I once
saw an Italian stab another fatally. I was on the opposite side
of the road, and I gave a yell or scream and rushed to take
the knife. That incident is always vividly before my eyes
when I see Tybalt stab Mercutio; and I have ever since,
when playing Romeo, used the "yell." I have noticed a
dead silence come over the house immediately, as if something beyond mere acting had happened. One of the audience told me the scream was so effective that he thought
the man was actually stabbed, and he was completely carried
away by the scene.' This seems at first sight like a perfect
example of 'emotion recollected in tranquillity.' But can Mr.
Boyne reproduce the cry, with certainty of effect, in perfectly cold blood? Does he not depend upon the emotional
tension of the scene to attune him for the effort? I confess
to a doubt whether Talma (who explicitly rejects Diderot's
theory)[9] could reproduce in perfect tranquillity the 'spasmodic vibration' of voice which he originally owed to over-
mastering emotion. There is nothing in his own account of
the matter to show that he could. Even the poet, though he
seldom writes under the first stress of passion or pain, must
summon up a certain 'fine frenzy' before he can recollect, or,
as Mr. Browning would say, 'recapture,' his grief or rapture.
As the *Westminster* reviewer aptly puts it, 'What comes of
being entirely tranquil, let the bulk of Wordsworth's own
verse testify.'

What, then, is the upshot of this part of our inquiry?
There can be no doubt that emotional experience, and the
study of emotion in others, are of the greatest value to actors.

[9] *Réflexions sur Lekain*, p. 40.

If this were not so, the mimetic art would not be mimetic. Even those of my informants who deny this are probably more dependent than they think on the unconscious action of their memory in registering real-life effects. Has not M. Sarcey recently been lamenting the passing away of the good old days of histrionic Bohemianism, urging that in their present state of domesticated respectability, actors and actresses are too much exempt from those crises of passion and rapture and despair which are necessary to the perfecting of their art? But whereas there is ample evidence of the tendency of personal feeling to mingle with scenic emotion of similar quality—as the vibration of one string will induce sympathetic vibrations in another tuned to the same pitch— there is comparatively little evidence of a tendency to store up in the memory particular ebullitions of personal emotion, and no evidence whatever that these ebullitions can be convincingly reproduced in cold blood. This the anti-emotionalists must prove—or rather they must prove that the ebullitions cannot be convincingly reproduced except in cold blood—before the case of Talma avails them one iota.

Chapter VII

THE PASSION OF LAUGHTER

Joy, in the civilised adult at any rate, has no such immediate and characteristic expression as grief or terror. The most stoical among us will scarcely receive a crushing blow without exhibiting some outward sign of dejection; but the best of good tidings (after, perhaps, a single exclamation of surprise) will hardly ruffle our outward calm. A state of high spirits, however, has certain characteristic symptoms, the chief of which is a proneness to laughter. According to Darwin,[1] 'Laughter seems primarily to have been the expression of mere joy or happiness'; and though it has become in a measure specialised as the expression of that complex emotion which we term amusement, it still, to some extent, fulfils its primary function. There is, therefore, a just instinct

[1] *Expression of the Emotions*, p. 198.

in the popular antithesis of 'laughter and tears' as the characteristic expressions of joy and grief. Having inquired into
the tendency of imagined sorrow to affect the physical
organism, I was anxious similarly to test the action of
imagined joy, and in order to do so I was compelled to
treat laughter as its proper expression. At the same time,
overestimating, perhaps, the degree in which laughter has
become specially associated with amusement, I conceived that
to treat it as a general manifestation of high spirits would
lead to misunderstanding; consequently I framed my questions thus:

In scenes of laughter (for instance, Charles Surface's part in
the Screen Scene, or Lady Teazle's part in the quarrel with Sir
Peter), do you feel genuine amusement? Or is your merriment
entirely assumed? Have you ever laughed on the stage until the
tears ran down your face? or been so overcome with laughter as
to have a difficulty in continuing your part? And in either of
these cases, what has been the effect upon the audience?

To this section a note was appended explaining that it
did not refer to laughter caused by chance blunders or other
unrehearsed incidents, but solely to that which forms part
of the business of the play.

The answers somewhat surprised me. For reasons to be
stated presently, I anticipated that there would be as great
a preponderance of testimony against the reality of stage-
laughter as for the reality of stage-tears. As a matter of fact,
the evidence is pretty evenly balanced, but deflects, if anything, on the side of reality. Were we to include among the
affirmative answers those which attribute genuine stage-
laughter to the reaction of the spectators' hilarity upon the
performer, the 'ayes' would have it by a large majority. Of
this class of answer, the following, from Mr. W. H. Vernon,
is a good specimen. 'I have often,' he writes, 'felt genuine
amusement in a scene, and an exhilaration of spirits caught
(doubtless) from an unusually responsive audience, which
has visibly reacted and produced the best possible effect. In
comedy the actor is more alive to his audience's humour
than in tragedy. The effect is instantaneous, and a good-
tempered house evokes the best qualities of a comedian by
placing him on good terms with himself.' Many other artists

practically echo Mr. Vernon, and must be classed as undecided. Mr. Toole, for example, says in his *Reminiscences,*
'Yes, I enjoy a rollicking farce. I laugh with the audience,
and get carried away by the fun of it.' The contagion of
laughter from an appreciative pit must certainly be potent;
so much so, indeed, that one actor tells me he has often had
to pinch himself or otherwise inflict physical pain in order
to repress this sympathetic hilarity. But it is not the hilarity
referred to in my questions. What I wished to ascertain was
whether the humour of a laughter-scene, unaided by the enjoyment of the audience, is apt to take such hold upon the
player as to make him laugh without any effort of will. The
two forms of laughter—laughter from sympathy with the
character, and laughter from sympathy with the audience—
must always tend to coalesce; yet I believe that an observant
artist must be able, up to a certain point, to distinguish between them.

'To me,' writes Signor Salvini, 'it is more difficult to compass mirth than sorrow. I have almost always wept from
real grief upon the stage, but I have never laughed with
conscious enjoyment. And in truth my simulated laughter
has never transfused itself into the audience, which has remained insensible to my gaiety.' There is nothing surprising
in this confession, unless it be its frank simplicity; and that
can surprise none but those who insist on regarding actors,
not as serious and self-respecting artists, but as mere childish
and morbidly egoistic triflers. Many actors who are not, like
Salvini, exclusive devotees of the 'grave cothurnate Muse'
agree with him in declaring their own stage-laughter 'an
artificial effort.' Among those who hold this view I may
mention Mr. and Mrs. Kendal, Mr. Boucicault, Mr. Pinero,
Mr. John Drew, and Mr. Wenman—all of them comedians
whose mirth, whether real or assumed, has awakened thou-
sandfold reverberations in many a crowded theatre. I have
little doubt, however, that even they, if the point were
specially suggested to them, would allow a certain effect to
contagion from the audience.

On the other hand, many witnesses of no less authority
maintain that their laughter is frequently, if not always, un-
forced. On such a question no one, surely, has a better right
to be heard than Mrs. John Wood. 'I am always genuinely

amused,' she writes, 'when I act a comic character, and my
laughter is frequently spontaneous. . . . I have noticed that
any point that is made spontaneously always has an electric
effect upon the audience, if it is in perfect harmony with the
scene.' Take, now, the testimony of Mr. Lionel Brough. 'In
playing parts like Tony Lumpkin, I feel that I *am* Tony
Lumpkin, and feel myself "full of laughter." I don't remember ever laughing until tears ran down my face, but
with a good audience I have laughed and enjoyed myself as
much as if I had been in the real situations.' The phrase I
have italicised indicates that Mr. Brough is to some extent
dependent on reaction from the audience. Indeed, this may
be taken for granted in all cases; though the ideal actor of
the anti-emotionalists should by rights be ready, if necessary,
to reel off his thoroughly-mastered lesson before 'a church-
yard full of gravestones'—to quote John Ryder's graphic
description of an irresponsive house. Macready, while form-
ing his Drury Lane company, wrote to Henry Compton
asking his opinion of a certain light comedian whom he
thought of engaging. 'He has some fun,' replied Compton,
'which I think does not amount to enjoyment. I never saw
him carried away by the exuberance of his spirits.' [2] Had
Macready been a believer in Diderot, he would have taken
this as a strong recommendation; but Compton (himself a
delightful comedian) clearly designed it as a reproach. 'My
heart is as much in laughter as in emotion,' Mrs. Bancroft
writes. 'Without a keen enjoyment of a comic situation my
laughter would be empty—a hollow imitation. All acting
must be an assumption at the start, but as I grow and advance with the play I become more and more influenced by
its argument, and therefore more absorbed in it. . . . I
have laughed on the stage till I cried, but not as a rule. All
emotions should be guided by discretion, or one would be
in constant hysterics.' As Mrs. Bancroft's irresistible laugh
is certainly not the least of her gifts, this testimony is extremely valuable. Mrs. Bancroft also tells how Mr. H. J.
Byron, who had of course studied her talent very carefully,
could detect in her laughter states of feeling of which she
herself was scarcely conscious. He would come round after
the performance and ask, 'Are you not well to-night?' 'Yes,

[2] Compton, p. 100.

quite well,' Mrs. Bancroft (then Miss Marie Wilton) would reply. 'There was something the matter with your laugh,' he would say—and on reflection Mrs. Bancroft would admit (what she had before scarcely realised) that some petty annoyance had been preoccupying her mind. So minute are the differences between what is absolutely true in art, and what (to the delicate sense) is perceptibly false!

Mr. John Coleman sends me some interesting notes on this point. He is all for the reality of laughter in such passages as the Screen Scene. 'I have often gone on the stage,' he writes, 'very nervous and depressed, but have forgotten all my troubles by the time I have arrived at the Screen Scene, and have entered thoroughly into the spirit of the thing. I am always physically exhausted at the end of the scene, and a little angry with myself for liking such a cad as Charles proves himself to be in this particular situaticn.' Mr. Coleman has a curious and very plausible theory as to the origin of the extraordinary 'Kch!' (like the sound of a saw) with which, according to stage tradition, Sir Peter Teazle and Charles Surface accompany the backward jerk of their thumbs to indicate the presence of the little French milliner behind the screen. Mr. Coleman believes that the original Sir Peter and Charles (King and Gentleman Smith) must have been very good laughers and that the absurd sound now considered indispensable must have originated in the mechanical imitation by inferior actors of their explosions of ill-suppressed merriment. It is certainly difficult to guess what sound in nature can have suggested the 'Kch!' of the traditional Charles. Mr. Coleman, too, relates a half-pathetic anecdote to show, as he says, 'how nearly akin laughter is to hysteria.' William Farren, the celebrated Sir Peter Teazle, Lord Ogleby, and Grandfather Whitehead, made his last appearance on the stage at Sheffield, under Mr. Coleman's management. 'He had suffered from paralysis of the vocal cord, so that his articulation was imperfect and frequently unintelligible. Notwithstanding, he looked noble and distinguished, and emitted flashes of his old fire. His character was Sir Peter, and the Joseph was a veteran actor who had been a captain in the army, and had acted with Kean. When the two old gentlemen commenced to laugh about the "little French milliner," the audience laughed with

them at first. Encouraged by this, they went on and on till
they became quite hysterical (producing a somewhat similar
effect on the audience) and at last collapsed altogether. In
vain the prompter prompted; in vain Lady Teazle urged
them to go on; deuce a word could they utter, good, bad, or
indifferent, until Charles spoke without, and sent the servant
to get Sir Peter off.'

We must go to France for other instances of inextinguish-
able laughter arising out of the business of the scene. It is
recorded of Mlle. Desmares, on the authority of Lesage,[3]
that she would often interrupt the action of a comedy 'pour
céder à une folle envie de rire [in order to indulge an unreasoning impulse to laugh].' Now Desmares was one of the
best soubrettes of her time, and so popular that the public
used to applaud even these extravagant accesses of mirth.
M. Lambert père writes: 'Je me suis amusé pour mon compte
beaucoup après m'être bien mis dans la situation et j'ai
réussi, grâce à ce moyen, à trouver des effets comiques inat-
tendus, maintenu par cette bonne humeur entraînée et en-
traînante qui se communique aussi vivement que le bâille-
ment. Je dois avouer, pourtant, qu'une fois je me suis pris
moi-même et qu'une idée si burlesque m'empoigna dans une
situation comique dont j'avais tiré de grands effets, que je
ris de telle façon qu'il me fallut quitter la scène—mais je
commençais le théâtre à cette époque et n'étais pas maître de
moi suffisamment.' [Greatly to my advantage, I have sometimes succumbed to hilarity after beginning a scene and have
thereby managed to hit upon unforeseen comic effects, prolonged by the unresisted and irresistible gaiety that is as
catching as a yawn. I must admit, though, that on one occasion I was my own victim. In the midst of a comic scene
in which I had scored some capital effects I was seized with
so wild a sense of the ridiculous that I laughed until I had to
get myself off the stage. But that was when I was still new
to the theatre and lacking in self-management.]

Many other artists—I may name Mr. Clayton, Mr. Beerbohm Tree, Mr. Wilson Barrett, Miss Alma Murray, Miss
Wallis, Mrs. Chippendale, and Miss Geneviève Ward—believe that stage-laughter is often genuine; and this, as I have
said, was at first a surprise to me. Every theatre-goer must

[3] Lemazurier, ii. p. 162.

have noticed the comparative rarity of good laughter on the stage. Tolerable pathos is far commoner than even moderately convincing merriment—so it seems to me, at any rate, and (I find) to many other observers. I imagined that the explanation of this lay in the very nature of laughter. Its causes and conditions are still moot questions, but I found all theorists agree in regarding suddenness and unexpectedness of impression as an almost essential factor in its production. Hobbes puts this very strongly in a well-known passage. 'Forasmuch,' he says,[4] 'as the same Thing is no more ridiculous when it groweth stale or usual, whatever it be that moveth Laughter it must be *new* and *unexpected*. . . . I may therefore conclude that the Passion of Laughter is nothing else but *sudden Glory* arising from a sudden *Conception* of some *Eminency* in ourselves, by *Comparison* with the *Infirmity* of others, or with our own formerly.' This analysis, though obviously incomplete, is generally held to be correct in its insistence on novelty as an important element in the ludicrous. Diggory, indeed, had laughed 'these twenty years' at Mr. Hardcastle's story of the grouse in the gun-room, but it may have been part of 'the constant service of the antique world' to suffer no amount of custom to stale a patron's jest. Now, the jests of the stage, whether they lie in dialogue or in situation, are necessarily familiar to the performer; and in this fact I thought I had found a reason for the infrequency of natural stage-laughter. But the answers I have just summarised show that stage-laughter may be, and often is, perfectly natural, in the sense of being produced by no deliberate simulative effort. Hence I conclude, on the one hand, that merriment retains, in almost unimpaired activity, its original function as a safety-valve for mere high spirits, not necessarily connected with any ludicrous idea; and, on the other hand, that the things which tickle our risible muscles need by no means be 'new and unexpected.' Everyday experience, indeed, is sufficient to show that 'the dearest jokes are the auldest jokes.' Which of us has not laughed a hundred times at Falstaff and at Dogberry, though we may know by heart every word they utter? Which of us can refrain from laughing when some passage of arms between Boswell and Johnson flashes upon the

[4] *Human Nature*, chap. ix. par. 13.

memory—the colloquy about the baby in the tower, for
example? or when we think of Sam Weller's skirmish with
Mr. Justice Stareleigh, or of Jos Sedley's heroism on the eve
of Waterloo? A few moments ago, some accident recalled
to my mind that sublime translation from Heine's *Wall-
fahrt nach Kevlaar* in an Anglo-German guide-book to the
Rhine:

> Many came hither on crutches
> Who now dance so stealthy,
> Many now play on the viol
> Who formerly were not healthy—

and though it has been a joy to me for years, I laugh as I
write it down. Age, indeed, is the chief merit of some witti-
cisms. We laugh at them because we have been in the habit
of doing so since our childhood; we should now be puzzled
to say where the humour comes in. Why, then, should not
a comedian laugh in the most hackneyed situations? To an
actor of mobile midriff, it may well be more difficult to restrain laughter in scenes whose humour depends on his
gravity than to summon it up when the action requires it.
If this be so, we may probably find an explanation of the
rarity of good laughers on the stage in the simple fact that
good laughers are no less rare in real life. We all know men
or women who are celebrated for a particularly pleasant or
hearty laugh, just as they might be for any other uncommon
physical charm. The ordinary laugh of the ordinary man,
if not unpleasant, is apt to be trivial, and a laugh which
would not specially annoy us in real life may become exas-
perating when transported to the stage. Thus, what with
unskilfully simulated laughter and unpleasant natural laughter, the merriment of the scene becomes, as a whole, unconvincing. It is only exceptional artists who either simulate
laughter to perfection or are happily endowed by nature
with musical and infectious glee.

Chapter VIII

NATURE'S COSMETICS

THE MUSCLES of the throat and even the lachrymal glands are more or less under the control of the will. However strong a probability we may establish, it is impossible absolutely to prove, in any given instance, that tears in the eyes or in the voice are the result of emotion. But can we find no symptoms of emotion which are utterly beyond the control of the will, and cannot possibly be simulated? If such symptoms of real emotion are found commonly to accompany the imagined emotion of the stage, will they not prove a very close analogy, at least, between the two phenomena?

Blushing and pallor precisely fulfill these requirements. If we could hear (for instance) of any Rosalind who blushes at the line 'Alas the day! what shall I do with my doublet and hose?' and turns pale when she hears of Orlando's wound, this would prove a curious degree of what may be called physical identification with the character, for the very reason that the actress could not possibly produce these changes by any voluntary effort. Physiological records may furnish cases of a power to blush and blench at will; but even if these exist (they have not come to my knowledge) we can only regard such a faculty as a freak of nature, much more abnormal than (for example) the power of moving their ears which some people possess. I have heard of, and seen, an instance in which a distinguished actor produces, by a mechanical device, a sudden and very striking pallor, which is of great value in one particular situation. But this effect depends upon morbid physical conditions, and does not in the least invalidate the general principle that changes of colour are beyond the control of the will. In Mr. Gilbert's *Comedy and Tragedy,* where Clarice breaks off her improvisation in an agony of dread, which is mistaken by the onlookers for part of her performance, Dr. Choquart alone exclaims, 'This is not acting. Her colour comes and goes!'

As a medical man, the worthy doctor knows that these functions of the 'vaso-motor system' are quite involuntary, and accordingly concludes (rightly enough, as it happens) that Clarice's agony is real. But had he examined into the matter a little more closely, he might not have been so confident. He would have found that imagined emotion may, and often does, approach so nearly to reality as to be accompanied by the very same symptoms, though probably in a minor degree. Of this the answers to the following question leave, I think, no possible doubt:

Do you ever blush (involuntarily) when representing bashfulness, modesty, or shame? or turn pale in scenes of terror? or have you observed these physical manifestations in other artists?

On this question I have two remarks to make. The first is, that when I formulated it I had neither read of nor observed cases of blushing and pallor on the stage. I must have come across one or two of the anecdotes to be quoted presently, but they had made no impression upon me. The question was entirely the result of an *a priori* process of reasoning. If my hypothesis as to the nature of mimetic emotion was the true one, these symptoms must certainly accompany it; but when I issued my interrogatory I was unaware of any positive evidence on the point. Thus the emotional theory, as I understand it, led me to a prediction, or rather anticipation, which subsequent inquiry has amply justified.

Secondly, it seems worth while to note that in the original edition of my interrogatory the word 'involuntarily' was omitted, so that this was not a leading but a *mis*leading question. Almost all my informants misunderstood its purpose, and, thinking to contradict my theory, unconsciously confirmed it. Supposing me to refer to voluntary changes of colour, they assured me that no one can blush and turn pale at will, and that at best it would be useless, since the changes would be practically invisible to the audience by reason of the actor's make-up. But the great majority of them (at least three-fourths) added either that they themselves *involuntarily* change colour, or that they have seen others do so; which was precisely the point I aimed at.

First among the witnesses to pallor as a possible effect of mimic emotion, I may place one who, if not a great actor, was at least a competent observer—William Shakespeare, to wit. He tells us how the First Player could

> Force his soul so to his own conceit
> That at her working all his visage wann'd;

and he evidently thinks no worse of the nameless tragedian for 'feeling his part' to this degree. It is surely not too rash to conjecture that he had seen in Burbage or Alleyn the changes of countenance which he attributes to the 'master' of the strolling company. As to Betterton, unquestionably one of the greatest actors that ever trod the boards, we find it positively averred that he not only changed colour but produced a great effect by so doing. The author of *The Laureat, or, the Right Side of Colley Cibber, Esq.*, writes as follows:[1] 'I have lately been told by a Gentleman who has frequently seen Mr. *Betterton* perform this part of *Hamlet*, that he has observ'd his Countenance (which was naturally ruddy and sanguin) in this Scene of the fourth Act, where his Father's Ghost appears, thro' the violent and sudden Emotions of Amazement and Horror, turn instantly on the Sight of his Father's Spirit, as pale as his Neckcloath, when every Article of his Body seem'd to be affected with a Tremor inexpressible; so that, had his Father's Ghost actually risen before him, he could not have been seized with more real Agonies; and this was felt so strongly by the Audience, that the Blood seemed to shudder in their Veins likewise, and they in some Measure partook of the Astonishment and Horror, with which they saw this excellent Actor affected.'

The following anecdote of Baron, the Betterton of France, would be still more valuable if we could altogether believe it; but I admit that it verges on the marvellous: 'Baron, après sa retraite, qui fut de plus de vingt années, remonta sur la Scène; elle étoit alors en proie à des Déclamateurs boursouflés qui mugissoient des vers au lieu de les réciter. Il débuta par le rôle de *Cinna*. Son entrée sur le Théâtre, noble, simple et majestueuse, ne fut point goûtée par un Public accoutumé à la fougue des Acteurs du temps; mais lorsque dans le Tableau de la Conjuration, il vint à ces beaux vers:

[1] 1740, p. 31.

Vous eussiez vu leurs yeux s'enflammer de fureur,
Et dans un même instant, par un effet contraire,
Leur front pâlir d'horreur, et rougir de colère,

on le vit pâlir et rougir successivement. Ce passage si rapide
fut senti par les Spectateurs. La Cabale frémit et se tût.' [2]
[Baron, after over twenty years' retirement, returned to the
stage, then under the blight of those windy elocutionists
that ranted their lines instead of just delivering them. He
opened in the the part of Cinna. His entrance, which was
dignified, restrained, majestic, was not at all to the liking
of an audience used to the tantrums of the contemporary
acting. But when in the oath scene he came to the splendid
lines

Their eyes you would have seen to blaze in instant rage
And, fast as thought 'twixt opposites can find a path,
Their brows to pale in horror and suffuse in wrath,

he was first seen to pale and then to flush. This instantaneous
transition had its effect on the audience; a shiver ran
through the hostile claque, and it fell silent.] It is possible, to
be sure, that the habit of 'forcing his soul to his conceit' may
have begotten in Baron an excessive mobility of the vaso-
motor system, placing it, in effect, under the control of his
will. In that case, this particular incident could not be cited
as a proof that the actor was, at the moment, under the influence of emotion; but, on the other hand, such a faculty
can only have arisen from the frequency of emotional
changes of colour, generating in the vessels of the skin a
peculiar, not to say unique, sensitiveness.

The flush of fury is not so directly germane to our argument as the blush of shame, for it can be mechanically
produced; yet the following note upon Barry's Othello
surely does not describe a mere muscular forcing of blood to
the head: 'When Shakespeare puts in the mouth of his enraged Moor . . . this great and soldier-like expression—

Had all his hairs been lives,
My great revenge had stomach for them all—

we see Mr. Barry redden through the very black of his face;
his whole visage becomes inflamed, his eyes sparkle with

[2] Dorat, p. 47.

successful vengeance, and he seems to raise himself above the ground while he pronounces it.'[3]

As to pallor, again, this passage from Davies' *Dramatic Miscellanies*[4] is very much to the point; and Davies, let me repeat, had excellent facilities for observation: 'Mrs. Siddons, very lately, in the third act of the Fair Penitent, was so far affected with assuming the mingled passions of pride, fear, anger, and conscious guilt, that I might appeal to the spectators, whether, in spite of the rouge which the actress is obliged to put on, some paleness did not show itself in her countenance. I think, too, that Mrs. Cibber, Mrs. Yates, Mrs. Crawford, and Miss Younge have given the same proof of consummate feeling in scenes of a similar nature.'

Writing of her first appearance as Juliet, Fanny Kemble tells how the part gradually took possession of her. In the first scene she was self-conscious and inaudible; in the next, the ball-room scene, she began to forget herself; in the third, the balcony-scene, she had done so entirely. 'For aught I knew,' she continues,[5] 'I was Juliet; the passion I was uttering sending hot waves of blushes all over my neck and shoulders, while the poetry sounded like music to me as I spoke it.' Fanny Kemble was then a beginner; but she repeatedly avers that a hot blush always 'bepainted her cheek' in the Balcony Scene. Miss Helen Faucit, one of the most accomplished artists of her day, bears emphatic testimony, not only to the fact of changing colour, but to its artistic value: 'The abuse of cosmetics on the French stage,' she writes, 'which was then [1845] habitual, has since been carried in many instances to excess upon our own. When the skin is covered with what is, in effect, a painted mask, the colour, which under strong emotion would come and go, is hidden under it, and the natural expression of the countenance destroyed.'[6] Whence proceeds the deadness of a too much made-up face, if not from the suppression of the natural play of colour? Though we may not, as a rule, be actively conscious of its presence, its absence necessarily makes itself felt.

Among the actors of to-day there is little conflict of

[3] *The Actor*, 1755, p. 9.
[4] Vol. iii. p. 58.
[5] *Record of a Girlhood*, ii. p. 60.
[6] *Shakespeare's Female Characters*, p. 437.

opinion on the subject of pallor. Salvini's evidence is included in his answer to my first question; but he adds that few actors have the power of so completely entering 'into the skin' of their characters. Ristori declares unhesitatingly that she both blushes and grows pale in accordance with the emotion she is portraying. Many artists who have never observed blushes on the stage have seen lips and cheeks turn white under the make-up, or have been told that their own countenances blench, in scenes of terror. 'I have never known my colour come and go, nor have I ever noticed it in any player,' writes Mr. Forbes Robertson; and Mr. Dion Boucicault notes with decision, 'No, never—don't believe in it.' These are almost the only thoroughgoing sceptics on the subject of pallor. Others (among whom I may mention Mr. and Mrs. Bancroft and Mr. and Mrs. Kendal) admit that they have noticed it, but regard it as exceptional. Mrs. Kendal remarks that she once produced a very convincing effect of pallor in the Screen Scene in *The School for Scandal,* but as that was due to a mouse running up the back of the screen, it is scarcely a case in point. Many, on the other hand, assert that the 'wanning' of the visage is a common and even habitual accompaniment of imagined terror and kindred emotions. Among these I may name Mr. Clayton, Mr. Beerbohm Tree, Mr. Wilson Barrett, Mr. Augustus Harris, Miss Geneviève Ward, Miss Bateman, Miss Achurch, Miss Dorothy Dene, and Miss Maud Milton. Mr. John Coleman writes, 'I have never known an artist, male or female, accustomed to the higher range of art, who was not subject to these outward manifestations of the inward emotions'; and an experience of forty years, in close association with most of the leading actors of that period, certainly entitles Mr. Coleman to speak with authority. 'I often turn pale,' writes Miss Isabel Bateman, 'in scenes of terror or great excitement. I have been told this many times, and I can feel myself getting very cold and shivering and pale in thrilling situations.' 'When I am playing rage or terror,' Mr. Lionel Brough writes, 'I believe I do turn pale. My mouth gets dry, my tongue cleaves to my palate. In Bob Acres, for instance (in the last act), I have to continually moisten my mouth or I should become inarticulate. I have to "swallow the lump," as I call it.' This testimony to the effect even of comic terror is extremely curious.

As to blushing, the evidence is less conclusive; and the reason is not far to seek. Laughter may or may not be 'a passion of sudden glory,' but blushing is certainly an effulgence of sudden shame. A carefully rehearsed humiliation or embarrassment necessarily tends to lose the vividness which whips the blood tingling to the cheeks. Blushing, too, depends on a certain delicacy of the skin which is probably not fostered by the habitual use of cosmetics. Nevertheless, several of my informants allow that they either blush themselves or have seen others blush. 'On the stage,' writes Fru Winterhjelm, 'I blush and turn pale according to the situation. It is therefore my custom to "make up" so lightly as to allow the natural colours to show through; and this, I have noticed, produces the strongest effect on the audience.' Miss Isabel Bateman, for instance, writes: 'I remember Miss Kate Rorke's blush in *Delicate Ground*—a charming flush that suddenly covered her face, and gave wonderful reality to the scene.' In the few months during which my attention has been specially directed to this point, I have myself noted several unmistakable cases of blushing on the stage. In the third act of *The Railroad of Love,* for example, I am very much deceived if a warm flush does not overspread Miss Ada Rehan's face at certain points of the boudoir-door scene between Valentine Osprey and Lieutenant Everett. One case of pallor, too, I witnessed distinctly, and that in no less a person than—M. Coquelin! It was in the scene in *Les Surprises du Divorce,* in which Henri Duval learns that his hated ex-mother-in-law has, by a horrible freak of fortune, become his step-grandmother-in-law. M. Coquelin threw into his rendering of this scene an almost tragic intensity, and his pallor at the moment of the awful discovery struck me forcibly. Still, I should not have ventured to bring it forward in evidence, had not my observation been confirmed by that of another spectator who asked me, without any suggestion on my part, whether I had noticed Coquelin turn pale at that particular point. Mr. John Drew, again, notes that he has 'known a good effect produced by the sudden, angry flushing of the face after a blow administered on it.' It might be argued that this flush was a direct result of the blow itself, apart from any emotional process in its recipient; but if so the buffet must have been unpleasantly realistic.

My next question was simply a following-up of the same line of thought:

A distinguished actor informs me that he is in the habit of perspiring freely while acting; but that the perspiration varies, not so much with the physical exertion gone through, as with the emotion experienced. On nights when he was not 'feeling the part,' he has played Othello 'without turning a hair,' though his physical effort was at least as great as on nights when he was bathed in perspiration. Does your experience tally with this? Do you find the fatigue of playing a part directly proportionate to the physical exertion demanded by it? or dependent on other causes?

The pores of the skin are still more completely beyond voluntary control than the capillary vessels which govern the complexion. We are accustomed to think of perspiration as attendant upon high temperature and violent bodily exertion; but everyone has also heard of, if not felt, the 'cold sweat' of terror. A like phenomenon accompanies even the most passive bodily agony and many other forms of intense feeling. 'When a man suffers from an agony of pain,' says Darwin,[7] 'the perspiration often trickles down his face; and I have been assured by a veterinary surgeon that he has frequently seen drops falling from the belly, and running down the inside of the thighs of horses, and from the bodies of cattle, when thus suffering. He has observed this, when there has been no struggling which would account for the perspiration. . . . So it is with extreme fear; the same veterinary has often seen horses sweating from this cause; as has Mr. Bartlett with the rhinoceros; and with man it is a well-known symptom. The cause of perspiration bursting forth in these cases is quite obscure.' Suppose, then, that an actor plays the same part on two successive evenings, the temperature and his physical exertion being the same in both cases: if on the one night he plays mechanically and without perspiration, while on the other night he 'feels the part' and perspires freely, this fact surely helps us to understand the

[7] *Expression of the Emotions*, p. 73.

precise condition of mind and body which he designates as
'feeling.' Since mere intellectual exertion has no tendency to
produce perspiration, the emotionless actor of Diderot's ideal
should perspire in exact proportion to the temperature and to
his physical effort. If this is not usually the case, it at least
follows that fews actors come up to the said ideal.

Unless the point were specially suggested to them, actors
would scarcely think of putting on record their experience in
this respect. Thus the evidence to be gathered from theatrical
biography is meagre. Here, however, is a curiously apt case
in point: 'Acted leisurely,' writes Macready (December 6,
1833), *without inspiration or perspiration;* still, I seemed
to produce an effect on the audience, but I was not identified
with Werner.' [8] When Henderson first played Hamlet at
Bath, says his biographer,[9] he discarded his predecessor's
velvet suit and dressed in black cloth. 'Extreme agitation oc-
casioned a perspiration. The coat was wet as if it had been
"immersed in the ocean." The performance ended, Hamlet
resigned his habit to the keeper of the wardrobe, who received it with astonishment and horror, hung it to the fire,
lifted up both hands and exclaimed ". . . Heaven bless us
all! . . . They may talk of Muster Lee, and Muster Lee, and
Muster Lee, but Muster Lee is nothing to this man—for
what they call perspiration." A person present observed that
the severest critics must acknowledge the young gentleman
had played the character with great warmth, if not with
spirit.' There are countless proofs, indeed, of the physical
exhaustion attendant upon emotional acting. Mrs. Siddons,
for instance, robust as she was, was frequently prostrated by
her bursts of passion. As an example, let me quote a curious
account given by Macready[10] of her collapse after playing
Arpasia in Rowe's *Tamerlane.* 'In the last act,' he says,
'when, by order of the tyrant, her lover Monesis is strangled
before her face, she worked herself up to such a pitch of
agony, and gave such terrible reality to the few convulsive
words she tried to utter, as she sank a lifeless heap before
her murderer, that the audience for a few moments remained in a hush of astonishment, as if awe-struck; they

[8] *Reminiscences,* i. p. 395.
[9] Ireland, p. 70.
[10] *Reminiscences,* i. p. 202.

then clamoured for the curtain to be dropped, and insisting on the manager's appearance, received from him, in answer to their vehement inquiries, the assurance that Mrs. Siddons was alive, and recovering from the temporary indisposition that her exertions had caused. They were satisfied as regarded her, but would not suffer the performance to be resumed. As an instance of the impression this great actress made on individuals who might be supposed insensible, from familiarity, to the power of acting, Holman turned to my father, when Mrs. Siddons had fallen, and looking aghast in his face, said: "Macready, do I look as pale as you?"' It is incredible that Mrs. Siddons in this instance was acting in cold blood, or that her exhaustion was due to the mere physical and intellectual effort of playing Arpasia, who appears in only three acts out of the five.

Among contemporary artists I find a more general agreement on the point suggested by this question than on almost any other. I may even say that all my informants, with one exception, who have had much experience of emotional parts are absolutely unanimous. 'One is never so exhausted as when acting well,' says Mr. Bancroft. 'Playing with the brain,' says Miss Alma Murray, 'is far less fatiguing than playing with the heart. An adventuress taxes the physique far less than a sympathetic heroine. Muscular exertion has comparatively little to do with it.' 'On a bitterly cold night in America,' writes Mr. Wilson Barrett, 'when the thermometer has been 15° below zero, and I have stood shivering at the wings waiting for my entrance in Hamlet, I have been in a profuse perspiration before I had half finished a scene.' 'Emotion while acting,' writes Mr. Howe, 'will induce perspiration much more than physical exertion. I always perspired profusely while acting Joseph Surface, which requires little or no exertion.' Similarly, Mr. Herbert Standing writes, 'I have had the honour of playing in *The Man of the World* with the late Samuel Phelps, and have seen him, while sitting quietly in his chair, bathed in perspiration.' 'Emotion and perspiration,' says Salvini, 'go together. There are characters which call for scarcely any physical exertion, and which are nevertheless most fatiguing: for example the part of Corrado in *La Morte Civile.*' 'Ce qui brise,' says M. Albert Lambert—and this is the one opinion that runs counter to my argument—'ce sont les colères non pensées, les cris froids, les déclamations oiseuses, à côté du sujet et en dehors de la nature.' [The things that exhaust one are the unreasoning rages, the unfelt outcries, the empty pomposities—the irrelevant and the unnatural.] That these should be very fatiguing to the actor, as well as to the audience, is comprehensible enough; but M. Lambert further remarks that by keeping 'le coeur chaud, la tête froide' [a warm heart, a cool head] the actor escapes exhaustion. 'I suffer from fatigue,' writes Mr. Forbes Robertson, 'in proportion to the amount of emotion I may have been called upon to go through, and not from physical exertion.' Mr. Clayton told me that after playing Hugh Trevor, a part which demands no unusual muscular strain, he has been so exhausted that he has lain down on the floor of his dressing-room and said to his dresser, 'Don't come near me for an hour!' feeling as though he had been thrashed all over. 'Though I have played Othello,' writes Mr. Coleman, 'ever since I was seventeen (at nineteen I had the honour of acting the Moor to Macready's Iago), husband my resources as I may, this is the one part, the part of parts, which always leaves me physically prostrate. I have never been able to find a pigment that would stay on my face, though I have tried every preparation in existence. Even the titanic Edwin Forrest told me that he was always knocked over in Othello, and I have heard Charles Kean, Phelps, Brooke, Dillon, say the same thing. On the other hand I have frequently acted Richard III. without turning a hair.' It is evident that the exceptionally exhausting quality of Othello does not lie in the physical effort it demands. Hamlet, Macbeth, and Richard III. must at least equal it in that. On the other hand, I think we can have no difficulty in recognising a peculiar poignancy in the emotions of 'the great brute gladiator,' as Mr. Traill calls him, 'fast in the toils of Iago Retiarius,' which (according to my theory) amply explains the overwhelming effect. More than any other of the great Shakespearean characters (except perhaps King Lear) Othello must be played with the heart rather than the head. His head, in truth, was not his strong point.

One or two of my informants are inclined to attribute perspiration and consequent fatigue to general nervousness rather than to the special emotion of a particular character. They dwell on the fact that the nervous excitement of a first night is a noted sudorific. This argument would be of great weight if the symptom were confined to first nights and other peculiarly nervous occasions. But we have no reason for supposing that the actor referred to in my question—Mr. Hermann Vezin—was more nervous one night than another; unless, indeed, we choose to argue in a circle and describe as 'nervousness' the very condition of mind and body which enables a player to enter into the emotions of his part. It is true that some great actors have confessed to feeling a certain nervousness, amounting almost to stage-fright, every time they faced the public; but they have always added that, the first plunge once over, this sensation passes off. We may readily admit that nervousness (in the ordinary sense of the term) heightens the tendency to perspiration on special occasions; but it cannot account for the whole phenomenon.

The following observation of François Riccoboni's may be quoted as the most plausible anti-emotionalist argument on this point which has come under my notice: 'Je ne dis pas qu'en jouant les morceaux de grande passion l'Acteur ne ressente une émotion très-vive, c'est même ce qu'il y a de plus fatiguant au Théâtre. Mais cette agitation vient des efforts qu'on est obligé de faire pour peindre une passion que l'on ne ressent pas, ce qui donne au sang un mouvement extraordinaire auquel le Comédien peut être lui-même trompé, s'il n'a pas examiné avec attention la véritable cause d'où cela provient.' [11] [I am not saying that the actor, when he plays the great tragic dramas, does not experience intense emotion; indeed, such pieces are the most exhausting of all. But his tension springs from the inevitable strain of depicting a passion that he does not feel—an exertion that has startling effects on the pulse and can hoodwink the actor himself unless he has closely analysed its true source.] Unless this chapter has entirely failed in its purpose, I think it establishes a fair probability that 'the comedian' may be right in his self-analysis, and Riccoboni wrong.

'But hold!' say the anti-emotionalists, shifting their ground to what may be called Diderot's second position; 'we do not deny that some, many, even most actors may exhibit

[11] *L'Art du Théâtre* (1750), p. 41.

symptoms of emotion which cannot be mechanically simulated. Our point is that the greatest artists do not feel on
the stage, and would not be great if they did.' Then Betterton, Baron, Mrs. Siddons, and Salvini must be relegated to
'the ruck of middling actors' ? That were a paradox indeed.

Chapter IX

'AUTOSUGGESTION' AND 'INNERVATION'

'I HATE to dissemble when I need not,' says Gatty to her
sister Ariana in Etherege's *She Would if She Could;*
' 'twould look as affected in us to be reserved now we are
alone, as for a player to maintain the character she acts in
the tiring-room.' Madam Gatty was an anti-emotionalist by
instinct. She had not considered whether it be necessary or
desirable for the player to attain and preserve a certain emotional level before and during the performance of an arduous part. It is to this point that the following groups of
questions refer:

G. H. Lewes relates[1] how Macready, as Shylock, used to shake
a ladder violently before going on for the scene with Tubal, in
order to get up 'the proper state of white heat'; also, how Liston
was overheard 'cursing and spluttering to himself, as he stood at
the side scene waiting to go on in a scene of comic rage.' Have
you experienced any difficulty in thus 'striking twelve at once'?
If so, how do you overcome it?

It used to be said of a well-known actor that he put on in the
morning the character he was to play at night; that on days
when he was to play Richard III. he was truculent, cynical, and
cruel, while on days when he was to play Mercutio or Benedick
he would be all grace, humour, and courtesy. Are you conscious
of any such tendency in yourself? or have you observed it in
others? In the green-room, between the acts, have you any tendency to preserve the voice and manner of the character you are
playing? or have you observed such a tendency in others?

Macready and Liston, it may be said, could not affect
their emotional states by shaking a ladder and spluttering,

[1] *Actors and Acting*, p. 38.

these being merely mechanical devices for producing extreme muscular mobility. This argument, however, ignores
the undoubted tendency of outward expression to react upon
emotion. 'He who gives way to violent gestures,' says Darwin,[2] 'will increase his rage; he who does not control the
signs of fear will experience fear in a greater degree. . . .
Even the simulation of an emotion tends to arouse it in
our minds.' Eduard von Hartmann, 'the Philosopher of the
Unconscious,' gives to this principle the hybrid name of
'autosuggestion' and treats it as one of the central secrets of
acting.[3] Lessing too, though he would probably have re-
belled at the word, was familiar with the thing. He discusses in his *Hamburgische Dramaturgie*[4] the respective
merits of the actor who has feeling (Empfindung) but little power of expression, and the actor who has great power
of expression but no feeling. The latter he declares, very naturally, to be the more useful of the two. By merely imitating
the emotional expression of others 'he will attain to a sort
of feeling, in virtue of the law that those modifications of
the soul which produce certain changes of the body, can,
conversely, be produced through the medium of these
changes. This sort of feeling cannot, certainly, have the persis-
tence and fire of that which takes its rise in the soul; yet
in the moment of performance it is powerful enough to
bring about in some measure those involuntary physical
changes from whose presence we can alone infer with certainty the presence of the inward emotion. Suppose that such
an actor has to express the utmost fury of wrath, and suppose that he does not even understand his part sufficiently
to know the reason of this fury. . . . If he has merely learnt
to imitate correctly the most obvious symptoms of rage as
expressed by an actor of native feeling—the hasty tread,
the stamping foot, the rough voice, now screaming, now
chocking, the play of the eyebrows, the quivering lips, the
grinding teeth—if he can imitate these things correctly, I
say (and that may be done by a mere effort of will), then
a dim feeling of wrath will infallibly seize upon his soul,
which, in turn, will react upon his body and produce those

---

[2] *Expression of the Emotions*, p. 366.
[3] *Philosophie des Schönen* (1887).
[4] May 8, 1767.

changes which do not depend upon our will alone. . . . In short, he will appear to be really enraged, when in truth he is nothing of the sort, and does not even understand "the motive and the cue for passion."' Lessing, I need scarcely point out, was a thorough-going emotionalist.

This principle of 'autosuggestion' explains Macready's practice, and the similar devices of other actors. It is of course conceivable that Macready may have kept his mind perfectly calm while he worked up the muscular tremor of fury; but the supposition is difficult. The most intimate correlations can by practice be overcome, just as a juggler can keep five balls in the air with his right hand while with his left he plays 'Home, sweet Home' upon the concertina. Diderot would tell us that Macready ought to have performed a similar feat, but there is no evidence that he did perform it. 'There is reason to suspect,' says Darwin again,[5] 'that the muscular system requires some short preparation, or some degree of innervation, before being brought into strong action.' Macready's primary object, no doubt, was to mobilise his muscles, but he probably knew very well that in doing so he mobilised his mind.

There is abundant testimony to the difficulty of 'striking twelve at once,' and many methods of overcoming it are on record. It is recorded of Baron[6] that before going on the stage in a scene of high excitement, 'il se battait les flancs pour se passionner; il apostrophait aver aigreur et injuriait tous ceux qui se présentaient à lui, valets et camarades de l'un et de l'autre sexe, et il appelait cela "respecter le parterre."' [. . . he belaboured himself to work up excitement, hurled rasping words and insults at everyone in the vicinity, whether underlings or colleagues of either sex; and this process he called 'paying respect to the house.'] Sticotti states the same fact in a different form. 'Baron dans la coulisse,' he says,[7] 'se pénétroit déjà des choses qu'il alloit dire; il paroissoit hors de lui-même; il s'interrogeoit, il gémissoit, il parloit aux autres de sa triste situation, comme si elle eût été bien véritable, et dans cet état, il entroit sur la scène; ce principe excellent est peu suivi des Acteurs médiocres.'

---

[5] *Expression of the Emotions*, p. 116.
[6] *Dictionnaire Larousse*, art. 'Baron.'
[7] *Garrick*, ed. 1770, p. 63.

[Baron, while still in the wings, was already supercharging himself with the speeches he was about to deliver. He would appear to be beside himself; he would put questions to himself, he would utter moans, he would talk to bystanders about his harrowing dilemma as if it were actuality; in that state he would make his entrance. This salutary practice is but little emulated by commonplace actors.] This was practically the system of Macready; and theatrical tradition tells of an actor-manager who carried the same method to a length which neither Baron nor Macready thought necessary. When going on in a particular situation of great excitement, he used to work himself up by kicking the property-man; it being understood that he should afterwards apologise and give the fellow a shilling. One night, when the house was very bad, the property-man planted himself at the wing to receive the accustomed kicking; but the canny actor-manager restrained himself, saying as he passed him by, 'Not to-night, Barkins; the treasury won't stand it.' This gentleman's respect for the property-man varied in the inverse ratio of his respect for the pit.

Many of my informants admit that, though they do not shake ladders or kick property-men, they adopt mechanical means of less violence in order to work themselves up before an excited entrance. They mumble to themselves through their clenched teeth, snap their fingers, hold up their hands and shake them rapidly with a loose wrist, or 'stand rigidly and rock the body to and fro with gradually increasing nerve-tension.' Mr. Arthur Cecil informed me that Phelps used always to stand muttering to himself before making his entrance. One night, during the run of *The Merry Wives of Windsor* at the Gaiety, Phelps lost his way in the intricate passages between his dressing-room and the stage, and was not to be found when his cue was given. The 'wait' was becoming noticeable, when Mr. George Belmore, who happened to be standing at the wing, bethought him to imitate the muttered thunder which used to announce the actor's approach. He thus kept the audience in the belief that the delay was an intentional effect, until the missing Falstaff was rescued from the labyrinth. In hand-to-hand combats such as the death-struggle of Macbeth or of Richard, tragedians have been known to hurl the most horri-

ble curses at each other under their breath. When Phelps
first encountered Macready on the battlements of Dunsinane,
he was astonished to hear the older tragedian overwhelm
him with savage obloquy. Thinking that no offence he could
possibly have committed could justify such treatment, he responded in kind, and 'gave as good as he got.' Great was
his surprise when, at the end of the play, Macready thanked
him cordially for the spirited way in which he had played
up to him in the combat. In a recent revival of Dumas's *An-
tony*, Paul Mounet and Madame Tessandier had recourse
to this device: 'Ils avaient intercalé dans une scène des
jurons, des injures que le public n'entendait pas, mais avec
lesquels ils se fouettaient les nerfs; ils emportèrent la scène
dans un mouvement de passion échevelée qui électrisa la
salle.' [8] [Into one scene they interpolated curses and insults, unheard by the audience, that served to get them
wrought up; and they carried off that scene with a surge
of abandon that overwhelmed the house.] There is a passage in *Rob Roy* where the bold outlaw, captured and pin-
ioned, stands writhing and foaming at the mouth, while
the other characters on the stage are singing the 'Tramp
Chorus.' In this scene Mr. J. B. Howard, the Rob Roy of
the modern Scotch stage, was in the habit of indulging in
such copious expletives, that an old dresser in the Edinburgh Theatre Royal, who used to be sent on among the
'supers,' begged Mrs. Wyndham to assign her a place on
the stage as far as possible from Rob Roy, 'for the language
he used made her flesh creep.' Since then, Mr. Howard has
learnt to do his swearing in Italian.

As a rule, however, mental concentration, rather than any
physical device, is resorted to in order to overcome the difficulty of 'striking twelve at once.' A favourite and of course
a very obvious method is to stand at the wing and drink in
every word of the dialogue leading up to the difficult entrance, in order to become impregnated with the spirit of
the situation. This was the method adopted by Mrs. Siddons,
as she herself tells us in a very curious study of the character of Constance in *King John*: ' . . . If the representative
of *Constance*,' she writes,[9] 'shall ever forget, even behind

[8] *Revue d'Art Dramatique*, March 1, 1887.
[9] Campbell, i. p. 213.

the scenes, those disastrous events which impel her to break
forth into the overwhelming effusions of wounded friendship, disappointed ambition, and maternal tenderness, upon
the first moment of her appearance in the third Act, when
stunned with terrible surprise she exclaims,—

> Gone to be married—gone to swear a peace!
> False blood to false blood joined—gone to be friends!

if, I say, the mind of the actress for one moment wanders
from these distressing events, she must inevitably fall short
of that high and glorious colouring which is indispensable
to the painting of this magnificent portrait. . . . Whenever I was called upon to personate the character of *Constance*, I never, from the beginning of the play to the end
of my part in it, once suffered my dressing-room door to
be closed, in order that my attention might constantly be
fixed on these distressing events which, by this means, I
could plainly hear going on upon the stage, the terrible effects of which progress were to be represented by me. Moreover, I never omitted to place myself, with *Arthur* in my
hand, to hear the word, when, upon the reconciliation of
England and France, they enter the gates of Angiers to rat-
ify the contract of marriage between the *Dauphin* and the
Lady Blanche; because the sickening sounds of that march
would usually cause the bitter tears of rage, disappointment,
betrayed confidence, baffled ambition, and, above all, the
agonizing feelings of maternal affection, to gush into my
eyes. In short, the spirit of the whole drama took possession
of my mind and frame, by my attention being incessantly
riveted to the passing scenes. . . . I have no doubt that
the observance of such circumstances, however irrelevant
they may appear upon a cursory view, were [*sic*] powerfully aidant in the representations of those expressions of
passion in the remainder of this scene, which have been
only in part considered.' It is perhaps worth noting that in
the Tubal scene, to which the anecdote of Macready refers,
no such process of 'abstraction,' as Mrs. Siddons calls it, is
possible, Shylock's entrance following immediately upon a
few words of trivial conversation between Salanio and Sala-
rino. Mrs. John Wood writes as follows: 'I once had a lesson that taught me the value of this concentration of mind,

and I have never forgotten it. The character I was playing was a wild, uncouth, ragged creature, who was devoted to the villain of the piece, he being the only person who had ever bestowed upon her a kindly thought. For this he became her idol. She watched his words and footsteps, and aided him innocently in his acts of villainy. At last she fancies that he loves the heroine, and, in her jealousy, imagines his love returned. She follows him; he meets the lady of his love; and she overhears him pour forth his passion. She does not wait to hear the heroine's reply, but rushes at her like a very tigress. The audience waited breathlessly for this supreme moment of the girl's fury, and the scene ended in a most pathetic manner, the sympathy of the public being greatly excited on this poor creature's behalf. I used conscientiously to listen to the preceding scene, and by so doing was really worked up to the right pitch of excitement when my cue came. One night, several of the company, convulsed with laughter, took off my attention by telling me of a great joke they were going to play off upon an unfortunate actor in the next piece. This thoughtlessness ruined my scene. I could not act up to the situation. I did not *feel* it. No amount of art can make up for the want of one real touch of nature. I then found out that they must be *combined* to produce an electrical effect upon your audience.' Miss Ellen Wallis, who has certainly done more than any other living actress to keep alive in the provinces the traditions of poetic drama, instances Isabella's entrance in the last act of *Measure for Measure* as a case in which she has found great difficulty in 'striking twelve at once.' Like Mrs. Siddons, she stations herself at the wing and listens intently to the opening speeches of the scene—the Duke's compliments to Angelo—thus working up her indignation for the great outburst of 'Justice, O royal Duke!' with which she flings herself at his feet. The effort of concentrating the attention is sometimes no less valuable in lowering than in heightening the vitality. Mrs. Kendal tells me that, in order to induce in the lines of her face, and in her whole person, the stony rigidity of Claire in *The Ironmaster*, she has often shut herself up in her dressing-room and deliberately fixed her mind upon all the 'old, unhappy, far-off things' she could think of—the pains, losses, and disappointments of her life.

Mr. Bancroft makes a similar statement with regard to the part of Orloff in *Diplomacy*. He used to prepare himself for the great 'scene of the three men' by the very process employed by Mrs. Kendal. Miss Geneviève Ward, again, writes: 'I find no difficulty in "striking twelve at once" in passionate or mirthful scenes; but before death-scenes I wish to be some time alone. My vitality is so strong that for quiet scenes I need to get my nerves under complete control.'

On the other hand we have anecdotes (though I can find but few) of great actors whose extraordinary natural mobility of mind and body enabled them to perform astonishing feats in the way of 'striking twelve at once.' A noteworthy instance is related by M. Coquelin. 'Talma,' he says,[10] 'jouait Hamlet un soir. En attendant son tour, il causait dans la coulisse avec un ami; l'avertisseur le voit souriant, distrait, s'approche:—"Monsieur Talma, cela va être à vous!" —"C'est bien, c'est bien, j'attends ma réplique." Sa scène, la scène du spectre, devait commencer dans la coulisse même et le spectateur entendre Talma avant de le voir. Il continue sa causerie, très-gai, la réplique arrive, il serre la main de son interlocuteur, et, le sourire encore aux lèvres, cette main amicale dans la sienne,

Fuis, spectre épouvantable!

et l'ami recule, effaré, et le frisson tombe dans la salle!' [Talma was playing Hamlet one evening. While waiting to go on he chatted with a friend in the wings. The call-boy sees him there smiling and oblivious, goes up to him, and says: 'M. Talma, it's almost time.' 'All right, all right; I'm waiting for my cue.' His next scene, the ghost scene, is to begin right there in the wings: the audience is to hear Talma before it sees him. He keeps on chatting vivaciously. Comes his cue: he presses his companion's hand and, with lips still smiling and the friend's hand still in his—

Avaunt, dread spirit!

The friend starts back appalled, and a spinal shiver runs through the house.]

Garrick, in private society, would often give the Dagger Soliloquy from *Macbeth* at a moment's notice. It is reported

[10] *L'Art et le Comédien*, p. 25.

of Kean and of Rachel that they would at one moment be
laughing and joking behind the scenes, and at the next moment on the stage, raving with Lear or writhing with Phèdre; while they had equal facility in stilling the ground-swell
of passion at the end of a trying scene. Even of Mrs. Siddons
Sir Walter Scott relates a similar story. In a drawing-room
one day, wishing to illustrate a peculiarity in John Philip
Kemble's manner, she placed herself in the attitude of an
Egyptian statue—her knees together, her feet turned a little inward, her elbows close to her sides, her hands folded
and held upright with the palms pressed together—and in
this attitude 'proceeded to recite the curse of King Lear on
his undutiful offspring in a manner which made hair rise
and flesh creep.' [11] On the other hand, it is said of Salvini
(who, by the way, speaks strongly of the necessity for 'innervation') that during a visit to America he was asked one
evening to give a short scene from the last act of *Othello,*
but refused, on the ground that 'it would be impossible for
him to present it acceptably without going through the entire play.' [12]

I need scarcely say that none of my informants confesses to 'putting on in the morning the character he is to
play at night.' That is simply a joke current among the supporters of a certain tragedian, who unhappily, played Richard too often for their comfort. There is a similar legend
about Mossop, who was said to 'order his dinner according
to the part he had to act: sausages and Zanga, rump-steaks
and Richard, pork-chops and Pierre, veal cutlets and Barba-
rossa.' [13] The same practice is attributed, on his own authority, to Mr. Walter Lacy, an actor of some eminence in
his day, who has now retired from the stage. 'Speaking of
some of his own performances,' says Mr. Bancroft,[14] 'he
thus related his different methods of dining: "When I
played Bluff Hal, sir (Henry of England), I drank brown
porter and dined off British beef; but if I had to act the
Honourable Tom Shuffleton, I contented myself with a delicate cutlet and a glass of port which resembled a crushed
garnet, and then sallied on to the stage with the manners

[11] Scott, i. p. 813.
[12] *The Voice,* x. No. 3.
[13] Doran, ii. p. 353.
[14] Bancroft, i, p. 421.

of a gentleman and the devil-me-care air of a man about town!" ' This method of tempering the gastric juices might be indefinitely refined upon. Mr. Irving ought to dine on devilled kidneys before playing Mephistopheles. When *Macbeth* is in the bill, haggis should reek on the tragedian's board, and hasty-pudding should put him i' the vein for Lear.

But if no one 'puts on in the morning the character he is to play at night,' almost everyone who is accustomed to highly emotional or even strongly marked characters admits the desirability of (so to speak) keeping the thread unbroken from first to last. 'My long experience of the stage,' says Macready,[15] 'has convinced me of the necessity of keeping, on the day of exhibition, the mind as intent as possible on the subject of the actor's portraiture, even to the very moment of his entrance on the scene.' And again:[16] 'Talma would dress some time before [the commencement of the performance] and make the peculiarities of his costume familiar to him; at the same time that he thereby possessed himself more with the feeling of his character. I thought the practice so good, that I frequently adopted it, and derived great benefit from it.' Burbage, according to Fleckno,[17] was 'a delightful Proteus, so wholly transforming himself into his parts, and putting off himself with his cloaths, as he never (not so much as in the tyring-house) assumed himself again until the play was done.' Anthony Aston tells us that *'Betterton,* from the Time he was dress'd to the End of the Play, kept his Mind in the same Temperament and Adaptness, as the present Character required.'[18] Salvini finds two or three hours of mental concentration an essential preliminary to entering with full conviction on such parts as Othello, Hamlet, or Saul; and the 'transmigration,' as he calls it, once effected, endures unbroken throughout the play. Junius Brutus Booth, who, in the maturity of his powers, was undoubtedly a magnificent actor, used to indulge in more than Salvini's two or three hours' mental concentration. 'Whatever part he had to personate,' writes Mr. Edwin Booth (and that excellent tragedian evidently

[15] *Reminiscences,* i. p. 115.
[16] P. 238.
[17] Malone, iii. p. 18.
[18] Aston, p. 5.

approves his father's practice), 'he was from the time of its rehearsal until he slept at night imbued with its very essence. If Othello was billed for the evening, . . . disregarding the fact that Shakespeare's Moor was a Christian, he would mumble sentences from the Koran. . . . If Shylock was to be his part at night, he was a Jew all day; and if in Baltimore at the time, he would pass hours with a learned Israelite, who lived near by, discussing Hebrew history!' [Matthews and Hutton, iii. p. 100.] The tendency to retain in the green-room the manner and voice of the character one is assuming appears to be common enough. 'I observed this tendency in Macready,' writes Mr. John Coleman, 'and Charles Kean had the same peculiarity in a less degree.' Mr. Kendal, too, used to notice this habit in Charles Kean and thought it an affectation. So it was, no doubt; but the affectation may have arisen, not from vanity, but from deliberate artistic purpose. Mr. Kendal himself admits that between the acts of such a play as *The Ironmaster,* in which he leaves the stage and returns to it in high emotion, he would not willingly lapse into levity, because it would cost him unnecessary trouble to regain the right pitch of feeling. Many actors assure me that it is common for tragedians to shut themselves up in their dressing-rooms between the acts of a play, and to reassume their personage immediately on being called, sometimes even timing their walk from the dressing-room doors to the wing, so as to be able to step upon the stage without a moment's pause. M. Albert Lambert writes: 'J'ai quelquefois conservé les allures et les grimaces typiques de quelques personnages, de ma loge au foyer, et du foyer à la scène. Par example pour Louis XI je conservais tant que je pouvais son sourire faux et sarcastique, son regard d'acier; pour Louis XIV son grand air impassible; pour Alceste son front rembruni et sa moue mécontente; pour Tartuffe sa marche glissante, son œil éteint, demi-voilé, son sourire onctueux et son geste officiant; pour Harpagon sa grimace inquiète et nerveuse. Mais seulement parce que ces masques sont historiques, universels, et qu'il faut les apporter justes devant les yeux du public.' [I have sometimes maintained the carriage and the mien that belong to particular characters all the way from my lodgings to the green-room and from the green-room to the stage. For example, I preserve as far as possible the mirthless, sarcastic smile of Louis XI and his steely expression; the kingly imperturbability of Louis XIV; the frowning brow and petulant mouth of Alcestis; the slinking gait, furtive beclouded eye, oily smile, and pious gesturings of Tartuffe; the restless, impulsive expression of Harpagon. But I do so only because these countenances are matters of tradition, common property, and must be presented to the public eye with accuracy.] Between Othello's exit and re-entrance in the third act Mr. John Coleman would always prowl up and down behind the scenes like a wild animal, the stage being kept clear in order that he might be safe from interruption. 'I always endeavour,' writes Mr. Wilson Barrett, 'to get a short time to myself, in my dressing-room, to think over my character and work myself into it, so to speak. It is a trouble and annoyance to me to converse on any subject while waiting to commence my work. I have noticed the same thing in other actors.' Miss Wallis tells me that between the acts of a heavy part she always retires to her dressing-room and maintains absolute silence, not speaking even to her maid if she can help it.

'Silence was the order my mother had given as the rule for my dressing-room,' writes Lady Martin[19]—'no talk to take my thoughts from the work I had in hand.' 'I was taken by my aunt early to the theatre,' Fanny Kemble writes,[20] 'and there in my dressing-room sat through the entire play, when I was not on the stage, with some piece of tapestry or needlework, with which, during the intervals of my tragic sorrows, I busied my fingers; my thoughts being occupied with the events of my next scene and the various effects it demanded.' Miss Wallis relates how she once visited Ristori in her dressing-room between the acts of *Maria Stuarda,* immediately after the scene between Mary and Elizabeth. The great actress received her, as it were, enthroned, and, though perfectly cordial, never once throughout the interview relaxed her queenly bearing. 'Affectation!' the reader may say; but again I add, affectation with an artistic purpose. 'Such an exaggeration,' Ristori writes to me, 'as identifying oneself all day with the character to be performed at night belongs to the conventions of the old

[19] *Shakespeare's Female Characters,* p. 125.
[20] *Record of a Girlhood,* ii. p. 69.

school. My father, an experienced actor, who trained me for the stage, used to impress upon me that I should be melancholy for a whole day before playing a pathetic part—but I never acted up to his precepts. The true artist, indeed, before attacking an important part, will avoid all frivolous distractions; but he need not meditate on mortality or weep like Heraclitus.' Let me mention in passing that Ristori, in her Memoirs, professes herself so thorough an emotionalist that she never could 'feel' the passage where Mary Stuart pleads guilty to the murder of Darnley, because her historical studies had convinced her that this was a mistake on Schiller's part and that Mary was innocent! [21]

These citations appear to me to prove conclusively that many distinguished actors have a difficulty in flinging themselves at one bound into the passion of a scene, and find it advantageous to keep themselves more or less completely in touch with their personage during the whole time of performance. On the other hand, there is no reason to doubt that some temperaments require less 'innervation,' to use Darwin's word, than others, or that, with a few, an infinitesimal space of time suffices. It is to be remembered, however, that if the keeping up of a character behind the scenes may be due to affectation, the total dropping of it may, in some cases, be no less affected. There is a motive (the avoidance of ridicule) for the latter affectation; none, except the artistic motive, for the former.

'Le véritable acteur,' says M. Coquelin, 'est toujours prêt. Il peut prendre son rôle à n'importe quel moment, et susciter immédiatement l'impression qu'il désire.' [The true actor is always prepared. He can pick up his rôle at any point whatever and promptly evoke just the impression he desires.] I think there is ample evidence that the veritable actor, in this sense, is a rare bird.

[21] *Etudes et Souvenirs*, p. 85.

Chapter X

THE BROWNIES OF THE BRAIN

THE REAL paradox of acting, it seems to me, resolves itself into the paradox of dual consciousness. If it were true that the actor could not experience an emotion without absolutely yielding up his whole soul to it, then Diderot's doctrine, though still a little overstated, would be right in the main. But the mind is not so constituted. If the night of the murder of Duncan had been a fit time for psychological argument, Macduff might safely have moved an amendment to Macbeth's proposition:

> Who can be wise, amazed, temperate and furious,
> Loyal and neutral in a moment? No man.

There are many 'brownies,' as Mr. Stevenson puts it, in the actor's brain, and one of them may be agonising with Othello, while another is criticising his every tone and gesture, a third restraining him from strangling Iago in good earnest, and a fourth wondering whether the play will be over in time to let him catch his last train. I was anxious to obtain authentic illustrations of this double, triple, and quadruple action of the mind, and to that end framed the following question:

Can you give any examples of the two or more strata of consciousness, or lines of thought, which must co-exist in your mind while acting? In other words, can you describe and illustrate how one part of your mind is given up to your character, while another part is criticising minutely your own gestures and intonations, and a third, perhaps, is watching the audience, or is busied with some pleasant or unpleasant recollection or anticipation in your private life?

It has been objected that the phrase 'must co-exist' begs the question; but is there really any question to beg? I looked upon the double action of the brain as a matter of universal experience, a thing to be assumed just as one assumes that the normal man has two legs. I did not regard it as a tendency peculiar to actors, but common to all men. It seemed to me, however, that acting must beget special forms of this multiple activity, and I hoped to obtain some clear and convincing illustrations of it.

Fanny Kemble's self-analysis[1] deserves to rank as the classic passage on this point: 'The curious part of acting, to me, is the sort of double process which the mind carries on at once, the combined operation of one's faculties, so to speak, in diametrically opposite directions; for intance, in that very last scene of Mrs. Beverley, while I was half dead with crying in the midst of the *real* grief, created by an entirely *unreal* cause, I perceived that my tears were falling like rain all over my silk dress, and spoiling it; and I calculated and measured most accurately the space that my father would require to fall in, and moved myself and my train accordingly in the midst of the anguish I was to feign, and absolutely did endure. It is this watchful faculty (perfectly prosaic and commonplace in its nature), which never deserts me while I am uttering all that exquisite passionate poetry in Juliet's balcony scene, while I feel as if my own soul was on my lips, and my colour comes and goes with the intensity of the sentiment I am expressing; which prevents me from falling over my train, from setting fire to myself with the lamps placed close to me, from leaning upon my canvas balcony when I seem to throw myself all but over it.' No less interesting is Miss Clara Morris's account of her triple consciousness: 'There are, when I am on the stage,' she writes,[2] 'three separate currents of thought in my mind; one in which I am keenly alive to Clara Morris, to all the details of the play, to the other actors and how they act, and to the audience; another about the play and the character I represent; and, finally, the thought that really gives me stimulus for acting. For instance, when I repeat such and such a line it fits like words to music to this underthought, which may be of some dead friend, of a story of Bret Harte's, of a poem, or may be even some pathetic scrap from a newspaper.' Miss Morris is here speaking of parts which from frequent repeti-

---

[1] *Record of a Girlhood*, ii. p. 103.
[2] Matthews and Hutton, v. p. 224.

tion have lost their first effect upon her. Her account of her method of working up emotion will be found on a later page.

Another excellent witness to the same effect is Paul Mounet, of the Odéon, who has described to M. Larcher[3] 'le dédoublement qui s'opère en lui quand il est en scène: il y a en lui *quelqu'un* qui le regarde et l'écoute: alors il joue véritablement de lui-même, comme un musicien joue de son instrument. Quelquefois l'artiste s'emporte: *l'autre* le voit, mais il se laisse griser délicieusement en sa compagnie. Ces jours-là, il dépasse la mesure et rentre mécontent dans la coulisse. Mais s'il est resté maître de lui, s'il s'est fait plaisir à lui-même, il est sûr de l'effet qu'il a produit: il a triomphé du public parce qu'il a triomphé de lui-même.' [. . . the dual process that is at work in him when he is on-stage. There is a someone inside him that is observing him, listening to him; at those times he can literally play out of his own substance, as a musician plays on his instrument. Sometimes the actor gets out of hand; that other perceives it, but lets himself slip into a pleasantly companionable intoxication. On such days the actor exceeds moderation and leaves the stage dissatisfied with himself. But if he has kept himself under control, if he has given himself pleasure, then he can be confident of the effect he has produced. He has triumphed with the public because he has triumphed over himself.]

M. Mounet's comrade M. Albert Lambert writes: 'J'ai connu un artiste ne jouant qu'avec la sensibilité et une émotion que ne dominait pas toujours l'Art, s'apercevoir au plus fort d'une scène, que sa femme causait avec le pompier de service, s'en plaindre tout bas à son partner et continuer sa scène dans le même mouvement et dans la même émotion. J'ai quelquefois écouté "chanter mes effets," mais ceci c'est la corde raide, un seul faux pas et l'on glisse.' [This I know: An actor, one who never failed to play his parts with a sensitiveness and a feeling not always found in the profession, observing at the emotional height of a scene that his wife was engaged in a cosy chat with the house fireman, murmured his resentment to his fellow player and kept right on acting without change of tempo or of emotional pitch. I sometimes hear talk about 'faking one's effects,' but to do

[3] *Revue d'Art Dramatique*, March 1, 1888.

that is to walk a tightrope: one little misstep, and down you go.]

There is an anecdote[4] of Talma, after a scene of violent emotion, meeting his dresser at the wing and proceeding to abuse him roundly for not having polished his boots; the implication being that he had noticed the man's remissness while at the height of his passion. An actor who once played Horatio to a very famous Hamlet tells me that in the last act he felt the shoulder of his cloak quite wet with the tragedian's tears at the line 'What! the fair Ophelia,' yet that Hamlet's first remark on leaving the scene was, 'That damned organ was playing too loud all the time!' Such instances could be cited by the score. Indeed I have already quoted several of them in speaking of self-control, which is nothing but a manifestation of this dual consciousness.

Many actors—a surprising number, indeed—seem to be quite unaware of any double action of the mind. Some resent the suggestion, as though it implied carelessness or unconscientiousness on their part. Others simply reply that the actor should be 'absorbed' in his character, and seem powerless to analyse the state they describe as absorption. Others, again, relate curious incidents of the freaks of consciousness or of memory which occur in the course of long runs. Mr. Dion Boucicault, for example, states that when he has been playing a part for many months his mind is always occupied with other matters during the performance; 'and this to such an extent that when, desiring for some special reason to act my best, I turn my thoughts upon my part, I forget the words, and, to recover them, feel obliged to think of something else.' Interesting as it is, this experience is not what I wanted to get at. Here the playing of the part has become quite automatic, leaving the mind free to occupy itself as best it may. The very complex movements of piano-playing have been known (says Dr. Carpenter) to become so purely automatic as to be performed in sleep; and many pianists who know a piece of music thoroughly by heart will go wrong when they attempt to play with the notes before them. There is sometimes a difficulty, of course, in distinguishing between automatic action and the conscious or subconscious mental activity to which my question refers.

[4] Lardin.

Here is a case in which this difficulty presents itself. 'Not long ago,' writes Miss Isabel Bateman, 'I had to give a recitation after the play, and, feeling rather anxious about it, I found myself repeating the poem (a long one) during the third act of the play. I went through the whole recitation while acting my part, not only repeating the words, but calling to mind the different effects I wished to produce. I confess this with a feeling of guilt, but I don't think anyone can have noticed a difference in my playing.' The question here is: Had Miss Bateman played her part so long as to have reached the automatic stage? If not, this is a most curious instance of dual action. Mr. Leonard Outram informs me that, in playing James Ralston in the third act of *Jim the Penman,* where Mrs. Ralston cross-questions her husband as to the cause of his nervous excitement, he finds himself reading, with full comprehension, odds and ends from a newspaper which he happens to have in his hand. Here again one would like to know how often Mr. Outram has played the part; but the passage is one of such complexity that it would certainly take a very long time to render the playing of it quite automatic.

'When working in earnest,' writes Mr. Forbes Robertson, 'I can only admit two strata, so to speak: one stratum, the part, the creature I am for the time; the other, that part of my mind which circumstances and the surroundings compel me to give up to all things coming under the head of mechanical execution. I have experienced the other strata after a long run, and always fight against them, for I know they only mean that my work is getting mechanical.' Even more to the point is the following reply from Miss Janet Achurch: 'The only double line of thought I like to have on the stage is a mental criticism on my own performance: "I got that exclamation better than last night," or "I'm sure I'm playing this scene slower than usual," and so on. I suppose no one can help doing this; but any thought that comes to my mind outside my part I always stamp out as quickly as possible.' This is precisely the form of experience I wished to get at. Salvini, on the other hand, declares that the careful self-criticism to which he subjects himself is strictly confined to moments of reflection after the performance is over. It may be questioned whether this does not imply an undercurrent of involuntary and unconscious self-criticism running parallel with the action. The most miraculous memory will scarcely reproduce a cry or an intonation so clearly as to allow of its effect being estimated to a nicety. An instinctive sense of approval or disapproval must surely accompany its actual utterances.

Some artists who profess themselves unconscious of any double action of the mind unintentionally bear witness to its existence. 'There is no better sponge for one's tears,' says an actor of great pathetic power, 'than the sight of an over-fed noodle asleep in the stalls'; and a very distinguished actress confesses to having 'played at' a peculiarly stolid and stony woman of fashion whom she observed among the audience, determined to move her or perish in the attempt. Here we have clearly an attitude of mind quite inconsistent with 'absorption' in the obvious sense of the word. Another leading actor mentions a curious circumstance which bears upon this point. If a momentary uneasiness causes him to make some slight gesture not essential to his part—for instance, if a twinge of neuralgia leads him to put his hand to his brow—he will often make the same gesture at the same point on the following night, without the recurrence of its cause: whereupon he immediately wonders why he did so, and recalls, by a distinct effort of thought, the sensation of the previous evening. In this case, what I have called the critical part of the actor's mind is evidently watching the executant part with great intentness. Another mode of consciousness which manifests itself in many actors may be called commercial rather than critical. 'I know people,' writes Mr. J. B. Howard, of Edinburgh, 'who, while on the stage, can count a well-filled house, and sum up the cash almost to a fraction.' This faculty seems to be not uncommon.

I am indebted to Miss Wallis for two most interesting illustrations of dual activity of mind. In a large provincial town, one day, she was advertised to appear as Juliet. A few hours before the time of the performance, her little daughter was taken suddenly and seriously ill. She sent to the theatre to say that she could not possibly appear; but, the doctor assuring her that the child was in no immediate danger, she eventually determined not to disappoint the public. Never, she says, did she enter more thoroughly into the part, and never did she play it with greater effect. She was strung up by excitement to a higher emotional pitch than she could ordinarily attain. And all the time the best part of her mind was with her child. Messengers were passing to and fro all the evening between her hotel and the theatre, and the bulletins, fortunately, were reassuring. She came out of the ordeal exhausted in body and mind, and would naturally be very loth to go through it again. Such an experience proves that two modes of intense activity may co-exist in the mind, each being, no doubt, resolvable into several subdivisions, if the memory could but reproduce them with sufficient distinctness. In the second case related by Miss Wallis a purely intellectual process of some complexity accompanied the performance of an exacting emotional scene. She was playing the title-part in Mr. Wills's *Ninon* at the Crystal Palace, where she had never appeared before. The moment she uttered her first speech she was conscious of a distracting echo in the theatre. She felt that if it were to continue she could scarcely get through her part, and she set to work to discover the right pitch of voice for this oddly-constructed building. She was somewhat consoled, before long, to find that the audience seemed unconscious of the reverberation, but she noticed that her fellow-actors were quite bewildered by it. Observing closely the effects produced by her comrades, and experimenting with her own voice, she at last hit on the right pitch, but not until the first act was nearly over. We have here a complex process of observation and reasoning running parallel with the playing of an arduous emotional scene. I should add that this was Miss Wallis's first appearance on the stage after a long period of rest, so that her performance of Ninon, so far from being automatic, must have involved a considerable effort of memory and attention. 'And a vivid emotional process,' Miss Wallis herself would add; but it is not essential to this part of my argument to determine whether the executant mode of mental activity, in any particular instance, is or is not informed by emotion.

This may be the fittest place to point out that the double or treble strata of consciousness afford a simple solution of one of the favourite anti-emotionalist difficulties. If the tragedian felt with Orestes or Œdipus, cries Diderot, 'his lot would be the most wretched on earth.' That he should feel with them as much as the spectator feels with them would clearly not involve a chronic state of 'wretchedness'; for the fact that we take positive pleasure in the most poignant imaginary woes, though a paradox, is also a commonplace. It is the foundation and justification of tragedy. But it is quite possible that the tragedian should habitually feel with his character far more vividly than the average spectator—that he should feel to the extent of actual unmetaphoric suffering—and yet should not be 'the most wretched' of men. Severe suffering on one mental plane is quite consistent with perfect contentment, nay, with absolute beatitude, on another. Happiness and misery reside in the deeps of consciousness; the upper strata are of small account. I have a three months' holiday; I put money in my purse and take passage for Naples in an Orient steamer. We encounter a capful of wind in the Bay of Biscay, and I am prostrated by seasickness for fifty or sixty hours. I probably suffer more agony than consumption or cancer could inflict in a similar space of time; yet I am not really miserable; my fundamental consciousness is one of delighted anticipation; for

> I shall see, before I die,
> The palms and temples of the South.

Conversely, the maxim 'Let us eat and drink, for to-morrow we die' is the veriest mockery unless we put a liberal interpretation on 'to-morrow.' Treat it prosaically—place our death-warrant in our napkin—and a banquet fit for Lucullus will have small savour in our nostrils. So may it be with the actor. The surface of his consciousness may be tormented and tempest-tossed while the depths are unruffled. It may even be that the more really and acutely he suffers—the more thoroughly he merges himself in his part—the greater may be his fundamental happiness; for he knows that he is triumphing, and his spirit is glad. I am far from arguing that mimetic woes ever attain, or ought to attain, the full poignancy of the real miseries they represent. All I wish to point out is that actors may quite well undergo states of feeling

which may fairly be described as suffering—genuine and
acute suffering—without being on that account the most
miserable of men.

Another section of my interrogatory was designed to
throw further light on this question of double consciousness,
especially with reference to Diderot's assumption that to
'feel' a part implies absolute and, so to speak, helpless absorption in it.

Diderot tells how Lekain, in a scene of violent emotion, saw
an actress's diamond earring lying on the stage, and had presence
of mind enough to kick it to the wing instead of treading on it.
Can you relate any similar instances of presence of mind? And
should you regard them as showing that the actor is personally
unmoved by the situation in which he is figuring?

The anecdote of Lekain is regarded by the anti-emotionalists as a tower of strength; but its foundations are sadly
insecure. Not that there is any reason to doubt the fact. On
the contrary, similar incidents have come within the experience of every artist. It is the interpretation that is more than
doubtful. Intense emotion, as I have already suggested, will
often act upon the mind, not as chloroform but rather as
curari. It places all the faculties on the alert, and stimulates
every function of mind and body. The apathy of mere dejection may beget that relaxation of the nerves which places
us at the mercy of trifling accidents; the excitement of violent feeling has rather the opposite effect. So far as the incident of the diamond is concerned, Lekain might even have
been labouring under the whole emotion of the real Ninias;
much more may he have been experiencing the similar
though less poignant emotional state—the agony *con sordino*
—begotten by the imagination.

A few of the artists whom I have consulted—I may mention Mr. and Mrs. Bancroft, Mr. and Mrs. Kendal, and Mr.
Clayton—hold that in certain crises of extreme emotional
exaltation, an actor would be incapable of such presence of
mind as that of Lekain. This, however, is a theoretical
opinion rather than a statement founded on positive experience. I am informed of a score of instances in which
jewels—even stage-jewels—have been adroitly rescued, but
no one has related a single case in which the merest trinket

has been sacrificed to the passion of the scene. My informants, moreover, are almost unanimous in holding that presence of mind in face of trifling misadventures by no means proves that the actor is personally unmoved. 'In a like case,' Mr. Forbes Robertson very aptly remarks, 'the second stratum of my mind would act for me without interfering with the first.' Mr. Beerbohm Tree takes precisely the view of the diamond anecdote which I have suggested above. He holds that Lekain's action may be just as rationally explained on the hypothesis of extreme emotional tension as on that of perfect placidity. Mr. Tree tells of an analogous case within his own experience, in which a young actress, of highly emotional temperament, exhibited even greater presence of mind. She was grovelling at the feet of a stony-hearted inquisitor, praying desperately for the life of someone dear to her, when a diamond fell from her hair. She noted where it lay, put her left hand to her brow for a moment, and then let it fall, as though in the lassitude of despair, precisely upon the stray jewel. The gesture was so appropriate that the audience suspected nothing, and the effect of the passage was, if anything, heightened. Yet there is not the smallest reason to suppose that this lady—a convinced emotionalist—was, on this occasion only, simulating in cold blood the violent emotion of the scene.

Salvini tells me that on one occasion, while playing Orosmane in *Zaïre,* he suddenly felt, in the middle of the fourth act, that the belt which sustained his Turkish trousers had given way. Horror of horrors! What was to be done? As if in an access of passion, he dashed at a tiger-skin which covered the divan and swathed it round his body. The public 'non fece motto,' and in this improvised kilt he finished the act. 'I was told,' he says, 'that I had never played the scene with greater intensity of rage, irony and despair.' 'I never lose my presence of mind,' writes Miss Bateman (Mrs. Crowe). 'I was once acting with a gentleman who played my lover, and in his death agonies his wig came off. Luckily I wore a long mantle, and was able to hide the mishap by throwing a corner of it over the gentleman's head. Dozens of such accidents have happened to me, and I don't remember once failing to meet the emergency.' An extreme case of adroitness under difficulties is related by an actor of great experience. He was playing the very stormy love-scene in *Peril,* which ends in the lover chasing the unwilling fair one round and round the room. The lady wore a girdle of large and costly artificial pearls, and, just as this culminating point was reached, the string broke, scattering the pearls all over the stage. 'We finished the scene,' writes my informant, 'without any hesitation or any change of business, and neither of us crushed a single pearl. This shows that we had not lost our senses—that's all.' I should add that the hero of this dramatic egg-dance is, on the whole, an anti-emotionalist; but the incident is none the less a striking example of dual activity of mind.

Historical instances of presence of mind are simply innumerable. Baron, in *Le Comte d'Essex,* noticing in the course of his scene with Cecil that his garter had come unfastened, heightened the effect of contempt at which he was aiming by coolly stooping to tie it without pausing in his speech.[5] Brizard, a great tragedian of last century, was playing an heroic part when the plumes of his casque caught fire. He remained unconscious of the accident until the audience called his attention to it, when, without interrupting his declamation, he calmly took off the burning headpiece and handed it to his confidant.[6] What the confidant did, history saith not. Such anecdotes as these meet us at every turn, but as they seem to me to afford no evidence, one way or another, as to the actor's emotional state, I do not think them worth collecting. More to the point, perhaps, are the common anecdotes of actors interpolating personal asides to their fellow-performers in scenes of high emotion. Diderot gives an elaborate instance of this in the shape of a conjugal quarrel between an actor and actress,[7] carried on under cover of a scene between Eraste and Lucile in *Le Dépit Amoureux.* How Diderot should be in a position to report their asides he does not explain, and in the absence of such explanation we cannot help suspecting the episode to be imaginary. But supposing it genuine, and supposing (a difficult admission) that Molière's dialogue was as effectively delivered as Diderot represents it to have been, we must still

[5] Lemazurier, i. p. 95.
[6] Lemazurier, i. p. 173.
[7] Pollock, pp. 28-31.

remember that the scene is not one which could in any case make great claims upon the emotions of the performers. More credible and more to the purpose is an anecdote of Garrick, which I find in the *Monthly Mirror* for 1807.[8] 'A medical gentleman of eminence,' it appears, once remarked to 'Tom King the comedian,' that Garrick must have suffered greatly from 'the exertion of his feelings.' 'Pooh!' replied the original Sir Peter Teazle, 'he suffer from his feelings! Why, Sir, I was playing with him one night in *Lear*, when, in the middle of a most passionate and afflicting part, and when the whole house was drowned in tears, he turned his head round to me, and putting his tongue in his cheek, whispered *Damme, Tom, it'll do!* So much for stage feeling.' A precisely similar story is told[9] of Edmund Kean when playing Brutus to the Titus of his son Charles in Howard Payne's tragedy of *Brutus*. 'The strong interest of the play,' says Charles Kean's biographer, 'combined with the natural acting of father and son, completely subdued the audience. They sat suffused in tears during the last pathetic interview, until Brutus, overpowered by his emotions, falls on the neck of Titus, exclaiming in a burst of agony, "Embrace thy wretched father"; when they broke forth into the relief of loud and prolonged peals of approbation. Edmund Kean then whispered in his son's ear, "Charley, we are doing the trick."' These anecdotes are so exactly alike as to arouse a suspicion that the second may be nothing but the first revamped, according to a principle familiar to students of (theatrical) comparative mythology. The incidents themselves, however, are so probable that both may quite well be genuine. But do they prove that Garrick and Kean were unmoved? Surely not. The executant section or stratum of their minds may have been wrung with emotion, while the observant section, conscious of the success thus attained, found a safety-valve for its excitement in a hurried whisper of self-congratulation. 'My cousin, John Mason,' writes Fanny Kemble,[10] 'the first time he acted Romeo with me, though a very powerful muscular young man, whispered to me as he carried my corpse down the stage with a fine semblance of frenzy,

8 New Series, i. p. 78.
9 Cole, i. p. 163.
10 *Record of a Girlhood*, ii. p. 28.

"Jove, Fanny, you are a lift!" ' There is a clear distinction between this playful whisper and the exultant asides of Garrick and Kean. Mr. Mason, in all probability, was really unmoved, and therefore, according to Diderot, possessed the first qualification for a 'sublime' actor. How many of my readers, I wonder, have so much as heard his name?

The anti-emotionalists, as I have remarked before, should let presence of mind alone, and rather adduce instances of the evil effects of that absence of mind which they hold to be one of the manifestations of 'sensibility.' Unfortunately for their argument, the total absorption in one mode of feeling which numbs the intellect and deadens the sense is of very rare occurrence in real life, and still rarer, of course, on the stage. If this were not so, we should hear every day of some mediocre Othello strangling his Iago, or some second-rate Juliet stabbing herself in sad earnest. The classical case in point is the manslaughter (or slave-slaughter) committed by the Roman actor Æsopus, as set forth by Plutarch in his *Life of Cicero:*[11] 'Yet it is reported notwithstanding, that for his [Cicero's] gesture and pronunciation, having the selfe-same defects of nature at the beginning, which *Demosthenes* had, to reforme them, he carefully studied to counterfeit *Roscius,* an excellent Comedian, and *Æsope* also a player of Tragedies. Of this *Æsope* men write, that he playing one day *Atreus* part upon a stage (who determined with himselfe how he might be revenged on his brother *Thyestes*) a servant by chance having occasion to runne suddenly by him, he forgetting himselfe, striving to shew the vehement passion and furie of this king, gave him such a blow on his head with the scepter in his hand, that he slue him dead in the place.' François Riccoboni's comment on this incident[12] is conceived in such a nobly antique spirit that I cannot forbear quoting it: 'Pourquoi ne tua-t-il jamais,' he asks, 'aucun des Comédiens qui jouoient avec lui? C'est que la vie d'un Esclave n'étoit rien, mais qu'il étoit obligé de respecter celle d'un Citoyen. Sa fureur n'étoit donc pas si vraye, puisqu'elle laissoit à sa raison toute la liberté du choix. Mais en Comédien habile il saisit l'occasion que le hasard lui présentoit.' [Why did he never kill one of his fellow actors? Because a slave's life did not count, whereas the life of a citizen had to be respected. His rage, therefore, was not so very genuine, inasmuch as it left his judgment its full freedom of selection. As an astute comedian, he seized the opportunity that chance held out to him.] There is no paltry humanitarianism about Riccoboni. Like many another actor, he doubtless deplored the pettifogging laws which forbid the occasional slaying of a 'super' when the situation demands, or the 'super' deserves, his quietus. The affair (to speak seriously) was doubtless a pure accident, like many other 'true tragedies' in the annals of the stage; or else it was a case of temporary insanity. Diderot, as in duty bound, declares Æsopus to have been but a middling actor.[13] Two generations of Romans thought otherwise; but their judgment was no doubt biassed by the fact that they had seen him.

Instances of helpless, somnambulistic absorption, such as would lead an actor to trample a valuable jewel under foot, are scarcely to be found. Two famous tragedians of the early French stage, Mondory and Montfleury, are both said to have died of their reckless self-abandonment to violent passion—the former out-Heroding Herod in La Mariamne by Tristan l'Hermite, the latter playing Oreste in the original production of Racine's Andromaque.[14] Both anecdotes, however, seem to be entirely apocryphal. Less doubtful is a fine instance of non-absorption afforded by the stately and stilted Beaubourg. In the character of Horace, he was pursuing Mlle. Duclos, as Camille, with sword upraised to kill her. In her haste to escape she tripped and fell; whereupon Beaubourg politely took off his helmet with one hand, helped her with the other to rise, and handed her gallantly off the stage, as a preliminary to assassinating her behind the scenes. Holman, according to Reynolds,[15] once gave himself up so rashly to the torrent, tempest, and whirlwind of his passion, that he missed his footing and fell headlong over the footlights into the midst of the astonished fiddlers. This catastrophe, however, was due to the unusual slope of a very small country stage. Mrs. Siddons, speaking to Reynolds, said, 'My brother John, in his most impetuous

[13] Pollock, pp. 70-71.
[14] Lemazurier, i. pp. 422, 426, 126.
[15] Reynolds, ii. p. 76.

bursts, is always careful to avoid any discomposure of his dress or deportment; but in the whirlwind of passion, I lose all thought of such matters';[16] and Boaden says quaintly, 'When Mrs. Siddons quitted her dressing-room, I believe she left there the last thought about herself. Never did I see her eye wander from the business of the scene—no recognisance of the most noble of her friends exchanged the character for the individual." [17] Rachel, like John Kemble, remained perfectly conscious of every fold in her robe; yet Fanny Kemble assures us that 'her wonderful fainting exclamation of "O, mon cher Curiace!" lost none of its poignant pathos' on that account. 'Criticising a portrait of herself in that scene, she said to the painter, "Ma robe ne fait pas ce pli-là; elle fait, au contraire, celui-ci." ['My robe doesn't fall into that fold: it falls into this one.'] The artist, inclined to defend his picture, asked her how, while she was lying with her eyes shut and feigning utter insensibility, she could possibly tell anything about the plaits of her dress. "Allez-y voir ['Come and see for yourself.']," replied Rachel; and the next time she played Camille, the artist was able to convince himself by more careful observation that she was right.' [18]

On the other hand, I shall quote in the next chapter an extraordinary instance of absorption in a part which Fanny Kemble relates from her own experience. 'Miss O'Neill,' said Macready to Lady Pollock, 'was a remarkable instance of self-abandonment in acting. She forgot everything for the time but her assumed character. She was an entirely modest woman; yet in acting with her I have been nearly smothered with her kisses.' [19] From the time of Æsopus downwards, however, I can find only one authentic instance of absorption carried to a dangerous pitch. It is recorded in Lady Martin's delightful series of autobiographical criticisms. Describing her first performance of Juliet, she writes:[20] 'When the time came to drink the potion, there was none; for the phial had been crushed in my hand, the fragments of glass were eating their way into the tender palm, and the blood

16 *Macready*, i. p. 149.
17 Boaden, ii. p. 289.
18 *Record of a Girlhood*, ii. p. 12.
19 *Macready as I knew him*, p. 29.
20 *Shakespeare's Female Characters*, p. 115.

was trickling down in a little stream over my pretty dress. This had been for some time apparent to the audience, but the Juliet knew nothing of it, and felt nothing, until the red stream arrested her attention. . . . This never occurred again, because they ever afterwards gave me a wooden phial.' On this occasion Miss Faucit would no doubt have trampled on the Koh-i-noor had it lain in her path; but then she was a child of thirteen, and it was her first appearance on any stage.

Before leaving this branch of my subject, let me illustrate by three anecdotes three different degrees of dramatic absorption. The first (related by Mr. John Coleman, who was present on the occasion) goes to show that some artists are apt on occasion to yield themselves up with painful completeness to the illusion of the scene. Mr. and Mrs. Charles Kean were one night playing *The Gamester* at Belfast. It was their benefit; the house was crowded, and the play went electrically. It closes with a piece of 'business' said to have been invented by Mrs. Siddons. After the death of Beverley, Jarvis and Charlotte attempt to lead Mrs. Beverley away; but she turns at the door, and, as the curtain falls, flings herself in an agony of grief upon the body of her husband. On this particular evening Mrs. Kean had become so absorbed in her part that she could not shake off the illusion even when the play was over, and astonished the bystanders by vehemently shaking her husband as he lay on his pallet-bed, and crying piteously, 'Oh, my Charley!—my poor darling—you are not dead; say you are not dead!' 'Deuce a bit, my darling!' responded Kean. 'But tell me so—tell me so, Charley!' 'I *am* telling you so, Nelly; but there, there—come and get dressed for Violante.' 'Good gracious!' exclaimed Mrs. Kean, immediately recovering herself, 'it's wonderful I should have forgot about *The Wonder;* Servant, ladies and gentlemen!' And so, with a stately curtsey, she made her way to her dressing-room.

My second illustration is more ambiguous. In the fifth act of *Othello,* while Emilia is knocking at the door, and the Moor, in anguish of soul, is half rueing the deed he has but half done, a celebrated tragedian is in the habit of seizing a moment, when he is concealed from the audience by the curtain of Desdemona's bed, to drink a glass of water held

in readiness for him by his servant! In some actors such a
device might fairly be taken as a sign of callousness. The
particular artist in question, however, is an uncompromising
emotionalist in theory, and, as I have ample grounds for believing, in practice as well. The just conclusion to be drawn,
it seems to me, is that the accomplished artist, even in the
very tempest and whirlwind of passion, retains sufficient self-
mastery to neglect no means of economising or reinforcing
his physical resources.

The third anecdote takes us to the opposite end of the scale,
illustrating that sublime perfection of self-command which
belongs to the actor of Diderot's ideal. Some years ago an old
playgoer went to see a popular drama in which a very popular actor played an heroic part. He noticed that the popular
actor not only shouted very loud, but kept on changing his
key in an eccentric fashion. Shortly afterwards he met one
of the supernumeraries, whom he happened to know, and
they fell to discussing the play. 'What did you think of Mr.
So-and-So?' asked the super. 'Magnificent!' replied the old
playgoer, diplomatically: 'but why does he shout in such
different keys?' 'Oh, don't you know the reason of that,
sir?' answered the super. 'That's to keep the men up to
their work. When he changes his key it's to show that the
limelight isn't on him!' If the *Paradoxe* were anything more
than a paradox, this actor should be among the greatest
of his age.

Chapter XI

'DAMNABLE ITERATION'

A NECESSARY corollary to the anti-emotionalist theory—and
Diderot was not the man to shrink from it—is that long
runs, far from being the bane of art, must be its salvation.
He speaks with admiration[1] of a Neapolitan company which
was drilled until the actors were 'épuisés de la fatigue de ces
répétitions multipliées, ce que nous appelons blasés [worn
out with constant rehearsals, or what we call 'used up'],'

[1] Pollock, p. 57.

and then performed for six months on end, 'while the Sovereign and his subjects enjoyed the highest pleasure that can be obtained from stage-illusion.' Since Diderot had thus committed himself, I was forced to put the following question, though the subject has been so often thrashed out of late that I could not hope to elicit any very novel or interesting evidence:

With reference to long runs: does frequent repetition induce callousness to the emotions of a part? Do you continue to improve during a certain number of representations and then remain stationary, or deteriorate? Or do you go on elaborating a part throughout a long run? Or do you improve in some respects and deteriorate in others?

The general tenor of the answers was a foregone conclusion. My informants are almost unanimous in holding the long run system noxious. Some suffer more than others from the frequent repetition of a part; some are more alive than others to the element of novelty afforded by the changing audiences; some have a greater tendency than others to keep on working at and developing a part, studying new refinements and attempting improved effects; but all agree that there is a limit even to these alleviations of the evil, and that ultimately they either deteriorate or have to make a painful effort to keep up to the mark. No one who has ever seen a play after its fiftieth consecutive night will have any doubt on this point. Some artists, indeed, assert that the emotional passages of a part never grow stale to them, though they admit that in lighter scenes their playing suffers. 'If I really feel a part,' writes Miss Bateman, 'I never get tired of it.' Miss Geneviève Ward believes in the possibility of improvement throughout a long run, but admits that after playing Forget-me-not more than 500 times, she 'passed through a period of apathy, lasting several months.' One or two other artists add qualifying circumstances to their condemnation of long runs, but no one seriously defends them.

The truth is that Diderot had no means of studying long runs and their effect. He cites from hearsay the Neapolitan practice, but he probably never saw a piece which had been played, by the same players, more than a score or so of times, and these not consecutive, but spread over months or years.

Had he seen *La Tosca* on its 99th night or *Our Boys* on its
999th night, he would probably have suppressed the passage
as to 'the highest pleasure that can be obtained from stage-
illusion.' The true anti-emotionalist position as to long runs
should be, not that they are positively beneficial, but that an
actor who is an automaton from the first suffers less than
one who begins by playing from the heart and gradually
hardens into automatism. At the same time (as we have already seen in the case of laughter), it is easy to overrate the
tendency of mere repetition to deaden the sensibilities. An
inordinate number of *consecutive* repetitions is necessarily
mischievous. 'In order to obtain the right mood,' says Miss
Clara Morris, 'after the part has become so familiar that the
woes of the personage cease to affect me, I am obliged to re-
sort to outside influence; that is, I indulge in the luxury of
grief by thinking over somebody else's woes, and when
everything else fails, I think that I am dead and then I cry
for myself!' [2] No one can go through the same series of
emotions six times in a week (or seven or eight times in the
case of matinées) for a series of months or years without becoming jaded. But with proper intervals of rest and change,
a great artist (of this there is plentiful proof) can enter into
the emotions of Othello and Juliet even unto seventy times
seven. 'After feeling a part intensely on one night,' says Miss
Wallis, 'the reaction makes it impossible to enter into it
thoroughly on the following evening. Therefore an alterna-
tion of parts, and especially of such parts as Juliet and Rosalind—tragedy and comedy—is a blessed, and even essential,
relief.' The system of every well-regulated theatre, in every
country save England and America, provides for the necessary rest and change, and it is only of late years in our own
country that the '500th consecutive performance' has become
the one goal of managerial ambition. 'Repetition, certainly,
had no effect,' writes Lady Martin,[3] 'in making the [po-
tion-] scene less vivid to my imagination. The last time I
played Juliet, which was in Manchester in 1871, I fainted on
the bed at the end of it, so much was I overcome with the
reality of the "thick-coming fancies." ' But then Lady Martin
had never played Juliet five hundred, or even fifty, times in

[2] Matthews and Hutton, v. p. 224.
[3] *Shakespeare's Female Characters*, p. 181.

succession. Nor has Salvini worn his Othello threadbare in this reckless fashion.

Chapter XII

THE SPUR OF THE MOMENT

IT IS generally assumed that the actor who, by nature or training, is superior to the foibles of sensibility, will have every smallest detail of his playing regulated in advance, even to the motion of a finger or the raising of an eyebrow. On the other hand, a tendency to rely on momentary impulse is one of the protean forms of sensibility discussed in the *Paradoxe*. Therefore I formulated the following questions:

Do you ever yield to sudden inspirations of accent or gesture occurring in the moment of performance? And are you able to note, and subsequently reproduce, such inspirations? Have you ever produced a happy effect by pure chance or by mistake, and then incorporated it permanently in your performance?

In my chapter on the *Paradoxe* I have discussed the limitations placed upon momentary impulse by the fact that the actor is part of a complex mechanism which would be brought to a standstill by any great irregularity in the action of one of its wheels. These limits are wide enough, however, to admit of very important variations, and it is interesting to study the practice of different artists in admitting or excluding the suggestions of the moment.

In an 'Introductory Discourse' to the second English edition of Luigi Riccoboni's *General History of the Stage*[1] we find some curious details as to the methods of the great actors of last century. The writer is anonymous, but the date, the style, and the fact of his anonymity suggest that he may have been none other than the author of *The Actor*. He emphatically recommends the English actors of his time to imitate the variety of the Italians. 'With us,' he says, 'the same Scene is always played in the same Manner, not only by the same Actor, but by every Actor who performs it: We know,

[1] London, 1754, pp. xiv-xx.

therefore, before it comes, all that we are to admire. Perhaps there never was a greater or a juster Piece of Action upon the Theatre of any Country, than that consummate Player Mr. *Barry* threw into his character of the Earl of *Essex*, when his Wife fell into a Swoon, and he was going to Execution; but 'twas every Night the same. In this Manner also that beautiful, though perhaps not proper, Attitude of *Romeo* at the Tomb, is always the same, not only in Mr. *Barry* and in Mr. *Garrick*, every Time each plays, but 'tis the same in both. [This probably refers to Romeo's then traditional gesture of threatening Paris with the crowbar.] On the contrary, let an *Italian* please ever so greatly once in his Scene, he never courts a second Applause by the same Attitude . . . these People having that true Enthusiasm to conceive themselves really the Persons they represent. . . . In the Tragedy of *Boadicea*, which but for this cloying Repetition would certainly have pleased more than nine Nights, we had an Instance of the Fault in the greatest player in the World. . . . Mr. *Garrick*, in the character of *Dumnorix* in this Play, drew his Sword on the first Night in the midst of a Prayer; and full of the Uprightness of his Cause, brandished it in the Face of Heaven: It was disputed whether this were proper; but there could be no Dispute whether a Repetition of it could be proper; that was impossible. The Suddenness of a virtuous Emotion might excuse him once in doing it; but nothing could justify the cold Repetition.' Mrs. Cibber and Mrs. Pritchard this critic praises for their variety—also, 'that new Actress named before, who, tho' always the same haughty, jealous, fond *Hermione*, never was twice indebted to the same Set of Attitudes and Gestures to express that Excellence.' This 'new actress' I take to have been a Mrs. Gregory.

Davies, on the other hand, asserts[2] that Garrick, 'of all players he ever knew, gave the greatest variety to action and deportment'; citing as an unaccountable exception to this rule the constant uniformity of his action at the close of the Play Scene in *Hamlet*. At the lines

> For some must watch, while some must sleep:
> Thus runs the world away,

'it was his constant practice to pull out a white handkerchief, and, walking about the stage, to twirl it round with vehemence.' It is said (though I can cite no good authority) that he always gave the handkerchief three twirls, and that it was once noted as an innovation that he twirled it a fourth time. His personal theory, given under his own hand and seal, not only left room for, but insisted on, the inspiration of the moment. 'What shall I say to you, my dear friend, about the "Clairon"?' he writes to Sturz in 1769.[3] 'Your dissection of her is as accurate as if you had opened her alive; she has everything that art and a good understanding, with great natural spirit, can give her. But then I fear (and I only tell you my fears, and open my soul to you) the heart has none of those instantaneous feelings, that life-blood, that keen sensibility, that bursts at once from genius, and, like electrical fire, shoots through the veins, marrow, bones and all, of every spectator. Madame Clairon is so conscious and certain of what she can do, that she never, I believe, had the feelings of the instant come upon her unexpectedly; but I pronounce that the greatest strokes of genius have been unknown to the actor himself, till circumstances, and the warmth of the scene, has sprung the mine as it were, as much to his own surprise, as that of the audience. Thus I make a great difference between a great genius and a good actor. The first will always realise the feelings of his character, and be transported beyond himself; while the other, with great powers, and good sense, will give great pleasure to an audience, but never

> Pectus inaniter angit,
> Irritat, mulcet, falsis terroribus implet
> Ut magus.[4]

[. . . who with airy nothings wrings my heart, inflames, soothes, fills it with vain alarms like a magician . . .

(Translation by H. Rushton Fairclough, in Loeb Classical Library)]

I have with great freedom communicated my ideas of acting, but you must not betray me, my good friend; the Clairon would never forgive me, though I called her an

---

[3] *Garrick's Correspondence*, i. p. 359.
[4] Horace, Epist. ii. 1, 211.

excellent actress, if I did not swear by all the Gods she was the greatest genius too.'

That this passage expresses Garrick's deliberate and enduring opinion, I am led to believe by a piece of evidence whose value the reader must estimate for himself. In the British Museum Library there is a copy of d'Hannetaire's *Observations sur l'Art du Comédien*[5] bearing the book-plate of 'T. Jolley, Esq., F.S.A.' On its title-page is written, doubtless in Mr. Jolley's hand, the words *'Garrick's copy';* and I find that Mr. Jolley bought it for two shillings at the sale of Garrick's library in 1823. In discussing the question of inspiration, d'Hannetaire observes:[6] 'Un bon maître, loin de jamais diversifier la manière de rendre les différens morceaux d'une Tragédie ou d'une Comédie, les débitera toujours invariablement de même, au bout de dix ans, comme au bout de deux heures.' [A finished actor, so far from ever modifying his interpretation of the various scenes of a tragedy or of a comedy, will reproduce them without fail always in the same way, whether after two hours or ten years.] Opposite this passage, in the margin, the word *'wrong'* is faintly pencilled; and four pages further on, where d'Hannetaire remarks,[7] 'qu'il n'est qu'une manière de bien dire, de bien réciter [that there is only one right way of speaking or reciting],' the same annotator interjects *'wrong again.'* There is only one other marginal note in the book: where[8] the author describes a dogmatic theorist on acting, the same hand has pencilled '[M]acklin's [Ch]aracter,' the bracketed letters having been cut away in binding. Now, I have very little doubt that these are Garrick's annotations. Making allowance for the difference between a fine pen and a blunt pencil, I think the handwriting greatly resembles his. The antecedent probabilities, too, seem to me very strong. No one but an actor would be likely to contradict d'Hannetaire on such a seemingly trifling point of theory; and we know from the letter to Sturz quoted above, that in 1769 Garrick held the opinion which (if I am right in my assumption) we now find him reiterating some time between 1776 and his death in 1779. The pencilled notes are certainly not in

[5] Paris, 1776.
[6] P. 45.
[7] P. 49.
[8] P. 70.

the same writing as 'Garrick's Copy' on the fly-leaf; and there is every reason to suppose, I think, that the book passed from Mr. Jolley's library to the Museum, without coming into other hands. The fact that part of one of the notes was cut off in binding before Mr. Jolley's book-plate was affixed to the cover, excludes the supposition that any reader at the Museum (in defiance of the regulations) can have recorded his private sentiments on the national property. The matter is of no great importance, for an opinion so deliberately expressed as that in the letter to Sturz can scarcely have been the whim of a moment. Yet, if I am right in my conjecture, Garrick's emphatic contradiction of two remarks and two only in d'Hannetaire's 487 pages of theory, proves that the artistic value of spontaneity was habitually and vividly present to his mind.

The criticism of Clairon in the letter to Sturz raises the question: Which of the rival queens of the French stage did Garrick most admire? the frigid, measured, automatic Clairon, or the fiery, spontaneous, dæmonic Dumesnil? These two actresses are held up by Diderot as types of what a great artist ought and ought not to be. 'Quel jeu plus parfait que celui de la Clairon?' he asks.[9] '. . . Elle sait par cœur, tous les détails de son jeu comme tous les mots de son rôle. . . . Il n'en est pas de la Dumesnil ainsi que de la Clairon. Elle monte sur les planches sans savoir ce qu'elle dira; mais il vient un moment sublime.' [What acting was ever more perfect than Clairon's? . . . she has every detail of her acting by heart, just as much as every word of her part. . . . Now with Dumesnil it is a different matter; she is not like Clairon. She comes on the stage without knowing what she is going to say; half the time she does not know what she is saying: but she has one sublime moment.] Upon this passage Talma remarks,[10] 'J'avoue que je préfère le jeu sublime au jeu parfait.' [I confess that I prefer sublime acting to perfect acting.] It was Dumesnil who, at the height of her frenzy in the part of Cléopatre, made the whole parterre (a standing pit no doubt) recoil several paces 'par un mouvement d'horreur, aussi vif que spontané' [by a start of horror, as thrilling as it was spontaneous]. It was she, too,

who first dared to run on the French tragic scene.[11] Playing
the part of a mother whose son is threatened with death, she
actually ran across the stage to ward off the fatal blow. Until then, says Lemazurier,[12] 'on marchait plus ou moins vite
sur le théâtre; mais personne ne croyait possible d'y courir
[they walked faster or slower on-stage, but no one found
it thinkable to run].' The effect was probably unrehearsed,
and it took the audience by storm. Now, which of these
great actresses did Garrick prefer? 'Dumesnil,' says Boaden
in his life of Mrs. Siddons,[13] 'was the *explosive* heroine, the
Clairon the profound calculator of all her effects'; and he
adds that Garrick gave the palm to Clairon. Lemazurier,
on the other hand, declares positively[14] that Dumesnil was
his favourite and that he said of Clairon, 'Elle est trop actrice.' ['She is too much the actress.'] Lemazurier does not
state his authority, but the remark accords so exactly with
the whole tone of the letter to Sturz that we can have little hesitation in accepting it as genuine. Fanny Kemble,
too, states that Garrick described Clairon as the greatest
actress of her age, but said of Dumesnil that in her he forgot the actress and saw only Phèdre, Rodogune and Hermione.[15] She does not give her authority for this statement,
which may very likely have been a tradition in her family.
Voltaire, according to Lemazurier,[16] was also at heart of
the Dumesnil faction: 'Il ne balança jamais à lui accorder
la préférence qu'elle méritait, et s'il donna plus de louanges
à Mlle. Clairon, c'est qu'il ne pouvait se passer d'elle dans
ses ouvrages, et qu'il redoutait son caractère, tandis qu'il
était bien sûr de n'avoir rien à craindre de Mlle. Dumesnil.'
[He never came around to granting her the priority that
she deserved; but if he praised Mlle. Clairon the more highly,
it was because he could not dispense with her in his plays:
he was intimidated by her personality, whereas he was
entirely certain that from Mlle. Dumesnil he had nothing
to fear.] It appears, then, that some respectable judges pre-

[11] Lemazurier, ii. p. 195.
[12] Vol. ii. p. 200.
[13] Vol. i. p. 219.
[14] Vol. ii. p. 106.
[15] *Record of a Girlhood,* iii. p. 91.
[16] Vol. ii. p. 200.

ferred the spontaneous sublimity of Dumesnil to the calculated correctness of Diderot's ideal Clairon.

How are we to reconcile the sameness Garrick is said to
have exhibited in certain cases with the spontaneity he certainly approved? Why, very easily—he accepted the inspirations of the moment, he did not rely upon them. It may
fairly be doubted whether Dumesnil herself ever went on
the stage without knowing clearly what she intended to
do, though she may have been less scrupulous than Clairon
in carrying out her exact intentions. Joseph Jefferson, the
incomparable Rip van Winkle, once remarked to Miss Mary
Anderson that inspiration produces the greatest effects on
the stage, but that one cannot afford to wait for it, and must
therefore have everything regulated in advance in case it
should not come. He himself, therefore, has his 'business'
prearranged down to pulling off each finger of a glove at a
given word of a given speech. I may add that Mr. Irving,
who has gone forth to battle with M. Coquelin on this very
subject of inspiration, is himself (as I am assured on all
hands) scrupulous in repeating night after night every minutest detail of attitude and gesture.

An often-quoted saying of Baron's places him clearly on
the side of spontaneity. 'Les règles,' he said,[17] 'défendent
d'élever les bras au-dessus de la tête; mais si la passion les y
porte, ils feront bien. La passion en sait plus que les règles.'
[Rules prohibit lifting the arms higher than the head, but
if a strong impulse raises them there, that is where they belong. The strong impulse is wiser about it than the rules.]
This chimes with the well-known anecdote of Voltaire tying
the hands of a novice with pack-thread to restrain her exuberance of gesture, but applauding when an irresistible impulse of passion forced her to burst her bonds. It is said of
Lekain, on the other hand, that 'ses gestes étaient toujours
les mêmes; apprêtés, compassés et mesurés géométrique-
ment; que sur chacun de ses rôles, il les avait scrupuleuse-
ment notés en marge; qu'il passait la matinée à les étudier
devant une glace, et que quiconque lui avait vu jouer un
rôle, pouvait annoncer, scène par scène, tous les gestes dont
il y ferait constamment usage.' [. . . his gestures were always the same—schooled, regularized, geometrically precise;

17 Lemazurier, i. p. 97.

that for every rôle of his he had made painstaking marginal notes of them; that he would put in the morning testing them in a mirror; and that anyone who had seen him in a particular rôle could tell in advance, from scene to scene, every one of the gestures that he invariably used.] Lemazurier throws doubt on this statement, arguing[18] that, were it true, Lekain would have been a bad actor; but what 'would have been' must yield before what 'was.' Anthony Aston tells us of Mrs. Verbruggen[19] that 'she was all Art, and her Acting all acquir'd, but dress'd so nice, it look'd like Nature. There was not a Look, a Motion, but what were all design'd; and these at the same Word, Period, Occasion, Incident, were every Night, in the same Character, alike; and yet all sat charmingly easy on her.' Mrs. Verbruggen, better known as Mrs. Mountfort, was one of the first actresses of her time. 'She was Mistress of more variety of Humour,' says Cibber, 'than I ever knew in any one Woman Actress.'

Dramatic records abound in instances of great effects produced 'on the spur of the moment.' One of the most remarkable, certainly, is Charlotte Cushman's creation Meg Merrilies. In the season 1840-41, she was an unknown 'utility' actress at the Park Theatre, New York. Braham, the great tenor, was appearing as Harry Bertram in *Guy Mannering,* when one day Mrs. Chippendale, who played Meg Merrilies, fell ill. The part was handed to Miss Cushman about midday, the intention being that she should read it. When the evening arrived, however, she knew it by heart. 'Study, dress, &c. had to be the inspiration of the moment. She had never especially noticed the part. . . . but as she stood at the side-scene, book in hand, awaiting her moment of entrance, her ear caught the dialogue going on upon the stage between two of the gypsies, in which one says to the other, alluding to her, "Meg—why, she is no longer what she was; she doats," &c. . . . With the words a vivid flash of insight struck upon her brain. . . . She gave herself with her usual concentrated energy of purpose to this conception, and flashed at once upon the stage in the startling, weird, and terrible manner which we all so well remember: Braham afterwards came to her dressing-room and said, "Miss Cush-

[18] Lemazurier, i. p. 362.
[19] Aston, p. 18.

man, I have come to thank you for the most veritable sensation I have experienced for a long time. I give you my word when I turned and saw you in that first scene, I felt a cold chill run all over me. Where have you learned to do anything like that?" ' [20] Afterwards, no doubt, Miss Cushman greatly elaborated the character, which was the chief triumph of her career; but the effect of her first performance proves that 'la fureur du premier jet' is not always to be despised.

A most interesting case of momentary inspiration is recorded by Lady Martin, in her account of the first performance of *The Lady of Lyons:* 'As I recalled to Claude, in bitter scorn, his glowing description of his Palace by the Lake of Como, I broke into a paroxysm of hysterical laughter, which came upon me, I suppose, as the natural relief from the intensity of the mingled feelings of anger, scorn, wounded pride and outraged love, by which I found myself carried away. The effect upon the audience was electrical because the impulse was genuine. But well do I remember Mr. Macready's remonstrance with me for yielding to it. It was too daring, he said; to have failed in it might have ruined the scene (which was true). No one, moreover, should ever, he said, hazard an unrehearsed effect. I could only answer that I could not help it; that this seemed the only way for my feelings to find vent; and if the impulse seized me again, again, I feared, I must act the scene in the same way. And often as I have played Pauline, never did the scene fail to bring back the same burst of hysterical emotion; nor, so far as I know, did any of my critics regard my yielding to it as out of place, or otherwise than true to nature.' [21]

Macready's rebuke to Miss Faucit is quite in character; for Macready was perhaps the chief of a host of actors who disprove Diderot's assumption that 'feeling' and 'study' are things incompatible. He was an uncompromising believer in real emotion—of that we have had ample proof—and his great intelligence, combined with his almost morbid habit of introspection, gives his judgment unquestionable weight. 'In reading, as in acting,' he said to Lady Pollock,[22] 'intense

[20] *Charlotte Cushman*, p. 15.
[21] *Shakespeare's Female Characters*, p. 205.
[22] *Macready as I knew him*, pp. 27, 50.

feeling must move the performer; any interruption that
checks the feeling, destroys the power'; and in the same delightful book we are told that he gave up the idea of teach-
ing elocution 'with the conviction that no man could teach
feeling; and to teach the rest without that, would only be
to engraft his own manner upon another.' Yet this double-
dyed emotionalist was never tired of insisting on the necessity for diligent study and minute elaboration of 'tones,
attitudes and looks.' He praises these methods in other artists; his diary abounds in evidence that he practised them
himself; and independent testimony from a score of different
sources represents him to have been a very martinet, both to
himself and others, in his insistence on exact pre-arrange-
ment of effects. What becomes, then, of the supposed antagonism between sensibility and study?

A curious passage in the *Correspondence and Table-Talk*
of Benjamin Robert Haydon[23] bears directly on the point
under discussion. Haydon, says his son, 'was once induced
by one of the family to go and see Macready in *Lear*. He sat
out the first act and then went away, saying he could not
stand any more of it. He afterwards ridiculed the whole
thing, comparing Macready to a machine wound up to go
through a certain representation, and every night in the same
part performing exactly the same movements and making
exactly the same noises. Edmund Kean, he maintained,
never played the same part twice in the same way. The same
thing was true, he also said, of Mrs. Siddons. Of John Kemble the machine theory was always true. Haydon had studied Edmund Kean, from his first appearance in *Richard
III.*, in all his great parts in his best days. Mr. Lewes,
who allows that he only saw Kean in his later and feebler
days, asserts,[24] on the other hand, that Kean never trusted
to "the inspiration of the moment." This is probably true
of Kean's later period, when his intemperate habits obscured his fine genius, and he could no longer rely upon the
advent of the divine afflatus at the right instant. But Edmund Kean (as he remembered him) and Mrs. Siddons
were Haydon's faith.' The value of this passage lies in Haydon's assertion that the acting of Kean and Mrs. Siddons

---

23 Vol. i. p. 180.
24 *Actors and Acting*, p. 7.

used to vary from night to night. Such variety, as I have tried to show, is not at all inconsistent with that assiduous study which George Henry Lewes was right in declaring to have been characteristic of Kean. As for Macready, it is hard to understand how, by seeing him once in one act of *Lear*, Haydon could discover that he was always the same. It is true that he was scrupulous in the pre-regulation of all such details as belong to stage-management, but his diaries contain abundant evidence that throughout his career he never (in stage slang) 'put a part to bed,' but was always restlessly experimenting with a view to self-improvement.

Macready said of Fanny Kemble that she 'did not know the rudiments of her profession'; and if self-control be one of the rudiments the following confession proves that, as she herself puts it, he was 'not far wrong.' 'In the last scene [of *Venice Preserved*],' she writes,[25] 'where poor Belvidera's brain gives way under her despair, and she fancies herself digging for her husband in the earth, and that she at last recovers and seizes him, I intended to utter a piercing scream; this I had not of course rehearsed, not being able to scream deliberately in cold blood, so that I hardly knew, myself, what manner of utterance I should find for my madness. But when the evening came, I uttered shriek after shriek without stopping, and rushing off the stage ran all round the back of the scenes, and was pursuing my way, perfectly unconscious of what I was doing, down the stairs that led out into the street, when I was captured and brought back to my dressing-room and my senses.' This is an excellent instance both of an unrehearsed effect and of inartistic, somnambulistic absorption; for Miss Kemble seems to have had precisely the characteristics which Diderot ascribes to Dumesnil. Her inability to rehearse a scream in cold blood contrasts with Rachel's careful 'study of her sobs.' Yet Rachel, too, seems to have been to some extent dependent, in spite of herself, on momentary inspiration. She was apt to play badly for the first few nights of a new creation; and on such occasions she said to Houssaye, 'J'enrage, car je me sens enchaînée.' 'Mais tout à coup,' Houssaye continues,[26] 'le dieu l'emportait et elle éclatait en miracles.' ['I am furious,

[25] *Record of a Girlhood*, ii. p. 86.
[26] *La Comédienne*, p. 150.

because I feel shackled.' But all at once the gods would take possession of her, and then she rained miracles.]

Almost all the artists whom I have personally consulted allow that within due limits they readily avail themselves of inspiration, and most condemn as false in principle the too rigorous sameness, even down to the movement of a particular finger at a particular word, which a few actors laboriously cultivate. Many very happy effects have certainly been suggested by the spirit of the scene and produced on the spur of the moment—perhaps never to be reproduced. 'The late Mrs. Charles Kean told me,' writes Mr. Frank Harvey, 'that while playing at the Princess's Theatre she once made a great sensation in a moment of nervous excitement, and afterwards could not even remember what she had done, far less reproduce it.' Salvini is emphatic in his assertion that the finest effects are often unpremeditated, and that such inspirations can sometimes be seized and reproduced. As to the respective merits of study and inspiration, he expresses himself in almost the identical words used by Garrick in his criticism of Clairon. I am assured by several observers that Salvini varies very much in his 'business' from night to night, even to the extent of delivering a particular speech now up the stage, now down, standing one night, sitting the next, and on the third, perhaps, lolling on a divan. Robson, too (as I learn on the authority of his widow), was very erratic in his movements on the stage.

'I have often,' writes Mrs. Bancroft, 'been inspired to introduce on the spur of the moment a new gesture or a new reading of certain lines. . . . The voice must be guided by the feelings and love of the subject. Emotion has a wide range, and the heart can produce many notes. These I play upon as the fit seizes me.' Mr. Bancroft adds that on the first night of *Sweethearts* Mrs. Bancroft spoke Jenny Northcott's last line with a delicate pathos of intonation which she never afterwards entirely 'recaptured.' Mr. Hermann Vezin, both in theory and in practice, leaves a wide margin for variation in gesture. One gesture, he says, is true to your way of feeling the situation on one night, another on another. He condemns, for instance, the three solemn taps on the brow with which Charles Kean always preluded the line, 'In my mind's eye, Horatio'; and he relates some curious examples of Frédérick Lemaître's variability in this respect. 'Je suis capable,' writes M. Albert Lambert, 'quelque empoigné que je sois par la situation, de me rappeler l'accent que j'ai trouvé, mais pas toujours de le reproduire; et c'est alors que je m'aperçois que la seule vraie sensibilité trouve la corde vibrante de l'effet. Le hasard m'a servi souvent, et l'inspiration de mes camarades aussi; et à ce propos, le plus grand des plaisirs est de jouer la comédie avec de grands comédiens—j'entends des penseurs, et non des acteurs. Leurs regards, leurs silences, leurs pensées vous donnent des répliques mystérieuses et de soudaines inspirations.' [However completely carried away by a dramatic situation, I am able to remember afterward the inflection that I hit upon, though not invariably to reproduce it; and then I recognise that only genuine feeling will find the string to pluck for the ideal effect. Mere luck has often served me; the inspirations of fellow-actors, too; and for that matter the supreme pleasure is doing comedy with great comedians—I mean the thinking ones, not the mere actors. Their expressions, their silences, their very thoughts give you indefinable cues and sudden inspirations.] Of M. Mounet Sully, again, M. Larcher, founding, evidently, on personal confessions, writes, 'Il est en état d'improvisation constante.' [27] [He is perpetually in the stage of improvisation.] Mr. Beerbohm Tree, at the commencement of his career, used to force himself always to make a given gesture at a given word, but was taught by experience to regard the practice as useless and embarrassing. Mr. Clayton related to me an amusing yet really valuable instance of inspiration. Salome, in *Dandy Dick,* has just read from the *Times* the paragraph announcing the Dean's munificent offer of 1,000*l.* to the Minster Restoration Fund 'on condition that seven other donors come forward, each with the like sum.' 'And will they?' cries Sheba eagerly; whereupon the Dean, who has been standing with his back to the audience, turns with an unctuous yet sickly smile, and replies, 'My darling—times are bad, but one never knows.' This smile was an inspiration. For some time after the production of the play Mr. Clayton used to speak the line gravely and meditatively,

[27] *Revue d'Art Dramatique,* March 1, 1887.

without producing any effect. One evening the smile—a really admirable trait—came to his lips almost before he knew what he was doing. The audience rose to it immediately, and from that day forward the speech, thus accentuated, remained one of the most successful in the piece. A somewhat similar story is told of Mr. John Hare. He was playing the bibulous Baron Croodle on the first night of *The Money-spinner,* when by chance a champagne-cork was heard to pop behind the scenes. Mr. Hare had the presence of mind to let his face light up with an expression of rapturous anticipation; and the result was so good that the incident was afterwards repeated every evening.

On the whole, there is every reason to believe that, within due limits, momentary impulse plays an important and legitimate part upon the stage. But it is none the less evident that the actor who 'trusts to inspiration' in the sense of going on the stage unprepared and uncertain of his own intentions, deserves the very hardest things that MM. Diderot and Coquelin can say of him. I may pick up a five-pound note in the street to-morrow; but I should be a fool to leave my purse at home on the chance.

Chapter XIII

TO RESUME

IN ORDERING this discussion, I have had a double difficulty to contend with, as the reader may by this time have discovered to his cost. In the first place, there were two questions at issue—a question of fact and a question of theory: do actors feel? and ought they to feel? In the second place, I had not the advantage of starting from an unencumbered base and building up my theory in my own way by a straightforward synthesis of evidence. The issue had been obscured (as it seemed to me) by rash overstatements on both sides, and by a general failure to recognise and define the comparatively few points on which rational dispute was possible. Thus my exposition was necessarily mingled with controversy, and I fear the mixture has not thoroughly clarified. If exhaustion have not supervened upon the reader's bewilderment, a brief recapitulation may help him to find his bearings.

Acting is of all the arts the most purely imitative. In this respect it stands at the opposite pole from music, with sculpture, painting, poetry, in intermediate positions. Music deals almost entirely in what may be called sound-patterns, which have no prototypes in external nature. Poetry, and indeed all literary art, leans in the same direction. Its matter may or may not be imitative; its medium must be a more or less rhythmic succession of sounds, which does not depend for its attractiveness on its resemblance to anything under the sun. Painting, in these latter days, tends more and more to the condition of colour-music, the very vocabularies of the two arts being, it appears, interchangeable. Even sculpture, without entirely deserting its function, may present a mere arabesque of curves and surfaces. But acting is imitative or it is nothing. It may borrow from all the arts in turn—from the arts of speech, of song, of colour, of form; but imitation is its differentia. Acting *is* imitation; when it ceases to be imitation it ceases to be acting and becomes something else—oratory perhaps, perhaps ballet-dancing or posturing. Everyone knows that the actor is not necessarily a mere copyist of nature; he may sing, for example, or he may talk alexandrines; but he must always preserve a similarity in dissimilarity; he must always imitate, though we may permit him to steep his imitation, so to speak, in a more or less conventional atmosphere. 'He plays naturally,' or, in other words, 'He imitates well,' is our highest formula of praise even for the operatic tenor or the French tragedian, who may not deliver a single word or tone exactly as it would be uttered in real life.

The actor, then, is a man who, through the medium of his own body, imitates the manners and the passions of other men. We are all actors in rudiment, the tendency to such imitation being part of the mechanism of animated nature. That is why the stage is besieged by incompetent aspirants, the general tendency being easily mistaken for special aptitude. Conversely, I believe, that is why some theorists seek to exclude acting from the dignity of art. They ignore the amount of labour and thought required to transmute, not only the general tendency, but even a very special aptitude, into accomplished mastery.

By far the greater part of the imitation of man by man which takes place off the stage is totally unconcerned with emotion. In real life the emotions of others are precisely what we do *not* imitate. A child learns to speak, to walk, to sing by imitating its elders: it wails before its eyes are fairly opened to the world. We are all conscious of a tendency to mimic the tics and mannerisms of our neighbours—their gait, their voice, their accent; but the mere muscular copying of emotional manifestations never occurs, except for purposes of ridicule. The grief or laughter of another may seize and overmaster us, through the action of sympathy, though we may know nothing of its cause; but this is not imitation: it is infection. It may be said that all imitation which is not absolutely deliberate partakes of the nature of infection. True; but the infection of feeling has this peculiarity, that it is *not imitative*. We weep our own tears, we laugh our own laughter, without the smallest conscious or unconscious tendency to reproduce the particular forms which these paroxysms assume in the person who has 'set us off.' Therefore I think there is a clear distinction between mimicking tricks or habits and yielding to emotional contagion. Roughly speaking, the one is an affair of the surface, the other of the centres.

The manners and passions of his fellow-men form, as we have seen, the actor's province. Over part of this domain unemotional imitation will carry him safely. The reproduction of manners, in themselves, is effected by a mere extension of that instinct which makes children the 'sedulous apes' of their elders, and causes some of us, even in maturity, to stammer after conversing with a stammerer and to wink and twitch after seeing a victim to St. Vitus's dance. In all characters there is a greater or less element of manner, so that in all characters this instinct of mere imitation is brought into play. A large part of every impersonation is, and must be, as mechanical as the putting on of a wig or the painting of crows'-feet under the eyes. But comparatively few dramatic characters consist of manners alone. It is passion that interests and moves us; therefore the reproduction of passion is the actor's highest and most essential task. By what methods, then, can this reproduction be most fitly accomplished?

The external manifestations of passion consist, on analysis, of changes in the face, the limbs, or the organs of speech, many of which can be mechanically imitated with more or less precision, just as one can imitate the limp of a cripple or an Irishman's brogue. For example, we can all contort our faces into the semblance of weeping, we can smile and laugh at will (though the voluntary laugh is apt to be a lugubrious effort), we can sob, we can tremble, we can gnash and grind the teeth, not quite convincingly perhaps, but so that an observer can easily guess what emotion we are simulating. On the other hand, some of the symptoms of those passions which tend to express themselves immediately, forcibly, and unmistakably—the passions of grief and joy, terror and fury —cannot be imitated by the mere action of the will upon the muscles and tissues. No one can blush and turn pale at will; some actors, as we have seen reason to believe, can shed tears at a moment's notice and without any real or imaginary cause; but this faculty is not common, and is the result of long practice. These involuntary symptoms, however, are of such a nature as to be almost imperceptible on the stage. If the more obvious traits are vividly reproduced, a theatrical audience is ready enough to take tears, blushes, and pallor upon trust. It is undeniable, then, that for the practical purposes of dramatic presentation, the symptoms of passion can be mechanically mimicked with tolerable precision, and there is no reason to doubt that exceptional artists have attained astonishing skill in such mimicry.

It is certain, however, that the faculty of mechanically mimicking the ebullitions of passion with anything like deceptive precision is a very rare one. We have seen that our innate mimetic tendency does not generally exercise itself upon these phenomena; perhaps for no more recondite reason than that they are of exceptional occurrence and do not force themselves on our observation with the importunacy of habitual actions. Be this as it may, it is clear that the mechanical mimicking of passions on the stage is not, like the mimicking of manners, a mere extension of an inborn instinct. On the other hand, we have also seen that the paroxysms of passion tend to communicate themselves to those not primarily affected, through that subtle contagion which we call sympathy. Little Mabel breaks her favourite doll and howls piteously over the remains. Her elder brother, Jack, though his sex and his years raise him far above the weakness of doll-worship, nay, though he may have a dim sense of Rochefoucauldian satisfaction in Mabel's misfortune, will very probably yell in concert, as lustily as though the sorrow were his own. He certainly does not suffer anything like Mabel's agony of soul; in a sense he cannot properly be said to suffer at all; and still less can it be maintained that he deliberately mimics his sister. All we can say is that by the mysterious action of sympathy Mabel's grief acts upon Jack's nerve-centres and begets in them a condition so analogous to her own that it results in similar outward manifestations. The difference between the two states might be tested by the exhibition of a counter-irritant. A chocolate-cream will probably dry Jack's eyes as if by magic, while a wilderness of lollipops will leave Mabel inconsolable. In this sympathetic contagion we have an instrument provided by nature for supplying the deficiencies of our power of mechanical mimicry in respect to the subtler symptoms of passion. The poet—say Shakespeare—fecundates the imagination of the actor—say Salvini—so that it bodies forth the great passion-quivering phantom of Othello. In the act of representation this phantom is, as it were, superimposed upon the real man. The phantom Othello suffers, and the nerve-centres of the man Salvini thrill in response. The blood courses through his veins, his eyes are clouded with sorrow or blaze with fury, his lips tremble, the muscles of his throat contract, the passion of the moment informs him to the finger-tips, and his portrayal of a human soul in agony is true to the minutest detail. His suffering may stand to Othello's in the quantitative relation of Jack's grief to Mabel's; but, so far as it goes, it cannot be called other than real.

The anti-emotionalists would have the actor abjure, at any rate in the moment of performance, the aid of this sympathetic contagion. It is too dearly bought, they argue. The accomplished player should be able mechanically to mimic all symptoms of emotion which are of any use in creating illusion in the audience, and he must run no risk of becoming extravagant, inarticulate, or feeble, by reason of the too vehement disturbance of his own nerve-centres. The emotionalists, as I understand their position, maintain that the mechanical mimicry of feeling, even at its best, lacks the clear ring of truth, and that in yielding to the sympathetic contagion the accomplished actor does not in reality run any of the risks on which their opponents are so fond of dwelling.

The two questions, then, which we have had to consider in this discussion—do actors feel? and ought they to feel?— may be restated thus: Do actors habitually yield to the sympathetic contagion? and do the greatest actors—those who have most powerfully affected their audiences—admit or reject this method?

My first three chapters were purely preliminary. I described the methods of investigation I had pursued; traced, historically, the genesis of Diderot's *Paradoxe;* and tried to narrow the issue by analysing the different meanings attributed in the *Paradoxe* to the term 'sensibility,' and rejecting some of them as unfair or irrelevant. The investigation proper began with the fourth chapter. In it we found that the shedding of tears—one of the most palpable symptoms of pathetic emotion—is common, and even habitual, on the stage. We learned from Cicero and Quintilian that the Roman actors frequently wept; and we ascertained, in most cases on unimpeachable evidence, that tears have been shed on the stage by Garrick, Mrs. Cibber, Barry, Peg Woffington, Mrs. Pritchard, Mrs. Siddons, Miss O'Neill, Miss Fanny Kemble, Mlle. Champmeslé, Mlle. Duclos, Quinault-Dufresne, Mlle. Gaussin, Frédérick Lemaître, Madame Dorval, Miss Neilson, Charlotte Cushman, Samuel Phelps, Benjamin Webster, Salvini, Mr. and Mrs. Bancroft, Mr. and Mrs. Kendal, Mr. Irving, Miss Ellen Terry, Madame Sarah Bernhardt, Miss Mary Anderson, Miss Alma Murray, Miss Achurch, Miss Clara Morris, Mr. Wilson Barrett, Mr. Beerbohm Tree, Mr. John Clayton, Mr. Hermann Vezin, Mr. Howe, Miss Bateman, Mr. Lionel Brough, and several others. It would not have cost much trouble to extend this list almost indefinitely, but it seems to me sufficient as it stands, both in numbers and in authority. The frequency of real weeping on the stage being thus established, I had next to admit that tears can, in certain cases, be mechanically produced, and that they do not, therefore, afford conclusive evidence of any particular emotional state. In order to show that they are not, as a rule, so fallacious as the anti-emotionalists argue, and at the same time to prove that there is a close analogy between personal and mimetic emotion, I collected, in my fifth chapter, numerous instances of the mingling and (in M. Coquelin's phrase) 'kneading together' of the two states, which we found to coalesce indistinguishably, sometimes to the advantage, sometimes to the detriment, of the actor's performance. On the other hand, in Chapter Six, we found scanty evidence of any tendency to mimic in cold blood particular ebullitions of emotion, whether observed or experienced, and no proof whatever that unemotional mimicry is more effective than emotional acting. In the following chapter, treating of laughter as the characteristic expression of joyful emotion, and thus the natural antithesis to tears, we found a rather wide divergence of testimony. Some actors declare themselves highly susceptible to the contagion of their character's mirth, others (of no less authority) are equally positive in asserting their laughter to be always a deliberate simulative effort. I confess myself unable to suggest any satisfactory reason why the contagion of merriment should be less potent and universal than the contagion of tears. Can it be that there is a pessimistic bias in human nature, rendering men, on the average, less prone to joyous than to mournful emotion?

Here let me interrupt this recapitulation to point out a fact which is apt to be overlooked. In the course of my interviews with the leading artists of to-day, I have more than once mentioned, say, to X.—an emphatic emotionalist—that a fellow-artist, Z., had declared himself of the same opinion; whereupon X. would shrug his (or her) shoulders sceptically and remark, 'Oh, Z.!—I don't believe *he* ever felt anything in his life!' The doubt in these cases sprang from the common error of thinking that sensitiveness to what we have called the imaginative contagion presupposes unusual sensibility in the ordinary affairs of life. A little consideration will show us that the fact is not so. The executioner in

Thackeray blubbered over *The Sorrows of Werther;* and no one will deny that this is a touch of nature. To take an example from real life, Macaulay, who met his personal sorrows in no unmanly spirit, could weep by the hour over a trashy novel. We must all have known people, stoical enough in their own troubles, and perhaps even hard-hearted towards the sufferings of others, who would yet become maudlin over the imagined sorrows of a personage in fiction or on the stage. Thus the actor who owns himself affected by the emotions of his character—the superimposed phantom of his imagination—does not thereby lay any claim to exceptional tenderness of heart in the ordinary relations of life. In that respect, I imagine, actors are very much like other men. Diderot, as we have seen, found them 'caustic, cold, selfish, alive to our absurdities rather than touched by our misfortunes.' This character certainly does not apply to the players of our nation and time, whose large and ready charity proves that 'they know what 'tis to pity and be pitied.' But even if Diderot were absolutely just in his general assertion of the heartlessness of actors, we should still have no difficulty in believing them susceptible to emotional contagion from the phantoms of their imagination.

Continuing my summary, I pass to Chapter Eight. Here we ascertained that three symptoms of acute feeling, which are utterly beyond the control of the will—blushing, pallor, and perspiration—commonly, and even habitually, accompany the stage-emotion of the greatest artists. In this, it seems to me, we have proof positive that mimetic emotion is not, as some people argue, a state of mere vague unspecialised excitement, but is closely analogous to the emotion of real life. In the next chapter we inquired into the practice, attributed to several great artists, of mechanically mobilising the nerve-centres by means of that reaction from external manifestations of passion which Hartmann describes as 'auto-suggestion.' This proceeding, in various forms, we found to be fairly common; while the habit of mental concentration upon a part during, and even for some time before, the period of performance, proved to be still more general. The rationale of these practices is obvious enough. The one assists the actor to clothe himself, as it were, in the phantom of his imagination, and to keep himself thoroughly enveloped in it; the other heightens the sensitiveness of his organism to contagion from the emotions of his personage. The next chapter was devoted to an inquiry into the multiplex action of the mind whereby the accomplished actor is enabled to remain master of himself even in the very paroxysm of passion. I was able to adduce many cases in which double and treble strata of mental activity were clearly distinguishable, but very few examples of that total and somnambulistic absorption in a part which the anti-emotionalists assume to be the normal condition of the emotional actor. The succeeding chapter touched upon the question of long runs. We saw reason, on the one hand, to reject Diderot's opinion that an actor must gain by reiterating a character until his playing becomes entirely automatic, and to believe, on the other hand, that an actor may repeat a character indefinitely without degenerating into automatism, if only he takes care to allow himself proper intervals of rest and change between the performances of any one part. Finally, in Chapter Twelve, we 'Reasoned high Of fate, free will, foreknowledge absolute'—I trust the reader will not complete the quotation, adding 'And found no end, in wandering mazes lost.' We learned that some actors are artistic Calvinists, insisting on rigorous predestination of every detail of position, attitude, gesture, and inflexion; while others, the Arminians of the stage, leave a wide margin for impulse, spontaneity, freewill. The latter sect is probably the more numerous and influential; but we also ascertained that the 'foreknowledge absolute' of the necessitarians is by no means inconsistent with the keenest susceptibility to the emotional influence of their characters.

At the very outset of this inquiry, I insisted on the distinction between the simple or primary emotions—grief, joy, terror, &c.—and the secondary or complex and habitual emotions—love, hatred, jealousy, &c.—which have no immediate and characteristic outward symptoms, and are rather to be called attitudes of mind. No one denies, I think, that the primary emotions of an imagined character do in fact tend to communicate themselves to the nerve-centres of the actor, and to affect his organs of expression. Let me add, parenthetically, that it is surely illogical to deny the 'reality' of this mimetic emotion, since all emotion, except that which arises from instant physical pleasure or pain, is due to the action of the imagination upon the nerve-centres. This, however, is a mere question of nomenclature. Be it real or unreal, this mimetic emotion tends, in the great majority of cases, to come into play; and the actor who avails himself of it clearly works on the line of least resistance. The anti-emotionalists must prove that this straightforward course is beset with the most fatal pitfalls ere they can hope to induce actors to follow the roundabout route, repressing the action of the imagination and cultivating mechanical mimicry. I have tried to show that the pitfalls from which the anti-emotionalists recoil are either quite imaginary or easily to be avoided. On the other hand, the more we look into the matter, the less are we inclined to believe that even the greatest virtuoso of mechanical mimicry can attain to the subtle and absolute truth of imitation which is possible to the actor who combines artistically controlled sensibility with perfect physical means of expression. 'Raised or lowered by the twentieth part of the quarter of a tone,' says Diderot, the utterances of feeling 'ring false.' But is it not just the intervention of imaginative sympathy that enables the actor to produce and reproduce this delicately true vibration? There is no doubt that the imagination can readily bring about minute yet expressive changes, muscular and vascular, which the unaided action of the will is powerless to effect. Blushing and pallor are the chief of these, but there must be many others. Darwin[1] notes that when two dogs fight together in play (that is, when they imagine and act the emotion of anger) their hair at once bristles up, just as in actual warfare. This is a type of many similar phenomena in the human economy. And it must not be supposed that these minute changes do not contribute appreciably to the illusion. We may not consciously note a blush, a sudden pallor, a particular quiver of the lip, distension of the nostril, or corrugation of the brow; but they produce their effect nevertheless. Mr. Kendal once suggested to me what I think a luminous illustration of the difference between mechanically simulated and imaginatively experienced emotion. 'A sign-painter,' he said, 'takes a pot of crude

[1] *Expression of the Emotions*, p. 102.

vermilion, and daubs the red coat of the Duke of Wellington or the Marquis of Granby. It is undeniably red, and yet
somehow it is all wrong. But look into a red robe painted by
Rossetti or Holman Hunt, and you will find it composed of
a hundred different hues, which blend, at the proper dis-
tance, into a true and living whole.' To translate the illustration into musical terms, a mechanically mimicked utterance of emotion is like a note without its harmonics. The
analogy may be fanciful, but I do not think it is wholly
misleading.

In the foregoing pages there are, no doubt, errors of
analysis and of inference which have escaped my ken. On
the other hand, no one knows better than I that the subject
of mimetic emotion is full of subtleties and intricacies into
which I have not penetrated. Some day, perhaps, a better-
equipped psychologist may thread the maze to its inmost
recesses. Meanwhile, in taking leave of what has been to me
a fascinating inquiry, I cannot but hope that it may aid the
contending forces in a lingering and somewhat futile controversy to arrive at a clearer understanding of the true
points at issue than they have hitherto attained. If each party
fully realised its own and its adversaries' position, I believe a
treaty of peace would very soon be signed. It was drafted by
Shakespeare three centuries ago, when, through the mouth
of Prince Hamlet, he counselled the players of his day to
acquire and beget a temperance even in the very torrent,
tempest, and whirlwind of passion.

KEY TO REFERENCES

KEY TO REFERENCES

[This is not a complete list of authorities, but merely a table of those titles which have been abbreviated in the foregoing pages in order to save space.]

Assézat = *Œuvres Complètes de D. Diderot. . . . Notices, Notes &c. . . .* Par J. Assézat. Paris, 1875-77.

Aston = *A Brief Supplement to Colley Cibber, Esq; his Lives of the late famous Actors and Actresses.* By Anthony, Vulgò Tony, Aston. London, 1747 or 1748.

Bancroft = *Mr. and Mrs. Bancroft On and Off the Stage.* Written by Themselves. London, 1888.

Boaden = *Memoirs of Mrs. Siddons.* By James Boaden, Esq. Second edition. London, 1831.

Boswell = *Boswell's Life of Johnson.* Edited by George Birkbeck Hill, D.C.L. Oxford, 1887.

Bunn = *The Stage, both Before and Behind the Curtain.* By Alfred Bunn. London, 1840.

Campardon = *Les Comédiens du Roi de la Troupe Italienne.* Par E. Campardon. Paris, 1880.

Campbell = *Life of Mrs. Siddons.* By Thomas Campbell. London, 1834.

Charlotte Cushman = *Charlotte Cushman.* By Clara Erskine Clement. (American Actor Series.) London (*no date*).

Cole = *The Life and Theatrical Times of Charles Kean, F.S.A.* By John William Cole. London, 1859.

Compton = *Memoir of Henry Compton*. Edited by Charles and Edward Compton. London, 1879.

Coquelin = *L'Art et le Comédien*. Par C. Coquelin. Paris, 1880.

Crabb Robinson = *Diary, Reminiscences, and Correspondence of H. Crabb Robinson*. Edited by T. Sadler. London, 1869.

Davies = *Dramatic Miscellanies, consisting of Critical Observations on several Plays of Shakespeare*. By T. Davies. London, 1784.

D'Heylli = *Rachel, d'après sa Correspondance*. Par Georges d'Heylli. Paris, 1882.

Dibdin = *Annals of the Edinburgh Stage*. By James C. Dibdin. Edinburgh, 1888.

Doran = *Annals of the English Stage from Thomas Betterton to Edmund Kean*. By Dr. Doran, F.S.A. Edited by Robert W. Lowe. London, 1887.

Dorat = *La Déclamation Théâtrale; Poëme didactique*. [Par C. J. Dorat.] Paris, 1766.

Everard = *Memoirs of an unfortunate Son of Thespis; being a Sketch of the Life of Edward Cape Everard, Comedian*. Edinburgh, 1818.

Gueullette = *Acteurs et Actrices du Temps Passé. . . . Notices*. Par C. Gueullette. Paris, 1881.

Hawkins = *The Life of Edmund Kean*. By F. W. Hawkins. London, 1869.

Houssaye = *La Comédienne*. Par Arsène Houssaye. Paris, 1884.

Ireland = *Letters and Poems by the late Mr. John Henderson, with Anecdotes of his Life.* By John Ireland. London, 1786.

Lardin = Lardin's Preface to Diderot's *Paradoxe* in the *Bibliothèque Nationale*.

Lemazurier = *Galerie Historique des Acteurs du Théâtre-Français, depuis 1600 jusqu'à nos jours.* Par P. D. Lemazurier. Paris, 1810.

Lowe = *A Bibliographical Account of English Theatrical Literature.* By Robert W. Lowe. London, 1888.

Ludlow = *Dramatic Life as I found it.* By N. M. Ludlow. St. Louis, 1880.

Macready = *Macready's Reminiscences, and Selections from his Diaries and Letters.* Edited by Sir Frederick Pollock, Bart. London, 1875.

Malone = Malone's Historical Account of the English Stage, in Prolegomena to Variorum Shakespeare. London, 1821.

Matthews and Hutton = *Actors and Actresses of Great Britain and the United States, from the Days of David Garrick to the Present Time.* Edited by Brander Matthews and Lawrence Hutton. New York (*no date*).

Morley = *Diderot and the Encyclopædists.* By John Morley. London, 1878.

Noctes Atticæ = Beloe's Translation. London, 1795.

Oxberry = *Oxberry's Dramatic Biography and Histrionic Anecdotes.* London, 1825 to 1827.

Pollock = *The Paradox of Acting, translated with Annotations from Diderot's "Paradoxe sur le Comédien."* By Walter Herries Pollock. With a Preface by Henry Irving. London, 1883.

Reynolds = *The Life and Times of Frederick Reynolds.* Written by Himself. London, 1826.

Scott = Miscellaneous Prose Works of Sir Walter Scott. Edinburgh, 1846. (See also *Quarterly Review,* xxxiv. p. 216, June 1826.)

Talma = *Réflexions sur Lekain et l'Art Théâtral.* Paris, 1856.

The Voice = *The Voice* (Newspaper). New York, March 1888.

INDEX

INDEX

235

DRAMABOOKS

HILL AND WANG aims to establish DRAMABOOKS as a permanent library of the great classics of the theatre of all countries, in an attractive, low-priced format.

Eric Bentley, Advisory Editor to Dramabooks, is Brander Matthews Professor of Dramatic Literature at Columbia University.

Published